The Logic of Compressed Modernity

The Logic of Compressed Modernity

Chang Kyung-Sup

polity

First published in 2022 by Polity Press

Polity Press
65 Bridge Street
Cambridge CB2 1UR, UK

Polity Press
101 Station Landing
Suite 300
Medford, MA 02155, USA

ISBN-13: 978-1-5095-5288-7 (hardback)
ISBN-13: 978-1-5095-5289-4 (paperback)

A catalogue record for this book is available from the British Library.

Library of Congress Control Number: 2021946662

Typeset in 10.5 on 12 pt Sabon
by Cheshire Typesetting Ltd, Cuddington, Cheshire

For further information on Polity, visit our website: politybooks.com

CONTENTS

FIGURES, TABLES AND ILLUSTRATIONS

Figures

Tables

Photos

Box

PREFACE

The dramatic nature of South Korea's societal transformations on all fronts – beginning with the political departure in 1948 as a highly advanced democracy in form and spanning to the "miracle-paced" capitalist industrialization and economic growth since the mid 1960s and the global cultural ascendance of Korean popular culture (dubbed "the Korean wave") in the twenty first century – has been substantially derived from the radically extensive and unprecedentedly condensed process of simulating, materializing, and utilizing the modern (reads Western or American) systems of political, economic, and sociocultural life. In finding and justifying the rationale of such compressed Westernization-cum-modernization, professional social sciences, as mechanically partitioned from humanities, have often taken the place of public sociopolitical debates and intellectual philosophical deliberations. However, the overwhelming materiality of "successful" modernization and development – usually measured in terms of the degree of temporal and substantive compression – has sided with social scientists in social influence and technocratic utilities, who thus keep intensifying their self-partitioned practice in research, education, and public advice.

Three decades of work as a social scientist at a South Korean university have induced me to think that local social sciences are no less quite a unique social phenomenon to be explained themselves than an academic task of explaining the supposed real-world social phenomena. This thought is inseparable from a judgment that the extremely compressed nature of South Korea's modernization and development and its actual conditions, processes, and risks constitute a highly essential scientific subject. Another decisive judgment is that compression in modernization and development has been as much global historical necessitation (or sometimes coercion) as purposive national achievement. In still another related judgment, compressed modernization and development, while South Korea is indeed an exemplary case, have been universal across the postcolonial world whether in reality or aspiration. Given these interrelated thoughts and judgments, reflecting on locally practiced social sciences, including my own scholarship, becomes a very interesting and productive experience, even leading to a wide array of crucial clues in understanding the (real?) social world as well. Every day at work has thus been an interestingly productive experience, and part of its outcome is the current book.

Apparently, this self-reflective sociology of knowledge has long been experienced by numerous scholars around me. In particular, many of my Korean teachers in sociology – including Kim Il-Chul, Kim Kyong-Dong, Han Wan-Sang, Kim Jin-Kyun, Shin Yong-Ha, Kwon Tai-Hwan, Han Sang-Jin, Lim Hyun-Chin, and Hong Doo-Seung – have endeavored to offer earnest realizations about the contested utilities of locally practiced sociology and its desirable innovations in coming to effective grips with South Korea's historico-social realities. Such valuable realizations, along with their substantive contributions about various social phenomena, have crucially benefitted me in developing many key questions on compressed modernity discussed in this book. In particular, my thesis on *internal multiple modernities* (presented in Chapter 4) is decisively owing to abundant rich observations and intuitive thoughts available in their scholarship.

In analyzing compressed modernity since the 1990s, I have been engaged in quite close exchanges and collaborations with many of the world's leading authorities in studying comparative modernities – in particular, Ulrich Beck, Bryan S. Turner, and Göran Therborn. The outcomes of such relationships are fully incorporated in this book as follows: Chapter 3 ("Compressed Modernity in the Universalist Perspective") drawing on the concurrence between Beck and me on "reflexive cosmopolitization"; Chapter 4 ("Internal Multiple Modernities") sharing Therborn's global structuralist perspective on modernities; and Chapter 5 ("Transformative Contributory Rights") extending Turner's conception of citizenship to South Korea's transformative politics. Besides these chapters, a section in Chapter 1 ("Compressed Modernity in Critical Modernity Debates") discusses details of these scholars' arguments and their systematic implications for compressed modernity.

Aside from the current book, I have produced numerous other collaborative publications with them. In particular, my association with Bryan S. Turner reached a totally unexpected level of coediting with him a gigantic five-volume set of a social theory encyclopedia in 2017 (*The Wiley Blackwell Encyclopedia of Social Theory*), in which I directed the two sections on modernity/coloniality/development and Asian social theory, respectively. I tried to organize both sections in a globally balanced and inclusive way. For the Asian social theory section, I tried very zealously to organize numerous key Asian scholars into selecting and writing many entries on Asian (and Eurasian) theories and realities from properly positioned Asian perspectives. These entries represent various essential components and aspects of Asian modernities, so the current book also reflects them carefully. Besides, I was invited by Ulrich Beck to contribute my work on compressed modernity to the special issues of *British Journal of Sociology* (2010) and *Soziale Welt* (2010) that he edited as guest editor. In these contributions, as discussed in this book as well, I tried to explain the common theoretical and analytical ground between compressed modernity and Beck's "second modernity" and "reflexive modernization."

On the other hand, a group of highly respectable scholars has awakened me about the potential relevance of compressed modernity in explaining a wide variety of social phenomena beyond my immediate attention. Above all, I feel greatly indebted to many investigators of various genres of Korean popular culture (now often dubbed "the Korean wave"), including Nancy Abelmann and David Martin-Jones in particular. Frankly speaking, until I came to read their analyses of Korean popular culture in terms of compressed modernity, I had not been quite conscious of the reflective analytical potentials of any type of social scientific research as to such deep yet nuanced cultural representations of South Koreans' life experiences and trajectories. In this regard, those domestic and overseas audiences who eagerly subscribe to the sociocultural forces of masterpiece films, dramas, songs, novels, and other genres from South Korea seem to constitute both a very interesting subject for sociological enquiry and an analytical community themselves engaged in a critical cultural reflection on complicated and contradictory social realities that I have tried to explain as compressed modernity. This awakening has even led me to think that popular culture could be an effective form of reflection on the personal and social conditions of compressed modernity.

A special research program of Chonbuk National University, South Korea, on "Personal Documents and Compressed Modernity" (2001–2017), led by Yi Jeong-Duk, investigated South Koreans' life trajectories and family relations under condensed societal transformations by examining personal diaries and other valuable forms of private documents. While I was once invited to speak on compressed modernity at an international conference of this research program, I mostly ended up learning greatly from their highly systematic investigation into the private world's radical transformations in the twentieth century. I am also indebted to Emiko Ochiai as well as Stevi Jackson for awakening me about multifarious manifestations of compressed modernity in the demographic change, family life, and gender relations of many Asian societies. While my inquisition about compressed modernity, from the beginning, has presumed that South Korea is its exemplary, not unique, case, a lack of real-life ethnomethodological acumen to other societies has detained me from internationally extending it as my own research. It was actually Emiko Ochiai at Kyoto University who offered me a decisive impetus by kindly inviting me for a series of collaborations in a major global research and education program on "Reconstruction of the Intimate and Public Spheres in 21st Century Asia" (2008–2012). As this program adopted compressed modernity as a heuristic analytical framework for comparing the temporal trajectories of social and demographic transformations in various Asian countries vis-à-vis Europe and North America, I came to learn critically from Ochiai and her co-investigators, Zsombor Rajkai in particular, on compressed modernity's global realities and patterns.

Given the experience as an early analyst of post-socialism in the Chinese context, I have increasingly been attracted to recent social changes in the so-called "transition societies" in East Asia and elsewhere. In this regard, I am very grateful to Laurence Roulleau-Berger at the University of Lyon, who has extensively researched Chinese social affairs and intensively interacted with key Chinese scholars and intellectuals, for enlightening me about various specific conditions of post-socialist compressed modernity as manifested in contemporary China. She even edited a special issue of *Temporalités* in 2017, on "'Compressed modernity' and Chinese temporalities," to which I contributed an article that appraises China as a post-socialist complex risk society. My inquisition to reflect such collaboration with Laurence Roulleau-Berger will continue in the coming years in terms of comparatively analyzing late capitalist versus post-socialist instances of compressed modernity.

I also wish to express my gratitude to many overseas as well as domestic colleagues who have offered encouraging responses and constructive inputs after examining various parts of my work on compressed modernity over many years. Among other overseas colleagues,

Takehiko Kariya, D. Hugh Whittaker, Roger Goodman, Sébastien Lechevalier, Lynn Jamieson, Chua Beng Huat, Anthony Woodiwiss, Eui-Hang Shin, Hagen Koo, Seung-Sook Moon, Erik Mobrand, Alvin So, Yong-Chool Ha, Youna Kim, Charles Armstrong, Angie Chung, Gi-Wook Shin, Pieter Boele Van Hensbroek, Kiyomitsu Yui, Brian Yecies, Bruce Cumings, Hiroshi Kojima, Haruka Shibata, Paget Henry, Shirley Hsiao-Li Sun, Teo Youyenn, Raymond Chan, Pei-Chia Lan, Hsiu-hua Shen, Yunxiang Yan, Piao Kuangxing, Do-Young Kim, Rajni Palriwala, and Boris Zizek are warmly acknowledged. It may be impractical to similarly thank all Korean colleagues in the same respect, but I should acknowledge at least the scholarly support and encouragement kindly offered to me by Kwon Hyunji, Kim Baek Yung, Kim Seok-ho, Park Keong-Suk, Bae Eun-Kyung, Suh Yi-Jong, Yee Jaeyeol, Im Dong-Kyun, Chang Dukjin, Jung Keun-Sik, Jeong Il-Gyun, Choo Jihyun, Park Myoung-Kyu, Song Ho-Keun, Chung Chin-Sung, Kim Hong-Jung, Kim Sang-Jun, Eun Ki-Soo, Hong Chan-Sook, Kim Hwan-Suk, Chung Soo-Bok, Lee Cheol-Sung, Kim Kwang-Ki, Lee Seung-Yoon Sophia, Kim Hyun Mee, Han Joon, Chung Moo-Kwoon, Kim Dong-Choon, Chin Meejung, Lee Jae-Rim, Sung Mi-Ai, Lee Chul-Woo, Yoon In-Jin, Kim Tae-Kyoon, Lee Hyun-Ok, Chang Dae-Oup, Shim Doo-Bo, Kong Sukki, Lee Joonkoo, Seol Dong-Hoon, Song Yoo-Jean, Lee Yun-Suk, Eom Han-Jin, Kim Chul-Kyoo, Kim Hung-Ju, Song In-Ha, and many others.

The final stage in completing this book manuscript was generously supported by the University of Cambridge, where I was a visiting fellow of Clare Hall (college) in 2019 and later became the college's life member. Both Clare Hall and the Department of Sociology at the university kindly arranged my seminars, in which I presented key materials from the current book. I am particularly thankful to Sarah Franklin, the head of Cambridge's sociology department, for considerately arranging my visit and seminar and even offering keen interest in my work. John B. Thompson, now an emeritus professor of sociology there (and the director of Polity Press), also offered great enthusiasm for this book. During this period, I was also invited by Hubert Knoblauch to Technische Universität Berlin for a special seminar on some key issues of this book. A lengthy discussion with Knoblauch and his colleagues in Berlin was extremely useful in polishing up many parts of the book manuscript. Shortly after my visit to Cambridge, I was invited by the Academy of the Kingdom of Morocco for a special lecture on South Korean modernization, in which I reflected on the book's main substances by discussing South Korea's compressed modernity, both as achievement and risk. El

Mostafa Rezrazi at the Academy kindly arranged my visit and even offered to publish an Arabic version of this book.

These activities and relationships have resulted in numerous publications, some of which are partially incorporated in the current book after revision and updating as follows: Chapter 2 draws on a few sections of my chapter, "Compressed Modernity in South Korea: Constitutive Dimensions, Historical Conditions, and Systemic Mechanisms" in *The Routledge Handbook of Korean Culture and Society: A Global Approach*, edited by Youna Kim, Routledge (2016). Chapter 3 is revised and updated from parts of my article "The Second Modern Condition? Compressed Modernity as Internalized Reflexive Cosmopolitisation" in the *British Journal of Sociology*, volume 61, number 3 (2010). Chapter 5 is revised and updated from parts of my chapter, "Transformative Modernity and Citizenship Politics: The South Korean Aperture" in *South Korea in Transition: Politics and Culture of Citizenship*, edited by Chang Kyung-Sup, Routledge (2014). Chapter 9 draws on a few sections of my article, "From Developmental to Post-Developmental Demographic Changes: A Perspectival Recount on South Korea" in the *Korean Journal of Sociology*, volume 49, number 6 (2015).

Given the abundant scholarly cooperation, interests, and assistance offered by so many supportive colleagues and institutions from across the world, I am deeply concerned about whether the quality of this arduously completed, though long overdue, book is meaningfully satisfactory to them. In a sense, all such scholarly interactions themselves have been a huge blessing to me, so I feel already rewarded much more than I deserve. The only excuse I can make now is that I am determined to work further on all remaining limits and defects. Since I am also preparing a companion book on "The Risk of Compressed Modernity," I hope this could help make up for the existing shortcomings of the current book.

Finally, I wish to express my sincere gratitude for devoted research assistance by Xu Xuehua and Kim Hee Yun at Seoul National University, and also for considerate and careful editorial support by Susan Beer, Julia Davies, and many other staff at Polity Press.

The research and writing for this book have been supported by the National Research Foundation of Korea Grant (NRF-2013S1A6A4016337). Also, Hanmaeum International Medical Foundation kindly offered a generous financial support to help cover some publishing expenses of this book.

Part I

Compressed Modernity in Perspective

— 1 —

INTRODUCTION

Purpose, Debates, and Subjects

1.1 Purpose

South Korean society is marked by quite a curious mix of extreme social traits and tendencies.[1] With a per capita GDP of more than thirty thousand U.S. dollars, many of the world's leading industries, and the world's highest level of tertiary education completion, South Koreans may certainly boast, to both foreigners and themselves, of their "miracle" economic and social achievements, which were built upon the debris from a total civil war, besides decades of colonial exploitation. By contrast, a long series of social problems at internationally scandalous levels keep afflicting and embarrassing South Koreans, such as household indebtedness, elderly poverty, suicide, and even tuberculosis infection at some of the worst levels among all industrialized nations. On the other hand, South Korean workers still work more than two thousand hours annually along with just a few other countries, South Korean students study far more hours than all their foreign counterparts in the world, and South Korean elderly keep extending their laboring years beyond any known level in the world. Demographically, South Korea's fertility, which is at the world's lowest level (e.g. a total fertility rate of 0.84 in 2020), and its life expectancy, which is rising at the world's fastest pace, are predicted to make its population to age more rapidly than that of any other society.[2] What I have viewed for many years as the country's *compressed modernity* is full of extreme social traits and tendencies that often appear mutually contradictory. Given contemporary South Korea's seemingly incomparable intensities, velocities, complexities, and contradictions in all aspects of social order and personal life, it is hard to imagine that this society

3

used to be called a "hermit kingdom" after it was first exposed to Westerners.

How can social sciences deal with this miraculous yet simultaneously obstinate and hystericalized society? South Korea's global prominence in developmental, sociopolitical, and cultural affairs has not only impressed overseas media and public but also motivated numerous internationally respectable scholars to analyze its experiences as a potential basis of new patterns or possibilities in postcolonial modernization and development.[3] Despite their persuasive accounts of diverse aspects of South Korean modernity, its general social scientific implications and influences have been relatively limited. Their findings and interpretations, despite various substantive contributions, have failed to develop into an inclusive disciplinary paradigm. This is not necessarily because South Korean experiences have been largely idiosyncratic and thus difficult to apply to other societies and/or to distill generalizable theoretical implications. Some of them have scientifically constrained themselves by attempting to explain South Korea's performances in modernization and development according to somewhat ideologically or normatively fused perspectives, respectively underlining Confucian values, colonial modernization, state interventionism, global liberal order, and so on. More crucially, most of them have failed to predict repeatedly degenerative tendencies in South Korea's industrial capitalism, democracy, grassroots livelihood, and even demographic reproduction. Their scientific and intellectual influence has fluctuated in accordance with South Korea's built-in instabilities in nearly all domains.

More conventional social sciences, whether at the international or domestic level, do not appear to have been more successful in systematically and effectively elucidating what genuinely constitutes universally appreciable Koreanness. In the so-called mainstream social sciences in Europe and North America, South Korea has largely been subjected to disciplinary indifference, if not ignorance. Paradoxically, South Korean universities have mostly relied on such lines of social sciences for education and even research. Social sciences in general have been imported from the West (especially, the United States) mainly through South Korean PhDs from major Western universities and dispatched to South Korean realities throughout the post-liberation era (Kim, J. 2015). Educational institutional modernization has thereby been achieved quite rapidly and even intensely, but their scientific contributions in systematically probing and theorizing South Korean realities have remained largely ambiguous (Park and Chang 1999). In certain disciplines, there is even a tendency for internationally established scholars to avoid South Korea as their research subject. Borrowed Western social sciences in the South Korean context, no matter how much adapted locally, have critically added to the complicated nature of South Korean modernity by inundating this society with hasty speculative prescriptions under the assumption of Westernization-as-modernization. Many domestically trained scholars have responded to this dilemma by proposing the construction of "indigenous social sciences" or "Korean-style social sciences."[4] However, South Korean society's distinctiveness since the last century seems to have consisted much more critically in its explosive and complex digestion (and indigestion) of Western modernity than in some isolated characteristics inherited from its own past.

In a stark contrast to the virtually *intended inefficacy* of conventional social sciences in analyzing South Korean realities, there are abundant cultural creations and productions that have most brilliantly captured and processed them into quite meaningful forms of aesthetic and intellectual experiences. In particular, many of South Korea's films, television dramas, novels, and various performing arts have quite admirably articulated what its people and society have gone through in the endlessly turbulent but frequently spectacular moments of its modern history. Their skillful mastery of South Korea's social realities and experiences often enjoys such praises from media and expert critics as would elicit strong jealousy from academic social scientists.[5] After all, their social appeal has been proved globally – that is, not only in South Korea but also nearly across the world – in terms of show attendance sizes, television viewer rates, numbers of film seers, digits of webpage visitors, and magnitudes of SNS followers that may have been even unthinkable before. Such global popularity of South Korea's cultural productions has necessitated a special term for symbolically denoting their Koreanness, namely, "the Korean wave" (*hallyu*). Given that most of the Korean wave productions substantively reflect South Korean realities and experiences, their global popularities attest to a sort of transnationalized (aesthetic) reflection on common or diverse conditions of human life and society in reference to the South Korean context.[6] This trend was epitomized by the Oscar-awarded movie, *Parasite*, which masterfully narrates underclass South Koreans' struggle in everyday realities of (what I analyze in this book as) compressed modernity and has thereby elicited fervent viewer reactions across the world.

On my part, since the early 1990s, I have tried to show what I holistically conceptualize and theorize as compressed modernity can help to construe, on the one hand, the extreme changes, rigidities, complexities, intensities, and imbalances in South Korean life and, on the other hand, analyze interrelationships among such traits and components. Fortunately, this line of effort has been significantly validated by the pluralist turn in international scholarship on modernity and coloniality (Eisenstadt 2000) and by many scholars' constructive reactions to my work on compressed modernity in studying South Korea and other Asian societies in particular. The research topics and focus areas of such studies include: family relations and individualization in East Asia (e.g. Ochiai 2011; Lan, P. 2014, 2016; Hao, L. 2013; Jackson 2015); life world and life histories in Korean modernity (e.g. Yi et al. 2017); care system and social policy in East Asia (e.g. Shibata 2009, 2010; Ochiai 2014); sociopolitical structure of risk and disaster in South Korea (e.g. Suh and Kim, eds. 2017); all genres of "the Korean wave" (e.g. Martin-Jones 2007; Paik, P. 2012; Keblinska 2017; Lee, K. 2004; Abelmann 2003; Jang and Kim 2013; Regatieri 2017; Kim, H. 2018); Asian modernity and development in general (e.g. Kang, M. 2011; Yui 2012; Yi, J. 2015); and so forth. Most recently, some scholars both in China and overseas have analyzed post-Mao China as an instance of post-socialist compressed modernity (e.g. Wang, Z. 2015; Zhang, L. 2013; Xu and Wu 2016).[7]

Many of these studies have utilized the concept of compressed modernity, despite its theoretical vagueness and substantive openness, as a heuristic theoretical and/or analytical tool for organizing and interpreting their empirical findings. Perhaps the utility of compressed modernity consists more in its broad intermediary function between researchers and realities than any theoretically specific explanatory function. For the reason explained just above, the theoretical and/or analytical adoption of compressed modernity in comparative cultural studies that attempt to decipher the Korean wave's social substances and messages is quite an interesting development. Compressed modernity in South Korean realities and experiences may have been crucially perceived, whether consciously or unconsciously, by cultural producers as a heuristic clue to the main conditions and characteristics of contemporary South Korean society.

In my work on South Korean/East Asian compressed modernity, I have quite actively incorporated international scholarship on comparative modernities as broadly defined (to include postcolonialism and postmodernism). This is of course to draw critical insights from the world's authoritative analysts and writers on the globally fundamental yet contentious issues of modernity and its various reconstructive and degenerative tendencies. At the same time, I have been keen to explore potential contributory possibilities in the

6

global debates on comparative modernities on the basis of Korean/ Asian experiences. These motivations have materialized into close discussions and collaborations with numerous distinct scholars on their key work as follows: Ulrich Beck (reflexive modernization and cosmopolitization), Göran Therborn (entangled modernities), Bryan S. Turner (citizenship as contributory rights), Hubert Knoblauch (refiguration), Emiko Ochiai (compressed demographic transitions in Asia), Laurence Roulleau-Berger (post-Western social sciences), Stevi Jackson (gender in East Asia), Nancy Abelmann (family and mobility in South Korea), Seung-Sook Moon (mobilizational citizenship in South Korea), Hagen Koo (class formation in South Korea), Chua Beng Huat ("pop culture" in Asia, the Korean wave), as well as many of South Korea's key experts.

Critically building upon these earlier efforts, I intend to present a new book on compressed modernity, in which I present a more formalized explanation of compressed modernity in the South Korean and comparative contexts, and elucidate a special set of topics on South Korea's compressed modernity as its essential systemic properties. More specifically, I hope to elaborate on the definitional and structural constitution of compressed modernity and discuss some of the most essential systemic properties of compressed modernity as manifested in the South Korean context. The primary purpose of the book is to provide a sort of soft treatise on compressed modernity as a generic category of modernity in the modern world history. On the other hand, various systemic properties of compressed modernity will be presented in analytical narrative built upon a wide range of empirical observations, both by myself and in literature. I hope the definitional and inclusive nature of the current book will be found useful by a wide range of international scholars interested or engaged in the issues of comparative modernities, social structure and change in South Korea/East Asia, citizenship of South Koreans/East Asians, Asian popular culture, Asians' family life and personhood, comparative social policy and care system, and so forth.

1.2 Compressed Modernity in Critical Modernity Debates

Compressed modernity is a critical theory of postcolonial social change, aspiring to join and learn from the main self-critical intellectual reactions since the late twentieth century as to complex and murky social realities in the late modern world. Such intellectual reactions include postmodernism (Lyotard 1984, etc.), postcolonialism

7

(Chakrabarty 2000; Ashcroft, Griffiths, and Tiffin 2002, etc.), reflexive modernization (Beck, Giddens, and Lash 1994, etc.), and multiple modernities (Eisenstadt 2000, etc.). Postmodernism forcefully argues that modernity has exhausted or abused its progressive potential, if any, only to spawn deleterious conditions and tendencies for humanity and its civilizational and ecological basis. Postcolonialism cogently reveals that postcolonial modernization and development have been far from a genuinely liberating process due to the chronic (re)manifestation of colonial and neocolonial patterns of social relations and cognitive practices in the supposedly liberated Third World. Reflexive modernization in late modern reality, as argued by Beck and Giddens, is a structurally complicated process of social change under the uncontrollable floods of choices that expose modern society and people to more risks than opportunities. The multiple modernities thesis emphasizes a comparative civilizational perspective that helps to recognize variegated possibilities and forms of modernities in the diverse historical and structural contexts for nation-making or national revival. As directly indicated or indirectly alluded to in various parts of this chapter, all of these critical debates on modernity have essential implications for the compressed modernity thesis.

The problem of time–space condensation here was presented as a core subject in David Harvey's (1980) seminal discussion of Western modernism and postmodernism. In essence, according to Harvey, the accumulation crisis of capitalism and the effort to overcome it led to the expansion of controllable space and the generalization of mechanical time, which ultimately engendered time–space condensation (or, in Harvey's wording, "time–space compression") *on the global scale*. In this regard, Harvey argues, there are fundamental similarities in the objects that modernism and postmodernism respectively try to explain and overcome. While his emphasis on "the annihilation of space through time" and "the spatialization of time" involves the complex functional interrelationships between time and space (Harvey 1980: 270), it by and large focuses on what I present here as *time–space condensation*. As compared to Harvey's view that time–space condensation (on the global scale) accompanies the accumulation crisis of capitalism at each stage and the aggressive effort to overcome it, the time–space condensation and compression in compressed modernity at national and other levels involve much more diverse historical backgrounds, factors, and initiators.[8]

In addition, the phenomena argued by main theorists of postcolonialism (such as cultural "hybridity," "syncrecity," etc.) can also be included in time–space compression (Ashcroft, Griffiths, and Tiffin

2002).[9] If this literary criticism-derived theory is extended to cover social phenomena in general, most authors of postcolonialism seem to acknowledge the status of politically liberated Third World grassroots and intellectuals as concrete historical and social subjects, but still think that their spiritual, material, and institutional lives have not fundamentally overcome colonial and/or neocolonial (Western) cultures and values, but have combined the latter with indigenous elements in diverse ways.[10] It is true that postcolonial culture can be both "oppositional" and "complicit" with regard to (neo)colonial order and that, in the former case, colonial (Western) cultures and values, if any, may be conceived as something to be criticized and overcome. Similarly, in the specific aspects of time–space compression in this study, the process by which various cultures and institutions positioned at dissimilar points of the two axes of time and space interact and intermingle is open to a possibility of being dictated by the ideology, value, and will of many people as concrete historical and social subjects. It needs to be pointed out, however, that the breadth of cultures and institutions that are subject to compression here is much wider than that suggested by postcolonialism so as to include even postmodern and global elements. It also needs to be pointed out that the facets of compression here are not limited to hybridity or syncrecity but involve competition, collision, disjointing, articulation, compounding, and so forth.

The diverse dimensions of compressed modernity are emergent patterns of social structure and change that can be analyzed only in concrete historical and societal contexts. Therefore, the formation and transformation of compressed modernity in any nation need to be explained under a systematic and comprehensive examination of its global historical and structural conditions. In so doing, Therborn's thesis of "entangled modernities" offers a highly useful hint at the social and institutional outcomes of complex interactions and interrelations between international and local agencies of modernity. According to Therborn (2003: 295), "[b]ecause of its modes of historical generation, modernity has to be seen as a global phenomenon" ... and requires a "global approach ... focusing on global variability, global connectivity, and global inter-communication." Therborn (2003: 295) goes on to point out two "general processes of the making of modernity," namely, "the constitutive entanglements of modernity and some tradition, coming out of the infinitely variable incompleteness of every modern rupture with the past, and out of the plasticity of most traditions" and "the geo-historical entanglements, of the very different but significantly interacting and mutually

9

influencing sociopolitical roads to and through modernity." Many nations' global historical and structural conditions of modernization clearly demonstrate that geo-historical entanglements – and sometimes modernity-tradition entanglements as well – tend frequently or chronically to induce a compressed nature in the thereby generated modernities. While Therborn's (2003) thesis on "entangled modernities" is a crucial epistemological progress, it should be carefully complemented by astute attention to the importance of concrete historical agencies (as opposed to abstract structural conditions) in analyzing wide varieties of political, sociocultural, and economic transformations under the global order of modernity. This theoretical-cum-empirical necessity is most persuasively argued in Bruno Latour's (2005) "practical metaphysics" about inexhaustibly diverse ontological manifestations of values, purposes, and resources in the (debatably) modern world. Postcolonial entanglement of modernities, in all instances, has involved critical human and institutional agencies that have, often self-consciously but not always successfully, conveyed, accommodated, abused, modified, intensified, and/or resisted such global structural relations. This should be understood as a crucial part of what John Urry (2003) analyzed as "global complexity."

This has been the case even when entanglements have involved fundamental civilizational or systemic discontinuities as suggested by Ulrich Beck (Beck and Grande 2010) and Anthony Giddens (1990). Giddens emphasizes the qualitatively distinctive nature of modern social institutions (as opposed to traditional social orders), whereas Beck highlights the discrete characteristics of late or "second" modernity" (as opposed to early or "first" modernity). To the extent that South Koreans, among others, have incorporated West-originated modern social institutions into their local life, the *discontinuitist* interpretation recommended by Giddens and Beck will be methodologically and theoretically indispensable. However, a more critical utility of the discontinuitist approach consists in the very fact that various versions of *Western* modernity have arrived in South Korea or elsewhere mainly through political coercions and decisions (that is, as direct effects of international power relations) rather than as evolutionary adaptations. When West-originated social institutions, values, and goals are attained in condensed manners, or when they are compressively compounded with traditional and indigenous elements, their discontinuous – or, more correctly, dissimilar – nature in the South Korean or other context cannot but be responsible for social confusion, conflict, and alienation. Paradoxically, it is also

10

true that such discontinuous nature can become useful for inducing, suppressing, or even deceiving potentially resistant local subjects and interests in strategically determined directions of social change. Abrupt institutional (or ideological) replacement is sometimes much more feasible than gradual institutional (or ideological) reform because local resistance is epistemologically and/or socioecologically more difficult in the former situation.

While the condensed and compressive nature of South Korean or other modernity has been induced and intensified by their particular historical and structural conditions, it needs to be pointed out that modernity in general has an intrinsic dynamism. Giddens (1990: 16–17) indicates three main conditions for such dynamism of modernity: namely, "the separation of time and space and their recombination in forms which permit the precise time–space 'zoning' of social life; the disembedding of social systems . . .; and the reflexive ordering and reordering of social relations in the light of continual inputs of knowledge affecting the actions of individuals and groups." These complex conditions cannot be reproduced identically in every society, but it is safe to say that they are thoroughly relevant in the South Korean context as well. In fact, such conditions seem to have been intensified due to the transnational superimposition of modernity in South Korea under Japanese domination and American influence and, more critically, due to the South Koreans' own drive for dependent modernization and globalization. Beck (Beck and Grande 2010) presents "second modernity" as a critical alternative to postmodernity, arguing that various (mostly negative) "side-effects" of first or classic modernity add up to a qualitatively different situation in which the fundamental values of classic modernity are still respected, but have to be pursued with radically different social means and institutions under a cosmopolitan paradigm. Beck disputes "methodological nationalism" in social theory and analysis and instead advocates "methodological cosmopolitanism." In a sense, compressed modernity is already based upon methodological cosmopolitanism since it directly acknowledges and reflects global processes and structures by which the nature of modernity in late-modernizing societies is critically determined. Therborn (2003) also shares this globalist conception of all modernities.

As discussed in detail later in Chapters 2 and 4, the multiple modernities thesis (Eisenstadt 2000) can be extended to the internal multiplicity of modernities across varying units or agencies of modernity in each national society such as individuals, families, secondary organizations, localities, as well as societal units. Such internal multiplicity on the one hand reflects the varying complexities of time–space (era–place) compression across different units of (compressed) modernity and, on the other hand, induces national modernity to take on an inherently complicated nature. Besides, the emphasis of Therborn's (2003) entangled modernities thesis on "not just the co-existence of different modernities but also their interrelations" is directly relevant for the inter-unit interactive variability of (compressed) modernities discussed here. The authoritarian attribute of many postcolonial states in leading dependent modernization as often induces or intensifies this internal multiplicity of modernities as reduces or integrates it (see Chapter 4 in this book). The recent globalization trend, despite its dominant neoliberal impetus, tends to necessitate subnational (and supranational) units to intensify their separate efforts and independent functions for actively coping with the floods of new risks and opportunities in the global age and thereby reinforce their status as units of compressed modernity (Chang, K. 2016a).

1.3 Subjects

This book consists of three parts, respectively entitled: "Part I. Compressed Modernity in Perspective"; "Part II. Structural Properties of Compressed Modernity"; and "Part III. After Compressed Modernity." Part I offers, besides the current introduction chapter, two chapters that respectively explain the definitional and universal aspects of compressed modernity. Part II includes six chapters that respectively deal with the internal multiplicity of modernities, the particular mode of citizenship under compressed modernity, the complexity of the cultural configuration of compressed modernity, the productionist bias and reproductive crisis in development, the social institutional deficits and infrastructural familialism, and the demographic configuration of compressed modernity. Part III concludes the current book with a chapter discussing South Korea's post-compressed modern condition loaded with the dual burdens arising from, on the one hand, the earlier risky schemes of compressed modernization and development and, on the other hand, the common dilemmas accompanying social and economic maturation (or saturation). Although these diverse topics already constitute a sizable monograph, there are numerous other theoretical and empirical issues that need to be covered in order to provide a reasonably self-contained scientific account of compressed modernity. Nonetheless, this book is presented as a tentative general treatise on compressed modernity. Each of the above-mentioned chapters is briefly summarized as follows.

In Chapter 2, "Compressed Modernity: Constitutive Dimensions and Manifesting Units," I intend to present a formal definition and core theoretical/historical components of compressed modernity. Compressed modernity consists of multiple dimensions constructed by all possible combinations of temporal (historical) and spatial (civilizational) manifestations of human social activities, relationships, and assets – namely, temporal condensation of historical change, spatial condensation of civilizational compass, compressed mixing of diverse temporalities (eras), compressed mixing of diverse spaces (civilizations), and interactions among the above. Compressed modernity can be manifested at various levels of human existence and experience – that is, personhood, family, secondary organizations, urban/rural localities, societal units (including civil society, nation, etc.), and, not least importantly, the global society. At each of these levels, people's lives need to be managed intensely, intricately, and flexibly in order to remain normally integrated with the rest of society. Compressed modernity is a critical theory of postcolonial social change, aspiring to join and learn from the main self-critical intellectual reactions of the late twentieth century as to complex and murky social realities in the late modern world, including postmodernism, postcolonialism, reflexive modernization, and multiple modernities.

In today's rapidly and intricately globalizing world, as shown in Chapter 3, "Compressed Modernity in the Universalist Perspective," the driving forces of radical scientific-technical-cultural inputs and monopolistic political economic interests operate across national boundaries without serious obstacles. The liberal system transition of former state-socialist countries has intensified the globalizing nature of such inputs and interests. However, the ecological, material, and sociocultural risks accompanying the latest capitalist offense are not unidirectional (from developed to less developed nations) any more. Even developed nations cannot pass up the cosmopolit(an)ized hazards and pressures generated in the very process of their global economic and political domination over less developed nations. Managing these challenges, as well as exploiting the associated opportunities, by individual nations implies that internalization of cosmopolit(an)ized reflexivity takes place both in developed and less developed (capitalist and post-socialist) nations. Through this process, societies (or their civilizational conditions) are being internalized into each other, thereby making compressed modernity become a universal feature of national societies in the late modern world. In fact, the same is also true of individual communities, organizations, families, and persons.

As explained in Chapter 4, "Internal Multiple Modernities: South Korea as Multiplex Theatre Society," modernity – and the process of modernization – can be plural not only across different national societies, as persuasively indicated in Eisenstadt's "multiple modernities" thesis, but also within each national society. Korea has been particularly distinct in such internal multiplicity of modernities, including colonial dialectical modernity, postcolonial reflexive institutional(ist) modernization, postcolonial neotraditionalist modernity, free world modernity under the Cold War, state-capitalist modernity, cosmopolitan modernity under neoliberal economic globalism, and associative subaltern liberal modernity. These internally diverse modernities reflect a series of overpowering international influences and related local upheavals and confrontations to which Korean society and its people have been subjected since the late nineteenth century. Each of these modernities is not uniquely or exclusively Korean because they have been embedded in the global structures and processes of modern social change. Nevertheless, South Korea is certainly remarkable in the volume of multiplicities of modernities, the dramatic and intense realization of each modernity, the protracted operation of each modernity, and the extremely complex interactions among such multiple modernities. With all such impetuses and forms of modernities permanently extending their lifespan as variously embodied in the identites and interests of different generations, genders, classes, sectors, and/or regions, South Korea has been socially configured and reconfigured as a *multiplex theater society* in which all possible claims of modernities are aggressively and loudly staged side by side and/or one after another, however, without a clear clue to civilizational or sociopolitical reconciliation among them.

As detailed in Chapter 5, "Transformative Contributory Rights: Citizen(ship) in Compressed Modernity," the life histories of most South Koreans since the mid twentieth century have been replete with dramatic institutional, developmental, sociopolitical, and ethnonational transformations and crises through which their nation and society have emerged with fully blown (compressed) modernity. In each of these drastic and fundamental transitions, South Koreans have had to confront not only the difficulties inherent in such radical transitions but, more critically, the troubles ensuing from the crude institutional conditions for managing them. While both

14

the state and civil society were unstable, with their own survival remaining in question, the internal conditions and international environments required them to embark on, among other changes, rapid institutional and techno-scientific modernization and aggressive economic development. In fact, such transformations were often pursued in order to strategically trounce the sociopolitical dilemmas stemming from the inchoate, dependent, and even illegitimate nature of the state machinery and dominant social order. There have arisen *transformation-oriented state, society, and population for which each transformation becomes an ultimate purpose in itself, the processes and means of the transformations constitute the main sociopolitical order, and the transformation-embedded interests form the core social identity.* In this milieu, a distinct mode of citizenship has been engendered in terms of *transformative contributory rights.* Citizenship as transformative contributory rights can be defined as *effective and/or legitimate claims to national and social resources, opportunities, and/or respects that accrue to each citizen's contributions to the nation's or society's transformative purposes.* As South Korea has been aggressively and precipitously engaged in institutional and techno-scientific modernization, economic development, political democratization, economic and sociocultural globalization, and, mostly recently, ethnonational reformation, its citizens have been exhorted or have exhorted themselves to engage intensely in each of these transformations, and their citizenship, constituted by identities, duties, and rights, have been very much framed and substantiated by the conditions, processes, and outcomes of such transformative engagements.

As explained in Chapter 6, "Complex-Culturalism vs. Multiculturalism," the literally explosive growth of transnational marriages between Korean men and mostly Asian women from the beginning years of the twenty-first century seemingly signals that South Korea has entered a genuinely new epoch of cosmopolitan existence and change. This unprecedented phenomenon has drastically reconfigured diverse corners and peripheries of South Korea into manifestly multi-ethnic entities. The national and local governments have been quick in initiating a comprehensive policy of "multicultural family support," whereas various civil groups, media, and even business corporations have echoed the governmental drive with their own multiculturalism initiatives. On the other hand, as agencies of what I define here as *complex culturalism*, South Korean institutions and citizens have instrumentally, selectively, and flexibly incorporated into themselves various historical and civilizational sources of culture

15

in order to expediently consolidate the postcolonial sociopolitical order and then to maximize socioeconomic development. In this vein, neither the legal acceptance and physical integration of rapidly increasing numbers of foreign brides into South Korean society, nor the accompanying governmental and civil drive for multiculturalism, implies that this society used to be culturally isolated, or that it only now wishes to convert into a multicultural or cosmopolitan entity. The mass presence of "multicultural brides" seems to have further reinforced complex culturalism by enabling South Korean citizens and institutions to conveniently interpret that their open accommodation and active support for the marriage migrants help make their cultural complexity a more self-contained civilizational property. However, the more their multiculturalism as part of their self-centered globalism is framed through arbitrarily staged experiences, the more the Asian marriage migrants will remain differentiated, if not discriminated, from native Koreans. What remains to be seen is if these foreign brides would permanently be asked or forced to preserve and display their home-country cultural characteristics as an indispensable condition for native South Koreans' still elementary multicultural experiences and feelings.

In South Korea (and other East Asian societies), as indicated in Chapter 7, "Productive Maximization, Reproductive Meltdown," compressed modernity is to a critical extent the process and outcome of the developmental(ist) political economy that has been forcefully initiated from above (i.e. by the state), yet actively accommodated from below (i.e. by ordinary citizens). Modernity was conceived in a fundamentally developmentalist or productionist manner, so modernization principally became the politico-social project of achieving time-condensed economic development and thereby joining the world rank of "advanced nations." Such purposeful approach to modernity in terms of condensed national development has been substantiated by various policies, actions, and attitudes that are designed to maximize economic production and, not coincidentally, to systematically sacrifice the conditions and resources of social reproduction. After decades of successful economic development, such asymmetrical approach to production and reproduction seems to have critically lost its instrumentality. In spite of their enviable façade, covered with hyper-advanced industries, physical infrastructures, services, and lifestyles, the civilizational and even economic progress of South Korean society is now crucially impeded by the disenfranchisement and demise of those classes, generations, communities, cultures, and wisdoms that have been treated practically as *disposables*, unworthy of social reproduction support, under the narrowly focused developmental political economy.

In a fundamentally family-dependent way, as emphasized in Chapter 8, "Social Institutional Deficits and Infrastructural Familialism," South Koreans have managed their modern history and made various internationally envious achievements. The compressed nature of their modernity is structurally enmeshed with various social infrastructural utilities of families. This feature of South Korean society has been derived not just from its traditional – say, neo-Confucian – heritage of family-centered life but, more critically, from the processes and manners by which South Koreans have coped with various modern sociocultural, political, and economic forces. Even after the state managed effectively to govern national economic development and social institutional modernization, South Koreans' reliance on familial norms, relations, and resources have remained unabated. In fact, the familialized nature of South Korean modernity has kept intensifying, albeit in continually refashioning modes, as the state and its allied social actors have found and consciously tapped various strategic utilities from ordinary people's eager effort to sustain their family-centered/devoted lives. This has been evident concerning nearly all major features and conditions of South Korean development and modernization, such as early Lewisian industrialization based upon stable supplies of rural migrant labor, universalization of high-level public education enabling constant improvements in human capital, and sustained common ethic for familial support and care buffering chronically defective public welfare. The state's own practically driven familialist stance is not reducible to sheer private family values, but represents a distinct line of technocratic deliberation, conceptualized here as *infrastructural familialism*. Conversely, the state's such utilitarian familialism has made individual citizens realize that their developmental and sociopolitical participation in national life is systematically facilitated through familial allegiance and cooperation. Infrastructural familialism has been upheld both from above and from below.

Since the early 1960s, as detailed in Chapter 9, "The Demographic Configuration of Compressed Modernity," South Korea has undergone extremely rapid and fundamental transformation in both demographic and developmental dimensions. The rates of migration/urbanization, fertility, and mortality all kept changing at such unprecedented and incomparable paces that also characterized those of economic growth, industrialization, proletarianization (occupational change from agricultural to industrial sectors), and so forth. This

17

dual transformation was no coincidence, as the country's developmental experiences directly involved critical demographic conditions, processes, and consequences. South Korean development, though dominated by state-business network, relied on human resources in extraordinary scopes and degrees; whereas South Korean citizens – quite often through demographically flexible familial endeavors – rendered their human resources a strategic platform for active developmental participation and gain. Conversely, South Korea's recent economic crisis and restructuring – namely, its post-developmental transition – have both required and caused drastic reformulation of human resources, family relations, and reproductive behaviors, so that earlier demographic trends have been further accelerated in some aspects (e.g. fertility, population aging, etc.) and suddenly slowed down or reversed in other aspects (e.g. natal sex imbalances, divorce, suicide, etc.). Through half a century of radical sociodemographic changes, the country has dramatically turned from a society known for very high fertility, universal marriage, rare divorce, etc., into one of "lowest-low" fertility, widespread singlehood, rampant divorce, etc. As these demographic transformations tend to fundamentally undermine the hitherto taken-for-granted material and cultural conditions for socioeconomic sustainability, the country has aggressively explored strategic measures for reversing or relieving demographic deficits and imbalances.

As pointed out in Chapter 10, "The Post-Compressed Modern Condition," South Korea's "miraculous" achievement of modernization and development has not exempted the country from what Ulrich Beck explained as the risks of "second modernity" – namely, the inherent dysfunctions and increasing failures of modern institutions such as capitalist industry, labor market, education system, science and technology, national government, middle-class family, and so forth. While these onerous risks are only now recognized, South Koreans are struggling with additional predicaments derived from the particular measures and processes of their compressed modernization and development. Conversely, at the very historical moment that South Korean society should embark on fundamentally redressing the costs of such risky measures of compressed social and economic transformations, its people are confronted with the globally common prices to be paid at the supposedly mature stage of development and modernization. This is South Korea's *post-compressed modern* condition, which appears no less challenging than its immediate post-colonial condition plagued with poverty and hunger, political rifts, and social conflicts and dislocations.

18

— 2 —

COMPRESSED MODERNITY

Constitutive Dimensions and Manifesting Units

2.1 Introduction

In a globally grounded comparative modernity approach, this chapter presents the formal definition, core theoretical components, and historical conditions of compressed modernity. This approach draws insights from various critical debates on complex and murky social realities in the late modern world, including postmodernism (e.g. Lyotard 1984), postcolonialism (e.g. Chakrabarty 2000), reflexive modernization (Beck, Giddens, and Lash 1994), and multiple and entangled modernities (Eisenstadt 2000; Therborn 2003). As broadly examined in the previous chapter, all of these critical debates on modernity have essential implications for the compressed modernity thesis. Compressed modernity is a critical theory of postcolonial social change, aspiring to join and learn from these critical intellectual reactions to modernity and its degenerative variations.

Compressed modernity is *a civilizational condition in which economic, political, social and/or cultural changes occur in an extremely condensed manner with regard to both time and space, and in which the dynamic coexistence of mutually disparate historical and social elements leads to the construction and reconstruction of a highly complex and fluid social system* (Chang, K. 2017a). Compressed modernity, as detailed subsequently, can be manifested at various levels of human existence and experience – that is, personhood, family, secondary organizations, urban/rural localities, societal units (including civil society, nation, etc.), and, not least importantly, the global society. At each of these levels, people's lives need to be managed intensely, intricately, and flexibly in order to remain normally integrated with the rest of society.

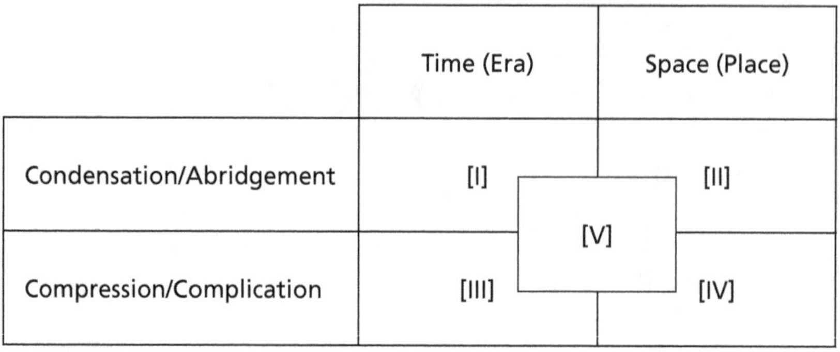

	Time (Era)	Space (Place)
Condensation/Abridgement	[I]	[II]
	[V]	
Compression/Complication	[III]	[IV]

Figure 2.1 The five constitutive dimensions of compressed modernity

Figure 2.1 shows that compressed modernity is composed of five specific dimensions that are constituted interactively by the two axes of time/space and condensation/compression. The time facet includes both physical time (point, sequence, and amount of time) and historical time (era, epoch, and phase). The space facet includes physical space (location and area) and cultural space (place and region). As compared to physically standardized abstract time–space, era–place serves as a concrete framework for constructing and/or accommodating an actually existing civilization.[1] Condensation/Abridgement refers to the phenomenon that the physical process required for the movement or change between two time points (eras) or between two locations (places) is abridged or compacted (Dimensions [I] and [II] respectively). Compression/Complication refers to the phenomenon that diverse components of multiple civilizations that have existed in different eras and/or places coexist in a certain delimited time–space and influence and change each other (Dimensions [III] and [IV] respectively). The phenomena generated in these four dimensions, in turn, interact with each other in complicated ways and further generate different social phenomena (Dimension [V]).

The above schema of differentiating time and space and separating condensation and compression needs a logical justification. In a non-Western historical/social context in which Western modernity is conceived as the core source of civilizational as well as politico-military superiority, the West stands not only as a discrete region but also as a discrete (but prospectively own) moment of history. Where indigenously conscious efforts for civilizational rebirth are defeated by external forces or frustrated internally, the West often becomes both a direction for historical change (modernization) and a contemporaneous source of inter-civilizational remaking (Westernization in

20

practice). The more condensed these changes become – that is, the faster modernization proceeds and the fuller Westernization takes place – the more successful the concerned countries tend to be considered (in spite of cultural and emotional irritations as well as political and economic sacrifices experienced by various indigenous groups). However, the very processes of modernization and Westernization endemically induce the cultural and political backlashes on the part of the adversely affected groups and, in frequent cases, systematically reinforce the traditional/indigenous civilizational constituents as these are deemed ironically useful for a strategic management of modernization and Westernization. Thereby compression becomes inevitable among various discrete temporal and regional civilizational constituents.

2.2 Constitutive Dimensions

The five dimensions of compressed modernity (in Figure 2.1) can be explained in terms of South Korean experiences in the following way. Time(era) condensation/abridgement (Dimension I) can be exemplified by the case that South Koreans have abridged the duration taken for their transition from low-income agricultural economy to advanced industrial economy on the basis of explosively rapid economic development. The rapid changes so often discussed in connection with South Korea – such as the "compressed growth" of the economy and the "compressed modernization" of society – belong to this dimension. (That is, compressed modernization is a component of compressed modernity.) Such compressed (condensed) changes are also apparent in the cultural domain, so that even postindustrial and/or postmodern tendencies are observed in various sections of society. South Koreans' pride that they have supposedly achieved in merely over half a century such economic and social development as had been carried out over the course of two or three centuries by Westerners has been elevated to the level of the state. The South Korean government has been busy publishing numerous showy statistical compilations that document explosive economic, social, and cultural changes for the periods "after liberation," "after independence," and so forth (NSO 1996, 1998).

South Koreans' success in condensing historical processes, however, does not always reflect the outcome of voluntary efforts but, in numerous instances, has simply resulted from asymmetrical international relations in politico-military power and cultural influence.

For instance, no other factor was as crucial as the American military occupation during the post-liberation period for their overnight adoption of (Western-type) modern institutions in politics, economy, education, and so forth. Nowadays, even the postmodern culture has been instantly transposed onto South Koreans through internationally dependent media and commerce (Kang, M. 1999). Even in those areas in which voluntary efforts have been decisive, the targeted end results alone do not tell everything. For instance, if one drives between Seoul and Busan taking ten, five, or three hours respectively, the driver (and passengers) will feel differently about the trip in each case and the probability of experiencing accident and fatigue from driving cannot but differ as well. We should analyze South Koreans' experience of overspeeding for development by focusing on the very fact of their overspeeding.

Space (place) condensation/abridgement (Dimension II) can be exemplified by the fact that the successive domination of South Korea by various external forces in the last century compelled the country to change in diverse aspects, ranging from political institutions to mass culture, under the direct influence of other world regions (societies), no matter what geographic distances and differences existed. After South Koreans were physically subdued by colonial or imperial external forces, many ideologies, institutions, and technologies engendered in dissimilar regional contexts were coerced onto them directly – that is, omitting or compacting the usual geographic or spatial requirements for inter-civilizational exchange and accommodation. Such geographic omission or spatial compacting constituted an abridgement or dismantlement of space. In particular, the Korean urbanization in the periods of colonial rule and capitalist industrialization was respectively a deepening process of external institutional imitation and economic dependency, so that the modern cities thereby created through space abridgement turned out to be utterly alien spaces disengaged from the indigenous civilization of Korea. As another customary evidence of space abridgement, most universities located in major cities function as the comprehensive, shopping mall-like outposts of the Western civilization.

The space condensation realized by South Koreans' own will was accelerated in the 1990s under the full forces of informatization and globalization. Especially, the splendid development of the so-called ICT industry has placed South Korea at the rank of a very leader in informatization. Now, the abridgement or dismantlement of space by electronic communication mechanisms is a catchword for national development in the twenty-first century. With these changes combined,

South Korea – a society where until only a few decades ago overseas travel used to be a luxury experience for a privileged minority – has enabled its citizens to have quasi-travel experiences of foreign (mostly Western) spaces even without moving overseas physically.

Time (era) compression/complication (Dimension III) involves the phenomena of intense competition, collision, disjuncture, articulation, and compounding between (post)modern elements (which have been generated as a result of time (era) condensation/abridgement and traditional elements (which have been either left unattended or intentionally preserved or reinstated) within a compact sociohistorical context. These phenomena, often dubbed "the simultaneity of non-simultaneous matters," are usually observed in ideology, culture, and other non-material domains that have fairly complex conditions and processes of change.[2] Particularly on the Korean peninsula where no indigenous social revolution helped to eradicate the feudal social structure, colonization and capitalist industrialization fell short of thoroughly permeating or replacing traditional values and culture. Besides, South Koreans' rapidly extended life expectancy as a core facet of social development has elongated the lifespan of traditional values and culture along with that of the old generations who wish to maintain such values and culture.

Consequently, traditional, modern, and postmodern values and cultures have come to coexist so as to bring about inter-civilizational compression among dissimilar time zones. Such inter-temporal compression is also found in the economic arena where the strategy of inter-sectoral "unbalanced growth" led to the coexistence of rapidly growing modern manufacturing sectors (in which the state has favorably supported modern industrialists) and stagnant traditional agriculture (in which only archaic family farming has been allowed legally). As a result, the articulation between dissimilar systems of production representing dissimilar historical epochs has become a core trait of the modern economic order. The everyday life, not to mention the lifetime, of South Koreans who are confronted with the compression of various historical epochs is filled with ceaseless "time travels." This is perhaps the most crucial ingredient of the South Korean television dramas and movies that have fascinated so many Asian nations under the rubric of the "Korean wave" (hallyu).

Space (place) compression/complication (Dimension IV) concerns the phenomena of intense competition, collision, disjuncture, articulation, and compounding between foreign/multinational/global elements (which have been generated as a result of space (place) condensation/abridgement) and indigenous elements (which have been either left unattended or intentionally preserved or reinstated) within a compact sociohistorical context. As diverse social elements generated from different world-regional contexts coexist and function within a same time–space, a hierarchical structure of dependency or (neo)colonial domination between them often ramifies. In the cultural realm, what Edward Said (1978) criticized as the West's "Orientalism" has frequently been internalized in postcolonial societies under the "internal Orientalism" (Schein 1997) of modernization elites or other culturally dependent local interests. According to Michael Lipton (1977), a similar hierarchical order has been observed in the form of "urban bias" in many Third World countries, sacrificing native agriculture, peasants, and rural society unjustly or irrationally. Besides, the early modernization theory, which induced self-abasement on to indigenous societies and peoples, was warmly welcomed by South Korean elites even if it reflected an external political effort to propagate the supposed superiority of the Western civilization into the politically subjugated territories (Kim, J. 2015).

Such a historical atmosphere has been crucially responsible for the extremely antagonistic conflict between indigenous cultures and institutions and foreign ones as have been vividly illustrated in the sectors of cultural production and medicine in South Korea.[3] Chronic bitterness characterizes the atmosphere among scholars of humanities (Korean history, philosophy, literature, etc.), specialists in traditional music and dance, and practitioners of indigenous medicine when their professional counterparts of Western specialties dominate society. However, thanks to the very historical context that Korean society was appropriated as a colony of industrial capitalism by an external force (Japan) and that, even after independence, South Koreans were pressurized to accept the political and economic order of Western standards by another external force (the United States), the remaining indigenous culture has sometimes claimed a significant historical and existential legitimacy regardless of its practical utility. The duality of South Koreans who have trodden, in practice, a highly extroverted developmental path and still show no hint of shedding their unreserved (ethno)nationalist pretense presents an easy clue that the modernity they have pursued is chronically afflicted with space-wise compression of dissimilar civilizations.

The social phenomena and cultural elements generated in the above four dimensions of compressed modernity are often put in intense competition, collision, disjuncture, articulation, and compounding among themselves, so that still more types of social phenomena and cultural elements are engendered. These can be considered the fifth, or all-encompassing dimension of compressed modernity. In fact, most social phenomena and cultural elements in South Korea involve this dimension. Given that the co-existence of past, present, Asia (Korea), and the West is a rather common trait of social phenomena and cultural elements engendered under compressed modernity, every civilizational component must have come into existence through various processes of hybridization. If anyone who lives in this type of society fails to develop and maintain a fairly complex mindset for incorporating such complicated social phenomena and cultural elements, he/she has constantly to risk the possibility of becoming a social dropout.

While understanding and responding to social phenomena that arise through condensed time and space is already a formidable task, comprehending and coordinating the complex interaction of such abruptly new social phenomena with traditional and indigenous ones constitutes an even more challenging undertaking. Such difficulties are particularly manifest in the complexities of social values and ideology systems. Family, firm, university, civil society, and even government exist as panoramic displays of diverse values and ideologies. These institutions, in which the values and ideologies from past, present, Asia (Korea), and the West do not simply coexist but keep generating new elements through constant interactions with one another, are "too dynamic" and too complex.[4]

2.3 Manifesting Units

There are various different units/levels of manifestation of compressed modernity in South Korea and elsewhere. Societal units (nation, state, civil society, national economy), city and community, secondary organizations, family, and personhood are all observable units of compressed modernity. These plural units/levels can take on compressed modernity in highly diverse configurations, ramifying what may be called *internal multiple (compressed) modernities*. Also, the primacy of certain units/levels over other units/levels in manifesting a society's compressed modernity constitutes a critical structural characteristic of the concerned society. On the other hand, different units/levels can exert mutually escalating (or obstructive) effects in compressed modernity. Let us discuss this issue in the historical and social contexts of South Korea and/or East Asia.

Societal units Societal units are most commonly discussed in regard to compressed modernity in South Korea (and East Asia). Economic catching-up and swift social and political modernization have been common national agendas in postcolonial contexts. Indeed, condensed economic, social, and political changes have commonly been experienced under the rubric of national development or revitalization. The nation is to flourish through economic, political, and social modernization, but its historical foundations need to be constantly reaffirmed through traditional/indigenous values, symbols, and memories. Besides, whether successful or not in such courses of (West-oriented) modernization, traditional and/or indigenous components of social, economic, and political orders will not vanish overnight. In this context, compression of traditional/modern(/postmodern) and indigenous/Western(/global) components of social, economic, and political orders almost inevitably ensue. It should be noted that, because of the internationally dependent and politically selective process of liberation (Cumings 1981), South Korea's modernization as a postcolonial national(ist) project has been a historically contested affair to date between the state and civil society. A sort of domestic Cold War has led civil society to assume an independent or rival status in South Korea's otherwise state-centered modernization and to actively pursue various progressive agendas ranging from labor rights to ecological justice (Chang, K. 1999, 2012a).

Regional (urban and rural) places East Asian countries not only boast of many historic cities of traditional governance, culture, and commerce but also have undergone explosively rapid (or condensed) urbanization in the course of sequential industrializations (from Japan to Taiwan to North and South Korea to China). In mega-size urban places, dense blocks of modern (if not altogether Western) life are juxtaposed with museum-like pockets of traditional/indigenous culture and politics. Overnight creation of huge bed towns and industrial cities is all too usual; so is overnight spread of modern and/or Western lifestyles. On the other hand, refined versions of middle-class consciousness and/or neotraditional forms of authoritarian political rule often help to both resurrect traditional/indigenous facades and incorporate cosmopolitan values and desires in private and public life (despite radically fast urbanization) (Koo, H. 2016). Condensed urbanization and compressive urban life, however, do not themselves constitute an honorable civilizational alternative, so that constant reconstruction of urban spaces becomes a built-in feature of East Asian urbanism. Urbanism here is not only "phantasmagoric" but also structurally ephemeral.[5] It should be noted that the urban-centered nature of East Asia's (compressed) modernity does not necessarily imply that rural areas have been left unchanged or frozen in their traditional characteristics and conditions. In a great historical paradox, South Korea's acutely urban-biased development has recently led villages and peasants to spearhead sociocultural globalization in the form of an abrupt increase in rural "forced" bachelors' transnational marriage with foreign brides from across Asia (Chang, K. 2018, ch. 6). There are a host of sociocultural and other affairs in which rural areas have turned out or functioned as central arenas of compressed modernity.

Secondary organizations   Secondary organizations such as schools and business firms have been hastily set up in massive numbers as instruments for modernization and development, but their organizational structure and culture are far from simple replication of those of Western societies. Traditional teacher–pupil relations still reverberate in authoritarian class rooms where cramming (condensed absorption) of modern/Western knowledge and technology is considered as an uncompromisable goal of education in the process of national economic and civilizational catch-up (Han, J. 1996). In South Korean sweatshop factories where the "economic miracle" was initiated from the late 1960s, work-line supervisors and company managers demanded that *yeogong* (women industrial workers) subserviently yet faithfully serve them as if they were elder kinsmen in a village (Koo, H. 2001). Modern industrial workplaces have often been reinvented as arenas for arguably communal interactions associated with paternalistic cultural traditions (Dore 1973; Walder 1986).

Families   Korean/East Asian familialism (or, broadly, family-centeredness) both as personal orientation and societal order is as much modern as traditional. Families function, on the one hand, like social battalions in which confusing and contradicting goals of societal processes (modern economy, polity, and civic life) are reorganized into strategic targets of everyday life and, on the other hand, like cultural reservoirs in which values and norms of diverse historical and social origins are absorbed and reproduced as guiding poles for personal life (Chang, K. 2010a). Family life in East Asia both appears as microcosmic of condensed and compressive societal processes, and buttresses such societal processes by tightly regimenting family members accordingly. In fact, most of South Korea's (and East Asia's) supposedly unique features of compressed development and modernization – such as labor-intensive industrialization, education zeal, family-reliant welfare, hyper-mobilization of (women's) gender,

27

and familial corporate control (*chaebol*) – are intricately enmeshed with various material and ideational functions and social institutional effects of familial relationships and organizations (Chang, K. 2010a; see Chapter 8 in this book). In an unprecedentedly rapid industrialization-cum-urbanization, most rural families have in fact internalized such development by sending some of their talented or motivated members to urban industries and schools and accordingly reallocating their material resources in order to actively support migrating family members' urban activities as a grand familial strategy. The public debate on *chaebol*'s effectiveness in their familial form of corporate ownership and management is still ongoing, despite many legal, political, as well as economic mishaps thereby committed. The developmental state's persistent dependence on women in flexible labor supply and stable welfare provision has been most essentially predicated upon (married) women's intense commitment to family. Considering the overwhelming share of parental financial contribution and moral commitment to public education, South Korea's unrivalled educational achievement is basically a familial accomplishment.[6]

Personhood If an ordinary Korean (or East Asian) adult hopes to secure a genteel image or position – or personhood in general – in everyday social life, he/she needs to be able to skillfully exhibit a highly complex set of values and attitudes that are finely tuned to diverse sociocultural, political, and economic contexts. To be considered as a good parent, teacher, and senior worker is a highly challenging and often confusing task since he/she is expected to successfully become a seemingly inconsistent or contradictory being in variegated contexts. To be considered as a good child, student, and junior worker is no less challenging and confusing. To be considered as a good spouse, friend, and colleague is another formidable and perplexing challenge. Life is further complicated along different stages of one's life course that demand constantly radical shifts in her/his social roles and relations in tandem with condensed and complicated societal changes. In a most crucial dilemma in this regard, various stages of one's life course can be influenced by mutually inconsistent – or, according to Beck and Grande (2010) and Giddens (1990), "discontinuous" – historical and societal factors, so that her/his youth, adulthood, and old age may easily lose logical sequences. Born in a traditional culture, raised in a modernizing/industrializing era, and surviving into a postmodern/postindustrial era, an ordinary Korean/East Asian adult must continually juggle with apparently illogical sets of values,

28

duties, and expectations in each stage of her/his life course. *Flexibly complex personhood* – circumspectly and tactfully being, or at least appearing, traditional-modernized-postmodernized on the one hand, and indigenous-Westernized-cosmopolitan on the other hand – is a civilizational requirement in this society.[7] Chronic possibilities for failing to be a flexibly complex social subject tend to induce Koreans/ East Asians to remain stressfully alert, whereas many energetic and resourceful individuals may try to lead highly colorful forms of life by tapping all sociocultural, economic, and political opportunities associated with compressed modernity.

Modernity has usually been conceived as the civilizational state of affairs in a national society. When postcolonial nations, upon liberation, embarked upon material, cultural, and/or institutional modernization often under state authoritarianism, many of their incumbent states were not able to justly represent or fully incorporate people(s) and society (societies) under their supposed jurisdictions. Within loosely, hastily and/or coercively defined national boundaries, certain regions, ethnicities, classes, professions (military in particular) or civil societies have frequently challenged the rule of the often self-established states by envisioning and pursuing alternative lines of modernization. At the grassroots level, individuals, families, and other intimate groups often implicitly defy the rule of any ineffective and/or authoritarian state in similar ways. Modernity (and modernization) can be plural not only across different national societies, as aptly indicated in the "multiple modernities" thesis (Eisenstadt 2000), but also within each national society. Such internal multiplicity and diversity of modernities/modernizations are critically predicated upon the varying complexities of time–space (era–place) compression across different units of (inherently compressed) modernity.[8] In an analogy to Bruno Latour's (1993, 2005) world view, we can think about a "practical metaphysics" of compressed modernities that are interactively generated by diverse social units and agencies.

Finally, while the above discussion on units of compressed modernity has focused upon various subjects within a national society, it should be pointed out that world regions and even the whole world can also be seen as potential or actual units of compressed modernity. This is far from difficult to discern empirically. Aside from the innumerable world conventions held by the United Nations and UN-affiliated global organizations, back-to-back global summits and inter-governmental conferences are being held in order to tackle ceaselessly arising global epidemics, economic crises, ecological havoc, etc. Through the WTO (World Trade Organization) framework, the political and economic elites of advanced capitalist countries envision the world as a fully integrated unit of economic modernity. While the world-system thinking led by Immanuel Wallerstein has already taught us that self-contained modernity can be meaningfully conceived only at the global level, the recent velocity of reflexive cosmopolitization, as analyzed in Chapter 3, certainly ratifies the necessity of probing "global modernity" much more frontally – above all, in regard to its increasingly compressed nature.[9]

Likewise, world regions are no less dynamically intensifying their unit status in political economy, culture, and even formal governance. The historic launching of the European Union as a formally legalized unit for political sovereignty as well as social and economic collaboration is certain to accelerate similarly targeted international efforts in other world regions. This European experience clearly evinces that the formal elevation of world regions as human existential units is not necessarily predicated upon the civilizational homogenization of involved societies. The extreme economic, sociopolitical, cultural, and even religious diversities within the European Union will be further complicated through now officially sanctioned reflective and reflexive interactions, engendering a wild new unit of compressed modernity (Beck and Grande 2007).

In recent decades, particularly after the global dissolution of the Cold War, Asia is following suit under the comprehensive socio-economic integration among Asian nations, peoples, and enterprises in autonomous and pragmatic terms (Chang, K. 2014). Apparently, Asia has been evolving into a transnationally organized industrial capitalism in tandem with its formation into a grand transnational labor market, a regionalized popular cultural zone, and so forth. These dramatic and fundamental changes seem to endow Asia with a historically unprecedented materiality, which allows for its recognition as a new regional unit of (compressed) modernity.

2.4 Discussion: From Theory of Modernization to *Theory of Modernitization*

Modernity has been conceived as the civilizational state of affairs in a national society that has been either evolutionarily engendered (as in some Western European nations) or simulatively constructed (as in all other nations exposed to Western European influences). Both processes have been conceptualized as modernization. In sociology and its derivative scholarships, the latter category of modernization has usually been discussed and understood in terms of domestically finding or developing certain cultural, sociopolitical, and economic conditions having "elective affinities" (Weber 1946) with modern entrepreneurship, democracy, and/or liberal community. In historical realities, modernization as such could have been hoped for and tried out, but no nation outside Western Europe has ever reached modernity this nationally enclosed way. They, instead, have *encountered modernity* through transnational politico-military, economic, and/or sociocultural dominations. Such encounters, from the very start, made modernity an issue of *relationalization* with West European (and, later on, Western) civilizations and political economies. (Relationalization – as compared to relation, meaning the objective state of being related – is defined here as the act of consciously envisioning, seeking, or imposing certain relationships.) Modernity as an epistemological property began to avail and even necessitate itself wherever its embodying nations reached "pre-modern" or "non-modern" peoples/societies with existentially threatening impacts. It even began to assume the status of a *meta-value* in the postcolonial world. This process was no exception to the now ex-European dominant nations in the "new" continents of Americas and Oceania. Although they would ultimately be able to actively add their own characteristics in deepening and expanding modern systems of politics, economy, and society, they, as migrant settler communities, initially had to encounter Western Europe as superior forces of motherly modernity. Such sentiment is not entirely absent even now.

If the concept of modernization should remain as it has conventionally been, we need an additional concept or theory to highlight the importance of the historical processes and structural conditions of supposedly modernizing nations' relationalization with the modernity of Western Europe (hereafter the West, considering the subsequently critical role of the United States in shaping modernity) as manifested politico-militarily, economically, and/or socioculturally. Under the epistemological condition or dilemma that modernity was already given as an inescapable historical necessity (with the implicit status of a meta-value) in the context of transnational relations of domination, modernization could not remain a natural (or indigenously realizing) social process, but became an *end-determining-cause* project with strong political elements. It is not so much modernity itself as the suppositionally proposed causes, whether relevantly effective (in achieving modernity) or not, that have decisively shaped the political, economic, social, and cultural conditions of a variety of postcolonial

31

nations. Such suppositions about causes of modernity have been presented practically by all individuals, groups, and institutions with any scientific, technological, political, social, journalistic, cultural, or even religious influences in the nation. Even when the question, if certain nations have actually been modernized, remains fundamentally ambiguous, it is crucially important to find and comprehend that they have been relationalizing themselves with modernity and its embodying forces in terms of predeterminedly organizing and managing basically all elements of nationhood according to variously understood, or asserted, conditions of modernity. Let me call this process *modernitization*, as differentiated from modernization. This concept/theory will critically help to analyze trans-social relations of modernity in the world order, comparable to social relations of production in Marxist class analysis. Modernitization can be seen when (West-derived) modernity is appropriated, simulated, adapted, reformulated, resisted, or rescaled by peoples and societies outside its originator region of Europe.[10] It will enable a proper emphasis on *the significance of concrete historical agencies* (as opposed to abstract structural conditions) in analyzing wide varieties of political, sociocultural, and economic transformations under the global order of modernity.[11]

Some historical varieties of modernitization on the national level may be identified as follows: (1) European settler colonies in the "new" continents that would become independent nations through civilizational appropriation and adaptation of European modernity; (2) proactive instrumentalist appropriation of European modernity by non-European nations such as Japan since the Meiji revolution and a majority of postcolonial nations; (3) intra-European spread and consolidation of modernity through mutual and interactive appropriation of national and local modernities; (4) "internal conversion" (Geertz 1973) in non-European societies and peoples in terms of inventive reappropriation of indigenous or traditional civilizations for (Western-)modern tasks and purposes, for instance, as argued in the Confucian modernity thesis; (5) socialist revolution, conversion, or alliance as a national development path alternative to capitalism or capitalist modernity; (6) dialectical self-reinvention of colonized peoples and societies as counterforce elements of colonial modern systems, for instance, (ethno)nationalist civil society and proletariat confronting the colonial(ist) state and capital (see Chapter 4); (7) internal colonialist unification/subordination of minor nations and ethnicities by Europe-modeled new modern states, such as Ryukyu under Meiji Japan and Tibet under communist China. In all these

32

instances, modernitization is a fundamentally compressed experience of modernity in the epistemological, civilizational, and/or political economic dimensions.[12] Compressed modernity has been a universal mode of modernitization across the postcolonial world.

Modernitization inherently involves compressed modernity. Above all, knowing, or being forced to know, modernity – as opposed to unconsciously growing into it – is an epistemological quantum leap. But the knowing process often involves unprecedented sufferings and sacrifices imposed by the initial modernizers on the rest of the world, often through invasion, colonization, or exploitation. Thus, achieving modernity as rapidly as possible and as greatly as possible became a historical exigency in order to minimize or remove such externally originated sufferings and sacrifices in the coming years. However, once political sovereignties and/or socioeconomic autonomies were lost under colonialism, the concerned nations often lost their status as a unit of modernity and, instead, incurred instantaneous incorporation into the transnationally reorganized modernity of invader nations. In all these simple occasions of modernitization, whether self-promoted or involuntarily coerced, modernity has been reasoned, pursued, or imposed in compressed manners. More complicated occasions of modernitization do not differ, as shown in the subsequent chapters in Part II of this book as to South Korean experiences.

— 3 —

COMPRESSED MODERNITY IN THE UNIVERSALIST PERSPECTIVE

3.1 Introduction

Seemingly, most of the main impetuses for social and economic transformations in the new century do not differentially or exclusively
apply to certain limited groups of nations. Consider the following:
global free trade and financialization, corporate deterritorialization
and transnationalized production, globalized labor use and class
struggle, globalized (or globally coerced by the IMF, etc.) policy
consulting and formulation, informatization and cyberspace, globally orchestrated bioscientific manipulation of life forms (gradually
to include human bodies), borderless ecological and epidemiological
hazards, transnational demographic realignments (migration of labor,
spouses, children), cosmopolitanized arts and entertainments and, not
least critically, globally financed and managed regional wars. There
are no permanent systematic hierarchies, sequences, or selectivities
by which different groups of nations – whether at different levels of
development, in different regions or of different races – are exposed
to these new civilizational and political economic forces in mutually exclusive ways. Wanted or not, they are every nation's concern
because they are structurally enmeshed with the new civilizational
process called "reflexive cosmopolitization" (Beck and Grande 2010;
Chang, K. 2010b).[1]

Recent world history seems to dictate that surviving, let alone
benefiting from, these new civilizational and political economic forces
requires every nation to actively internalize them. Isolationist efforts
– whether spoken in terms of trade protectionism, religious funda-
mentalism, media and internet control or else – are readily subjected
to international *moral* condemnations (in particular by neoliberals).

34

In fact, accepting or refusing these forces remains beyond willful political or social choice because they are *globally reflexive* – that is, compulsively occurring through "the autonomized dynamism of (second) modernization" across national borders (Beck 1994: 5). Rephrasing this issue in terms of involved risk, Beck emphatically indicates the arrival of "world risk society" as follows:

> To the extent that risk is experienced as omnipresent, there are only three possible reactions: *denial, apathy,* or *transformation.* The first is largely inscribed in modern culture, the second resembles post-modern nihilism, and the third is the "cosmopolitan moment" of world risk society.
>
> (Beck 2006: 331)

At the level of each national society, the above forces of reflexive cosmopolit(an)ization have been and have to be incorporated frontally in order to maintain its civilizational integrity as well as material and physical stability. Through this process, societies (or their civilizational conditions) are being internalized into each other, thereby making *compressed modernity* – a form of modernity I have so far analyzed with regard to externally oriented and rapidly overtaking modernizers in (pre-crisis) East Asia – become a universal feature of national societies in the second modern world (see Chan, K. 1999, 2016).

In this chapter, I intend to (1) theoretically discuss the new stage of compressed modernity as nationally ramified from reflexive cosmopolit(an)ization, and, then, (2) comparatively illustrate varying instances of compressed modernity in advanced capitalist societies, un(der)developed capitalist societies, and (from socialist to capitalist) transition societies. Let me begin by briefly elaborating on Beck's concept/theory of "second modernity," proceed to undertake the above two main tasks. This will be followed by a complementary indication of the declining status of national societies as the dominant unit of (compressed) modernity and the interactive acceleration of compressed modernity among various different levels of human life (namely, the globe, world regions, subnational localities, families, individuals as well as national societies) and, finally, a special observation of East Asia as the world's most dynamic arena of reflexive cosmopolitization and concomitant compressed modernities.

3.2 Variations of Compressed Modernity as Internalized Reflexive Cosmopolitization

Under reflexive cosmopolitization (of the world risk society), "second modernity" (Beck and Grande 2010) becomes ubiquitous, albeit with very diverse motives, processes, extents, and consequences. *Relatively speaking*, advanced capitalist societies may be characterized more often by second modernity of their own construction in that most of the driving forces of scientific-technological-cultural inputs and political economic interests for radicalized reflexivity originate from their own intent and power. By comparison, late developing and underdeveloped capitalist societies and (formerly socialist) transition societies may be characterized more often by "second modernity by dependency," in that these societies become subjected to risks of radicalized reflexivity largely due to their political and/or economic subordination to advanced nations and global actors (such as transnational business) or due to their own efforts at learning or seeking assistance and cooperation from such nations and actors.

Societies of relatively autonomous second modernity, in turn, may be differentiated in terms of earlier systemic characteristics of first modernity – i.e. liberal, social democratic, and developmental societies.[2] The processes, natures, and consequences of second modernization may involve potential differences (as well as similarities) associated with such systemic characteristics. Societies of relatively dependent second modernity, in turn, may be differentiated in terms of earlier extents and complexities of first modernity vis-à-vis traditionality, and in terms of systemic complexities concerning socialist vis-à-vis capitalist institutions. This latter group of second modern societies constitutes an overwhelming majority of nations in the world. Their internal diversities are beyond any easy classification. Nevertheless, they are commonly characterized by partial realization of second modernity (because of the protracted existence of pre-modern, first-modern, socialist-modern components), and such partially realized second modernity can sometimes produce devastating impacts due to its structural dissonance with indigenous social orders and principles.

Thus, relatively dependent second modern societies may be described also in terms of (cosmopolitized) compressed modernity. However, even relatively autonomous second modern societies also take on compressed modernity to the extent that they are subjected to cosmopolitized risks as well as opportunities generated from relatively dependent second modern societies. In sum, internalization of cosmopolitized opportunities and risks takes place both in relatively autonomous and relatively dependent second modern societies, so that compressed modernity becomes inseparable from reflexive cosmopolitization and thereby ubiquitous as well. Besides, to the extent that such cross-influencing takes place in a cosmopolitized process of reflexivity, a virtual simultaneity characterizes the temporal relationship between second modernity and compressed modernity.

It is however important to point out the different extents and impacts of compressed modernity between relatively autonomous and relatively dependent second modern societies. The former can be characterized by *low-order* compressed modernity because the usual impacts from the latter (through specialized trade, international migration, cross-border pollution, etc.) are likely to be more indirect, contained, monitored, and thus manageable (or presently tolerable) than their own impacts on the latter (through selectively free trade, transnational organization of production, financial invasion, neoliberal structural adjustment programs, bioscientific manipulation of local agriculture, cultural-ideological framing, etc.).[3] Thus, the latter can be characterized by *high-order* compressed modernity. In Western societies under low-order compressed modernity, the modern cultural-institutional-technological configurations are less compressed because they have more often evolved from the internal (or endogenous) historical processes with the external influences incorporated in a carefully managed manner; whereas in non-Western societies under high-order compressed modernity, the corresponding configurations are more compressed because they have more often been superimposed, borrowed or instantly adapted from outside with the internal civilizational elements subjugated willingly or unwillingly. In the latter, the suddenness and involuntariness of second modernity and its conflictual relations with indigenous interests and values, despite its globalized context, do not fundamentally differ from the classic situation of colonial modernity. Terrorism appears to be an extremist effort at bypassing such asymmetrical relations, whereas military invasion is not infrequently used in order to reinforce the asymmetry.[4] However, it is also true that such asymmetry keeps losing meaningfulness because the absolute magnitude of the impacts of relatively dependent second modern societies (including such demographic giants as China and India) on relatively autonomous second modern societies is growing at an unprecedented speed. Paradoxically, such international asymmetry itself seems to be one of the critical factors for this unprecedented velocity because it is directly linked to corporate and national possibilities of economic gain.

3.3 Advanced Capitalist Societies

The Historical Nature of Early Modernization

European modernization was a fairly diverse and uneven process across various sections of the continent. The post-World War II portrayal of (Western) Europe as a set of institutionally stable and economically affluent units of modernity has often arbitrarily extrapolated into the regional past histories, so that the arduous efforts of most European societies – many of them yet to be consolidated into independent or unified nation-states – to physically survive the aggressions of a handful of pioneer modernizers and to catch up with them by expeditiously learning their technological, economic, and institutional-political knowhows have remained insufficiently recognized.[5] The fierce intra-regional competition and rivalry embedded in European modernization was critically responsible for the two "world wars" fought over the politico-military (and civilizational) hegemony of the region (Hobsbawm 1994). For most European nations, *modernity was a nationalist international project involving both civilizational condensation and compression* amid plural sources of new knowledge, culture, and power (see Figure 2.1). That is, *compressed modernity* has characterized the civilizational nature of most European societies since the late eighteenth century.[6] Furthermore, the transcontinental political economic and demographic expansion of Western Europe into America and Oceania led to an overnight *transplantation of modernity* after indigenous nations were completely subdued or almost exterminated. However, differential reactions to various crisis tendencies of capitalist modernity and to domestic and international socialist influences engendered the divergence between Anglo-American liberal (and neoliberal) and North European social democratic systems of political economy and social policy (Turner 2016).

The non-European catching-up modernizers, particularly in East Asia, have been engaged in the same nationalist international project of modernity, however, through intercontinental (and interracial) transactions of commodities, technologies, scientific and cultural knowledge, and social institutions. The mercantile nationalist motivation has been most distinct among these Asian modernizers, who have shown impressive capacities for intercultural learning as well as neotraditional organizational rehabilitation.[7] The so-called developmental states in East Asia have proved to be both the most forceful vehicle of compressed capitalist development and the most tenacious conveyer of neotraditionalist democracy centered on political and social familialism (see Chang, K. 2010a). Besides, the "Cold War liberalism" in East Asia orchestrated by the United States against the next-door communist superpowers ideologically enshrined (transplanted) capitalist modernity and politically guarded the neotraditionalist authoritarian regimes in the region.

Compressed Modernity in Advanced Capitalist Societies as Internalized Reflexive Cosmopolitization

As David Harvey (1980) insightfully indicates, *the spatial integration and temporal condensation of political economic and cultural activities on the global scale* already became a generic feature of capitalist modernity in the early twentieth century, and has intensified to such an extent that national societies have increasingly become dubious as units of self-contained modernity.[8] However, since nation-states continue to be the dominant regulatory unit of economic life and sociopolitical citizenship, it is still epistemologically justifiable to conceive of national-level modernity (or modernities) whether it is endogenously shaped or not. In fact, as explained above, even Western modernity has never been a self-contained evolutionary experience for most countries in the region. Nevertheless, the unprecedented global velocity of time/space condensation and compression has forced even advanced capitalist nations into such chaotic civilizational conditions as to crucially debilitate various technological instruments and social institutions of national modernity (Beck and Grande 2010). This roughly corresponds to what Beck seems to consider the second modern condition under cosmopolit(an)ized reflexivity.

Substantively, late or second modernity in advanced capitalist nations has been characterized by such diverse tendencies as deindustrialization (multinational relocation of industrial production), corporate deterritorialization (transnationalization of business), informatization, national and global financialization, knowledge trading, industrial scientization (NT, BT, ICT), bioengineering, international ecological incursion and governance, post-rationalist and transnational cultural production, cosmopolit(an)ization of class relations and civil activism, cosmopolitan engagement in regional wars, transnational demographic realignments (migration of labor,

39

children, spouses), religious pluralism, and so forth.[9] While describing the details of these tendencies is not feasible here, it is safe to say that none of them can be effectively accommodated or countered by national societies as mutually independent entities. That is, second modernity is a wild world of borderless civilizational experimentations and inestimable social interdependencies. However, most nation-states still have tried actively to manage such experimentations and interdependencies supposedly for their exclusive national interests. This has led to a seemingly universal process of *internalization of reflexive cosmopolitization*, thereby engendering compressed second modernity in each national society.

And, as statist political economists have shown, some states have been exceptionally successful in economically riding the tide of second modernity (Weiss 1998). For instance, such remote nations as Iceland and Ireland suddenly became global star economies mainly on the basis of global financialization. Even the United States once seemingly regained its economic hegemony by manipulating its financial leverages internationally. In the information and communication industry, Finnish and South Koreans have dwarfed traditional industrial powerhouses such as Japan, the United States, and Germany. Americans, on the other hand, have aggressively pursued the bioengineering of agriculture in order to reinforce their dominance in the world's grain and meat markets. All these late capitalist achievements, however, have been accompanied by devastating incidents of economic, social or ecological hazards one after another – most symbolically, the near financial collapse of Iceland, Ireland, and the United States in the 2008–2009 global economic crisis.

Regardless of mutually diverse configurations and achievements of second modernity among the advanced capitalist nations, basically all of them have collaboratively attempted to engage the rest of the world in this new phase of capitalist modernity. This attests to their firm self-conviction as the upper hands of second modernity. The maximum utilization of old global institutions (such as IMF) and the creation of new global/international institutions (such as WTO, etc.) have all been dictated by the collusive league of advanced capitalist nations. Their intent is simple and clear – i.e. restructuring the world for the sake of maximum exploitation of existing and new forms of profit. The rampant expansion of global inequalities and socio-ecological hazards since the late twentieth century is no accident to this ruling league.[10]

However, exactly through the same historical process, the rest of the world has abruptly infiltrated into the basic economic, social, cultural, and ecological fabrics of the advanced capitalist nations. Under the chronic pressures of unemployment and insufficient income, workers in deindustrialized capitalist societies have ironically become the main consumers of industrial commodities from newly industrializing countries whose price competitiveness is often predicated upon potentially hazardous materials and technologies as well as socially problematic labor relations.[11] The demographic reproductive squeeze in European and, more recently, East Asian capitalist countries has been complemented by the sustained influx of various forms of temporary and permanent migrants from neighboring poor countries, whose presence entails multicultural and multi-ethnic reconfiguration of the societies concerned.[12] The postmodern and/or post-rationalist turn in Western academia, art, and literature has been accompanied by a strong inflow of theories and philosophies from the hitherto intellectual and cultural peripheries.[13] The industrial divestment by local business in advanced capitalist countries has sometimes been accompanied by corporate takeover or new industrial investment by the capital from developing countries as well as competing developed countries.[14] All these tendencies clearly attest to the critical fact that, under second modernity, advanced capitalist societies increasingly experience the civilizational internalization of hitherto peripheral others and thereby become compressed modern themselves.

3.4 Un(der)developed Societies

The Colonial and Postcolonial Conditions of Modernity

For most Third World countries, modernity initially *happened* as an international political incident. Whether through the coerced economic and social opening of parts of the nations to Western imperialist forces or the complete colonial occupation by Western countries, Third World countries came to confront modernity as a totally alien civilizational entity under which their indigenous systems of politics, economy, society, and culture had to be suddenly reconceived as obsolete or even unjust. For Third World societies, the already emergent modernity was to be arrived at by radically breaking way from, not by gradually building upon, their past. The Western colonial rulers, while inculcating and reinforcing such defeatist historical perspectives on the minds of colonized people, pursued *modernization of Westerners, by Westerners, and for Westerners* in their unilaterally declared new territories. Local figures hired or utilized by colonizers

41

for various auxiliary modern organizations and professions remained politically and culturally disarticulated from the rest of their nation, so their marginal position from both sides often induced them to try to existentially vindicate themselves by practicing or demonstrating exaggerated versions of modernity in a theatre-like social context (see Geertz 1973).

Upon liberation, unless it had been achieved through an anti-colonial and anti-feudal social revolution, many of these former colonial functionaries or collaborators were promoted into the political and cultural leadership and then embarked upon West-oriented modernization in an unquestioned manner (Fanon 2004). As the Western colonizers left behind the political systems and economic structures as radically deformed but not modernized, modernity arose as a substantively justifiable national(ist) project. However, modernization as a national project led by the former colonial collaborators was self-defeating because their vested material interests tended to preserve, first, the structural dependencies on the West of their only nominally independent nations and, second, the local structures of inequality interwoven with such (neocolonial) dependencies (Baran 1957; Frank 1967). Modernization, before long, became narrowly redefined as (capitalist) economic development – or, more precisely, as economic catch-up – for which the political and social ingredients of modernity would be compromised in accordance with various versions of Third World particularism in modernization as argued in Rostow's (1959) developmental stage theory and Huntington's (1968) functional authoritarianism thesis, etc. Condensed economic development, as a component of compressed modernity, became an almost universalized national goal, so that the developmentally promoted or justified practices in political governance, social mobilization and control as well as economic management continued to critically shape the actual patterns of modernity in the postwar Third World.[15] (As discussed below, the Cold War intervention by the United States and its allies further reinforced this developmentally excused distortion of Third World modernity.) The worst historical tragedy in the modern world consists in the fact that with all such sacrifices of political and social goals, economic development at meaningful levels and for sustained periods has been achieved only by a tiny minority of (formerly) Third World nations.

Compressed Modernity in Un(der)developed Societies as Internalized Reflexive Cosmopolitization

In spite of the protracted developmental failure of most Third World nations (and, for that matter, their failure in the national project of first or classic modernity), they have not been waived from the radical new world of second modernity. At the same time, in an all-encompassing process of civilizational transformation, global neoliberal economic restructuring has most directly and manifestly swirled un(der)developed nations into the vortex of second modernity. In fact, the concepts of modernization and modernity, much refuted in both un(der)developed and developed nations since the 1970s, have suddenly been relinquished in the recent global interactions between them. Paradoxically, this came to relieve the developed world of its hitherto noisily publicized duty of guiding and supporting the modernization project of less developed nations. Neither national modernization nor economic self-reliance is publicly encouraged anymore for un(der)developed nations in the global North–South interactions and dialogues.[16] The direct industrial and financial investment by advanced capitalist economies has replaced the local process of "learn-and-practice" industrialization. At the same time, in order to reduce the risk of such financial operation, the ruling league of advanced capitalist countries, through what is called the Washington consensus, decided to discipline un(der)developed nations to become responsible debtors.[17] Besides, their new economic initiatives linked to various monopolistic/oligopolistic commodities based upon not-yet-vindicated scientific, technological, and financial experiments have been coerced upon un(der)developed nations in the framework of global free trade (i.e. the WTO system).[18] Interestingly but tragically, the neoliberal propensity of subordinating all political, social, cultural, and ecological concerns to economic interests has intensified the already chronic imbalances between economic and noneconomic concerns in un(der)developed nations. Through this economically skewed and politically un(der)governed process of globalization, each un(der)developed country has become a cosmopolitan arena for late modern political economic interests and commercialized social and cultural relations (Henry 2020) – another ostensible instance of compressed (second) modernity as reflexive cosmopolitization.

It appears quite instructive that the sudden change of heart by the United States and its allies concerning the modernization project of (capitalist) un(der)developed countries happened at a critical juncture of Cold War politics. By the early 1980s, the economic and social

43

sustainability of the socialist systems across the world became highly questionable, even to socialist political leaders themselves, including Mikhail Gorbachev and Deng Xiaoping. The internal systemic failure of socialist modernity induced the leader states of the capitalist bloc to seriously reconsider the political utility of subsidizing the capitalist modernization process of numerous client nations.[19] In retrospect, the Cold War was another global regime of modernity, under which a political and ideological room for an autonomously reflective (not reflexive!) pursuit of modernity was flatly denied to most Third World countries (see Chapter 4 for the South Korean case). The capitalist modernity recommended by the West was a readymade civilizational system, and its local realization – in an extremely condensed fashion – was strategically supervised and supported by the West as an effort to curb the international political expansion of socialist influences. In this way, the American influence on local politics exacerbated the already acute rigidity of the Third World's illiberal capitalism and thereby incurred endemic anti-American sentiment. As the global Cold War was nearing an end, even such paternalistic political support for the (condensed) modernization project of many Third World countries was instantly terminated, giving way to an aggressively new but *underreflective* paradigm of global neoliberal economic restructuring. In this sense, the neoliberal restructuring of Third World political economies is a post-Cold War regime of cosmopolitized reflexivity in economic (mis)management. Interestingly, most of the Cold War foes of the so-called Free World have ended up volunteering to enter such cosmopolitized reflexivity in their post-socialist transitions.

3.5 (Post-Socialist) Transition Societies

Socialist Modernization

State socialism, as pivoting around planned heavy industrialization, was a modern system of condensed economic development based upon the politically dictated maximum mobilization of national resources into producer goods industries. In most state socialist countries, the historical establishment of such political economic systems, in turn, was a highly condensed, top-down process of copying or emulating the Soviet model (Kornai 1992; Riskin 1987). This was in clear contrast to some earlier social revolutions in which the carefully crafted alliance between local grassroots interests and communist ideals and strategies had enabled a self-reflective and indigenously

44

propelled process of social and political transformation.[20] Whether welcomed or not by local grassroots, the state socialist economic systems proved to be extremely successful in producing the initially desired outcomes in the economic structure and output. Such early economic performance of state socialist countries served the United States and its capitalist allies a serious cause for political anxiety, and thus intensified the civilizational war between socialist versus capitalist modernity. In the long run, however, it turned out to be a blind or impulsive run into an unsustainable state of economic and social affairs (Kornai 1992). Paradoxically, it was the frontrunner state socialist countries, such as Russia, some Eastern European countries, and North Korea, which first began to confront structural economic depression and social demoralization. However, virtually no other state-socialist country managed to avoid the structural economic and social crisis attending on the failure of the endlessly self-reflexive command economic system (Riskin 1987).

Compressed Modernity in Transition Societies as Internalized Reflexive Cosmopolitization

After fierce internal ideological and political struggles, China and the Soviet Union openly embarked on the post-socialist system transition to the market economy (and, in the Russian case, to representative democracy, in form, as well). Subsequently, almost all other socialist countries followed suit, seemingly completing the process of (capitalist) reflexive cosmopolitization. Just like the earlier transition to state socialism, the system transition (or reform) to a market economy has been a highly condensed process, at this time, of following or imitating the already existing institutions and practices of advanced capitalist societies. All of a sudden, industrial capitalism has become an object to catch up with by former ideological adversaries. But such systemic transferrals have been plagued with three types of inherent risks – namely, risks intrinsic in any capitalist or market economic system, risks ensuing from the gross unfamiliarity and/or ideological-emotional antipathy of (former) socialist citizens with the capitalist or market economic system, and risks associated with the poor resource endowment of citizens and enterprises due to national economic depression.[21] When these risks have been conflated any further due to political instabilities or malefactions surrounding the system transition, as has been the case in numerous transition societies (including Russia as a particularly troublesome case), human suffering and social costs have devastated the basic social fabric of the concerned

45

nations (Rajkai 2016). Some liberal – and thus radical in the context of transition political economies – Western advisors paradoxically considered these complex risks as a main reason for recommending the so-called "big bang" approach which would hopefully generate a shock therapy effect in terms of minimizing the duration of institutional confusions and human suffering.[22] Unfortunately, the Russian big bang approach only amplified the above risks, whereas the Chinese gradualist approach allowed a much more stable progress toward material affluence and ideological-institutional rebirth. The Chinese case seems to deserve some special attention.

China's gradualist (and thus less condensed) system transition, dubbed "reform" (*gaige*), has implied a protracted cohabitation of socialist, capitalist, and even (neo)traditionalist components of political economy, thereby imposing an ultra-complex (compressed) modernity on Chinese life.[23] Interestingly, some socialist institutions, practices, and legacies have turned out to be quite useful for market-based development – for instance, highly educated and disciplined labor being fully utilized for explosive labor-intensive industrialization, powerful local states orchestrating aggressive yet flexible programs of local economic development, the public ownership of scarce resources (such as land) preventing speculative rent-seeking activities and thereby facilitating the rational and fair allocation of economic inputs, the rigid residential control between urban and rural places helping to check or slow down the otherwise explosive exodus of poor peasants into already job-insufficient cities, and so forth (Chang, K. 2020). Against these seemingly accidental utilities of socialist legacies, various negative impacts and impediments engendered by the same or other socialist legacies have to be added.[24] It also needs to be recognized that, from the very beginning of reform, China has tried to accommodate the full spectrum of modern and late modern industries led by Western capital in what they have designated as "special economic zones" (SEZs or *jingjitequ*). This may be called an institutional framework of *enclave compressed modernity*. Dreaming of potential gold rush-type economic opportunities in the world's would-be largest market, capitalist enterprises from all advanced industrial economies began to flock into offshore Chinese SEZs and, responding to desperate urges of other local state units, into various interior regions. This trend has made China an internally cosmopolitized economic entity, directly exposed to both benefits and risks of the radical new world economy. Conversely, China's internationally oriented developmental success in the post-socialist era linked with a variegated set of institutional and sociocultural factors has exposed the world to both benefits and risks of China's complex modern political economy – the entire world having become, on the one hand, perplexed consumers of cheap, functional but hazardous Chinese products and, on the other hand, anxious sellers to voracious Chinese buyers of natural resources, technologies, and enterprises (Chang, K. 2017c).

Eastern European countries constitute still another group of post-socialist (second) modernity. Their individual post-socialist transitions, by and large closer to the Russian shock therapy approach than the Chinese gradualist approach, have initially demanded their populations to go through utmost confusion and distress (Rajkai 2016). But their geographic adjacency and historical/cultural connection to Western Europe have ramified a sort of "jumpstart" effect of (first and second) modernization or development – East Germany, of course, being the most direct example of this phenomenon, due to its practical economic and social incorporation into West Germany.[25] No doubt, the recent completion of political and economic unionization in Europe has been radically amplifying such jumpstart effect, so that compressed modernity as reflexive cosmopolitization has effectively encompassed another critical world region. East Germans' highly ambivalent feelings in the post-unification era, as an unfailing index of compressed modernity, would increasingly become a broad East European phenomenon in this second modern era.

The above account of developed, un(der)developed, and post-socialist countries under second modernity clearly evinces that reflexive cosmopolitization in the second modern world has ramified varying patterns of national-level compressed modernity in virtually every corner of the globe. This finding, however, should be qualified in the following two aspects. First, national society has rapidly lost its salient status as the unit of modernity, whereas other human existential domains or levels such as individual, locality, and world region have become seriously competing units of modernity. Second, and relatedly, these competing units are also increasingly characterized by compressed modernity, again in conjunction with reflexive cosmopolitization. These trends do not imply that national societies or states which govern them are left to themselves with nothing much to do. In fact, as convincingly indicated by many statist political economists, (second) modern states are entrusted with ever expanding and challenging functional duties. So are individuals, families, localities, regional blocs, and the entire world community. Under reflexive cosmopolitization, the functional relationship between national societies (and states) and other human existential domains or levels does not remain in a zero-sum structure, but assumes a dynamic of mutual escalation. Likewise, compressed modernities of different existential domains or levels tend to intensify reciprocally.[26]

3.6 Discussion: East Asia and Compressed Modernity

While this chapter's discussion of various historico-systemic instances of compressed modernity shows its fundamentally universal nature in the modern world, East Asia merits particular attention in some special aspects. The twenty-first century as the supposed "Asian century" in the world's political and intellectual discourses very much reflects a region-wide manifestation of compressed economic and socio-institutional advances, in particular including the highly successful developmental performances of post-socialist transition societies such as China and Vietnam. Needless to say, their (compressively) industrialized capitalist neighbors such as Japan, South Korea, Taiwan, and Singapore continue to perform strongly in economic and social affairs. (Although Asia's regional developmental velocity is also joined by most Southeast Asian nations, India, etc., let us focus on East Asia here.)

It is still debatable whether and how much the condensed liberal systemic transition of China and Vietnam, in terms of the market economy, privatized production, wage labor, and so forth, has enabled their spectacular economic development and concomitant sociopolitical stability. But many close observers believe that their post-socialist reforms have been very much motivated by the compressed developmental and other performances of their politico-ideological foes – in particular, Japan, South Korea, and Taiwan (Whittaker et al. 2020). When they finally decided to give up the isolationist attachment to the rigid state-socialist systems of production and governance, their new departure was not predicated upon any autonomously devised package of socioeconomic policies and programs, but crucially reflected a desperate aspiration for emulating their industrialized capitalist neighbors' developmental compression and its socio-institutional conditions. It was in this context that China and Vietnam began to send numerous delegations of technocratic, industrial, technological, and scientific personnel to these forerunners in capitalist industrialization and concomitant institutional transformations, leaving all ideological and historical considerations behind.[27] That is, compressed modernity – developmental compression in particular, but indispensably accompanied by various condensed socio-institutional transitions – has fundamentally characterized not only each East Asian nation's domestic socioeconomic transformations, but also the way they have perceived and utilized each other.

As a highly interesting historical episode of such regionally associative compressed modernity, East Asia's compressed capitalist industrializers have shown these post-socialist transition nations that many of their socialist-era political structural and socioeconomic institutional features – namely, the interventionist state's industrial engagement, sociopolitically organized mobilization of labor force, authoritative public allocation of social resources in strategic purposes, and so forth – can be recycled in emulating the successful late-capitalist developmental states' governance in rapid industrialization and concomitantly condensed social transformation (Chang, K. 2020, 2012a). While the current work cannot offer further details on such political and social institutional affinities between post-socialist and late capitalist societies in compressively achieving various national, communal, and individual goals, it is obvious that compressed modernity crucially characterizes both individual East Asian nations (and their subnational social units) and their strategic mutual relationships.

It should be clarified that such individual and relational significance of compressed modernity among East Asian societies structurally obstructs, if not preempts altogether, their collective civilizational or ideological formation of distinctive Asianness or Asianism. As a result of their common experience or achievement of developmental and other compressions, they have actually become cosmopolitized more than ever in nearly all economic and sociocultural spheres – including academic social sciences that are supposed to study such phenomena.[28] In a further paradox, such multi-front cosmopolitization reflects and glorifies strong nationalist sentiments and purposes shared between each state and its respective citizenry.[29] For instance, East Asians' increasingly mutual cultural consumptions, ranging from tourism to pop culture (above all, the so-called Korean wave represented by BTS), do not clearly help to dilute such growing nationalism.

Retrospectively, this nationalist paradox of compressed modernity characterized the very beginning of East Asia's new or modern international order in the late nineteenth century. It was Japan, a hitherto isolationist nation in the premodern East Asia pivoting on China's hegemony, that pioneered in compressed Westernization-cum-modernization through the famous Meiji revolution and thereby asserted itself as a regionally dominant and globally competitive political economic force. Those societies and peoples subjected to Japan's harsh colonial encroachment and exploitation would ultimately end up implicitly aspiring to get even by emulating Japan's miracle history in compressed modernity, as documented in numerous memoirs, biographies, and scholarly accounts of their national(ist) elites.[30] Japan's Meiji revolution was a West-reflexive radical systemic transition, but its grand purpose and basic process constituted an unprecedentedly central state-centered structure of political economic and socio-ideological order that would be frequently replicated elsewhere whether consciously or unconsciously, up until the very twenty-first century (Chang, K. 2012a).

Part II

Structural Properties of Compressed Modernity

— 4 —

INTERNAL MULTIPLE MODERNITIES

South Korea as Multiplex Theater Society

4.1 Introduction

The thesis of "multiple modernities" presented by Shmuel Eisenstadt (2000) emphasizes a comparative civilizational perspective that helps recognize variegated possibilities and forms of modernities in the diverse historical and structural contexts for nation-making or national revival. In this chapter, I additionally argue that modernity – and the process of modernization – can be plural not only across different national societies (as explained by Eisenstadt), but also within each national society. As already explained in Chapter 2, an internal multiplicity of modernities can be documented across varying units and agencies of modernity in each national society, such as individuals, families, secondary organizations, localities as well as various societal units (state, civil society, ethnonation, etc.). Such internal multiplicity induces national modernity to take on an inherently complicated nature. Furthermore, the multiple agencies of modernity/modernization can have mutually competing, stimulating, suppressive, nullifying or substitutive relationships and thereby engender what may be called the inter-unit interactive variability of internal multiple modernities.[1]

The internal multiplicity of modernities/modernizations can also be documented as to diverse historical manifestations of *modernization* (see Chapter 2). Since the late nineteenth century, Korean society (then Chosun) and people have been subjected to a series of overpowering international influences and related local upheavals and confrontations. These occurrences were fundamentally different from Koreans' previously experienced wars and conflicts reflecting mostly the structure and change of regional politico-military

53

relations. In the late nineteenth century, Japan invaded Korea as a global force after its successful reflexive self-transformation into a West-derived modernity.[2] Japan's colonization of Korea had a highly interesting implication about the new world order of modernity in the making – namely, Koreans' subordination to Western modernity through its surrogate agency. Japan's defeat to the United States in the Pacific War brought about another unique civilizational experience to (South) Koreans as this hegemonic liberal power practically ordered them to be incorporated into the so-called Free World pivoting around the American systems of politics, economy, and society. Despite their inescapable accommodation of American modernity in terms of reflexively liberal institutionalization and allied anti-communist stance (Mobrand 2019), South Koreans also tried to shape their modernity in culturally and economically self-asserting manners. Culturally, a sort of neotraditionalist modernity was instantly generalized among virtually all South Koreans as they tried to match their modern sociopolitical status as equal citizens with an equally dignifying cultural status of (traditionally aristocratic) Confucian subjects mainly in familial relations and rituals. Economically, a sort of state capitalist industrialization was initiated under Park Chung-Hee for swift and autonomous national development, engendering not only a remarkable collective economic outcome but also a highly unique system of political economy. South Korea recently entered the latest era of neoliberal globalization as an industrialized nation with numerous special features in its economy, society, and politics, and its proactive position in the newly forming world order has been based upon a complicated set of domestic socioeconomic risks and costs. All these earth-shattering transitions have reshaped South Korea into a remarkable political economic and civilizational entity attracting worldwide attention, but its social integrity and stability are still being tested, or reconstructed, with the sequentially disenfranchised groups of subaltern citizens accounting for a majority of its population.

Through the above historical transitions and accompanying civilizational and political economic changes, South Korea has become a nation of internal multiple modernities. It now appears a kind of multiplex society subjected to diverse yet coexisting regimes of modernities. Each of these modernities may not be particularly or exclusively Korean as they have been embedded in the global structures and processes of modern social change. Nonetheless, South Korea is certainly distinct in the volume of internal multiplicities of modernities, the dramatic and intense realization of each modernity, the unbounded prolonging of each modernity, and the extremely

54

complex interactions among such multiple modernities. While the thesis of internal multiple modernities is discussed here at the societal level, it is also relevant across other units and agencies of modernity (such as individuals, families, secondary organizations, localities, and national regions).[3] The social ecological complexity of internal multiple modernities is literally boundless.

If modern South Korea has been oversaturated with such diverse modernities, its still apparent Confucian traits in numerous aspects and domains should be seen as quite a remarkable phenomenon. What is later analyzed in this chapter as *postcolonial neotraditionalist modernity* offers part of the clue to such a phenomenon, but a much broader and lengthier understanding of traditional Korea (Chosun in particular) and its modern transformations and deformations is required. The sociopolitical significance of Confucianism in Korean history is almost as essential as in Chinese history. In particular, Chosun was established in 1392 explicitly as a formal Confucian state, in which Confucian order exhaustively defined and regulated sociocultural and political relationships, spanning from filial piety and friendship to royal authority over citizenry and even Chosun's tributary relationship with imperial China. From the sixteenth century, Chosun's Confucian aristocratic class of *yangban* tried to further bolster their social hegemony by adopting and then intensifying Chinese neo-Confucianism centered on familial religious rituals and relationships (Lee, K. 1990). The hegemonic authority of Confucianism was so intense and pervasive that Chosun's socioeconomic disintegration paradoxically resulted in widespread, often fake, *yangbanization* of ordinary commoners, who thereafter began to observe or pretend to observe Confucian social norms and rituals (Kim, S. 2003). After Japan colonially occupied Korea in the early 1990s, it reinventively utilized Koreans' Confucian norms and relationships for efficient control and exploitation of them, often by hybridizing Japanese sociopolitical rules with Confucianism.[4] Finally, as specifically analyzed later in this chapter, when Koreans were liberated from Japan on its defeat to the United States in the Pacific War, virtually all of them instantly tried to socioculturally dignify themselves by taking on Confucian norms and relationships mostly at the familial level in spite of – or, thanks to – their universal attainment of modern democratic political rights and sovereign citizen status (also see Chang, K. 2018). Relatedly, what is explained later (in Chapter 8) as *infrastructural familialism* would help Confucianism's practical influence rapidly spread into various social (extra-familial) domains and relatonships – in particular, labor and gender relations in society. These sequential

reinforcements and applications of Confucianism in traditional, colonial, and postcolonial Korea infallibly imply that whatever modern
encounters, transformations, and institutions have arisen must have
complexly reflected and affected Koreans' Confucian order and culture. It will require a serious separate study to concretely qualify
each of South Korea's internal multiple modernities with regard to its
potential Confucian traits, but one may safely judge that contemporary South Koreans' Confucianism cannot but be multifarious and as
much modern as traditional.

Subsequently in this chapter, the following regimes/types of modernities are discussed: colonial dialectical modernity; postcolonial
reflexive institutional(ist) modernization; postcolonial neotraditionalist modernity; the Cold War and Free World modernity; state-capitalist
modernity and national developmentalism; neoliberal economic globalism and cosmopolitan modernity; and subaltern liberal modernity
in the making. Then, various interactions and contradictions among
these internal multiple modernities are examined. The chapter will be
concluded by highlighting the unique sociocultural nature of South
Korea as a multiplex theatre society in which radically diverse claims
of modernities are aggressively and loudly staged side by side and/
or one after another without a convincing prospective for mutual
reconciliation.

4.2 Colonial Dialectical Modernity

Japan's colonization of Korea (then Chosun) for about four decades
in the first half of the twentieth century basically reflected a process of
transnationally reorganizing its capitalism with the ultimate goal of
becoming a pan-Asian capitalist empire. Japan's such ambition only
led to a devastating defeat in a major war against the United States
(whose influence in the Asia-Pacific region had been felt unwelcome
by Japan), leaving Korea to be divided and controlled by the United
States and its war ally, Soviet Union. South Korea's exceptionally
swift economic development in the subsequent few decades had been
hotly debated as to its major factors, including a possible positive
impact of Koreans' experiences as Japan's colonial subjects. Such
experiences have often been conceptualized as Korea's "colonial
modernization" under Japan. However, given Japan's obvious intent
to rule Korea as a permanent part of its imperial political economy
(Schmid 2010), it was essentially an *expanded modernization of
Japan, by Japan, and for Japan* as realized in a captured overseas

territory.[5] Japan's colonial rule in Korea, embodying its capitalist imperialism, was based upon a sort of *fish farm modernity* in that institutional-legal, ideational, and technological modernizations in colonized Korea were supported or implemented in such directions as to facilitate the maximum mobilization and exploitation of Korean resources. On the other hand, it has remained underspecified under what conditions and in what processes Koreans' colonial experiences have been utilized into serviceable social resources for national development and modernization in the postcolonial era.

If modernization did take place for Koreans under Japan's colonial capitalist rule, it was a fundamentally class-based process. Koreans became either peripheralized into structurally subordinated peasants (Shin, G. 1997; Kim, D. 2007) or transformed into a sort of *colonial precariat* in urban tertiary and industrial sectors (Kim, K. 1992; Shin, Y. 2001).[6] By executing the controversial Land Survey Project (*tojijosasaeop*), Japan illicitly appropriated a great part of Koreans' communally owned (and thus formally unspecified in ownership) land and converted ordinary villagers from communal moral economic subjects to individualized cultivators with class interests in the politically manipulated market economy (Kim, D. 2007). Colonial industrialization, a politically framed process of economically annexing Korean population to Japanese capital and technology, almost completely bifurcated industrial class relations according to ethnonational divisions (Kim, K. 1992). Under such processes, Koreans began to develop a socialist (ethno)nationalism with strong subaltern class consciousness (Cumings 1981).[7] This would function time and again as a staunch moralized ideology for (ethno)nationalist struggle against all capitalist ruling forces in succession, namely, Japan, the United States, and the U.S.-backed South Korean state and its client capitalists (Han, H. 2002).[8] This phenomenon may be conceptualized as *colonial dialectical modernity*, not simple colonial modernization. Capitalist modernity is often heedlessly equated to bourgeois ideology and status, but nowhere have a majority of the capitalist system-incorporated population ended up becoming bourgeoisie.[9]

Another instance of colonial dialectical modernity is the generation of a fervently (ethno)nationalist civil society under Japan (cf. Shin, Y. 2001).[10] During Japan's colonial rule, the Korean population as a whole constituted a *de facto* civil society vis-à-vis the authoritarian colonial authority as a surrogate state. Even without having developed a systematic ethos of liberalism (against the feudal state), Koreans' subjugation to the ruthlessly suppressive and exploitative rule of the Japanese colonial government induced them to conceive themselves

57

as a collective social subject to confront and resist the invader state (Shin, Y. 2001).[11] On March 1, 1919, for instance, Koreans launched a remarkable nation-wide protest, by non-violence means, to demand the termination of Japan's colonial rule. The Japanese colonial state, by racist abuse and exploitation, immediately awakened Koreans about their precarious ethnonational status in the global political order and unintendedly helped to form a contentious modern civil society whose impact would, on the one hand, spread to other societies under colonialist encroachment and, on the other hand, last even into the twenty-first century's politics in the Korean peninsula.

Even postcolonial politics could not fully do away with such (oppressively felt) external influence because the United States briefly established itself as a quasi-colonial state authority and then helped install the U.S.-backed governments or tried to ensure the pro-American position from the otherwise established state leaderships until quite recently (Cumings 1981; Park, T. 2008). Unfortunately, most of these U.S.-associated regimes, as well as the American occupation authority itself, remained or turned out highly hostile to civil society, helping deepen the (ethno)nationalist sentiment of civil society. Conversely, South Korean (ethno)nationalism has usually assumed an inherent civil society-orientation, consolidating a sort of (ethno)nationalist liberal modernity. Such (ethno)nationalist liberalism would long remain a central intellectual influence, competing against the above-mentioned (ethno)nationalist socialism and the subsequently explained (ethno)nationalist state capitalism under Park Chung-Hee and his successors.[12]

4.3 Postcolonial Reflexive Institutional(ist) Modernization

In numerous postcolonial societies, modernization began as a *reflexive* process (Giddens 1990; Beck, Bonss, and Lau 2003; Chang, K. 1999) in that their initial critical self-appraisal was usually focused upon their weaknesses and deficiencies vis-à-vis Western forces that had ruled and exploited them, hence leading to an open decision to emulate the West in institutional modernity and economic system (capitalism or socialism).[13] While the reflexive modernity thesis was initially offered mainly as an account of late modern social change in Western societies, a more explicitly corresponding process was taking place as a postcolonial world order, enabling the West to be honorably repositioned from an invader-exploiter to a civilizational model. Such reflexive modernization engendered two situational consequences. Internationally, some former colonial exploiters in the capitalist West thereby became postcolonial tutors and sponsors in modernization, whereas some rival powers assumed similar statuses by sponsoring alternative lines of modernization (socialism in particular). Domestically, mutually competing forces (such as the state, civil society, social classes, etc.) often ended up sociopolitically identifying themselves with their counterparts in the West and promoting broadly similar or common goals for development, modernization and/or reform.[14]

For Koreans, however, its former colonial ruler, Japan had been militarily defeated by the United States, which then imposed various fundamental reforms on Japanese politics, economy, and society broadly in accordance with American liberal principles and practices (Chang, K. 2012a). It was such American systems of politics, economy, and society that began to serve as reflexive standards for South Korean modernization and development.[15] In a way, given the fact that South Korea was subjected to the uninvited, if not unwanted, military occupation by the United States for a few years, its postcolonial reflexive modernization began as a sort of neocolonial process (Cumings 1981; Park, T. 2008). South Korea and other societies under American politico-military influence were induced or forced to transform into the "modern" (reads American) political, economic, and social systems, by which they would ultimately be incorporated into the new global political economy under American leadership and interest. Such neocoloniality was not evenly welcomed or tolerated among different sections of South Korean polity and society, but the Korean War came to effectively help disempower critical positions and voices within civil society.

In South Korea and elsewhere, postcolonial/neocolonial reflexive modernization usually took on an institutionalist nature in that most of its related efforts were centered upon institutional emulation or replication of the politico-legal, economic, and social systems of *seonjinguk* (advanced nations). Reflexive institutional(ist) modernization is a sort of modernization by institutional declaration whether through parliamentary legislations, government decrees, professional organizational statutes, civilian communal proclamations, or even dictatorial orders. In all such procedures, it has basically been a process of transnational knowledge transactions, for which West-modeled local universities have played an essential role.[16] In particular, academic social sciences have played a key instrumental role as embodied in the career paths of so many scholar-cum-politicians/administrators/ activists, often with academic degrees from Western universities (see Table 4.1).[17] These knowledge experts, however, have largely failed in helping to construct the robust social materiality of such transnationally imported or adapted institutions – in particular, embedding institutions in concrete social interests and relations, organizing resource flows for effective and sustainable institutional operation, and so forth.[18] Perhaps, such tasks are as much direct missions of politics, administration, and social activism as side duties of academics, but many involved academics, after all, have served as politicians, administrators, and civil activists as well.

In the area of public governance, however, the defective social materiality of reflexively established institutions seems to have been critically complemented by the historical memories of and references to the traditional systems of state management and local governance. Despite the feudal, or premodern, conception of social and political sovereignty, Chosun ruled the nation with the government structure, budgetary mechanism, and notion of citizenship that are remarkably correspondent to those of the modern era.[19] Even Koryo was not too different (Yi, K. 1984). To most South Koreans – except those academic, legal, and technocratic experts directly involved in West-oriented reflexive institutionalization – their mediated memories about the traditional states were a more availably significant cultural basis for understanding and accommodating the deluge of reflexively established institutions, than any public declarations or academic explanations about their foundations and relevance. Such available historical references to feudal state institutions were substantively limited and logically spurious because of the liberal foundation of the adopted reflexive institutions, but would turn out, as a paradox, epistemologically convenient when South Korean democracy was degenerated into a series of authoritarian statist rules with neotraditionalist appeals (Cumings 2005).[20]

Under the widespread and chronic deficit in the social materiality of transnationally derived institutions, postcolonial/neocolonial reflexive modernization has remained, in numerous public and civilian spheres, at a stage or state of what can be characterized as *cuttage modernity*. Shallowly planted branch-like social and legal institutions could not have effectively functioned for a long while, whereas their immediate (ab)use in complex postcolonial realities has often decelerated or even inhibited a stable growth into a firmly rooted tree-like condition. This dilemma has been most clearly and painfully manifested by the turbulent fluctuations of South Korean democracy (Choi, J. 2002). Besides such stultification of institutional modernity, the immature operability or malfunctioning of cuttage-level

Table 4.1 Major origin countries of South Koreans' doctoral degrees by disciplinary groups for the period of 1945–2013 (unit: accumulated degrees for 1945–2013; % of all foreign degrees by disciplinary group)

Rank	Social sciences			Engineering			Humanities			National sciences		
	Country	Num	%	Country	Num	%	Country	Num	%	Country	Num	%
1	US	5,881	62.8	US	5,261	63.8	US	2,217	33.4	US	3,400	70.3
2	Germany	846	9.0	Japan	1,965	23.8	Germany	962	14.5	Japan	698	14.4
3	Japan	817	8.7	UK	297	3.6	Japan	786	11.8	Germany	251	5.2
4	UK	569	6.1	Gemany	248	3.0	France	664	10.0	UK	164	3.4
5	China	325	3.5	France	197	2.4	China	640	9.6	France	102	2.1
Sum of top 5	–		90.1	–		96.6	–		79.3	–		95.4

Source: Abridged and translated from Table 3 in the Press release of the Korea Higher Education Research Institute (KHEI). 2014. "57% of the Overseas Doctoral Degrees between 1945 and 2013 are American Degrees" (http://khei.re.kr/post/2099).

institutions has often induced or allowed other types of institutions to be used as surrogates – a widely observed phenomenon describable as *institutional functional conflation*. When some organizational inertia and/or structural interests are consolidated by surrogate institutions, they tend constantly to threaten or complicate the normal growth and operation of the supposedly proper institutions in charge and, no less seriously, distort their own original institutional functions. For instance, the intense and lengthy politicization of South Korea's military and media have crucially hindered the consolidation and stabilization of normal political parties, while retarding and deforming their own institutional evolution.[21]

A seemingly contrasting phenomenon is a widespread and chronic tendency of inter-institutional segregation and isolation. Reflexive institutional modernization usually takes place through a process of civilizational or systemic *reverse engineering* in that each of core social institutions comprising an advanced civilization or social system is simulated or adapted by a separate division of functionaries socially entrusted and/or legally licensed.[22] The initially pragmatic practice of *compartmentalized institutional simulation* has gradually been degenerated into a stiff structure of mutually isolationist divisions of institutional simulation, with the academia being one of the worst instances.[23] Compartmentally simulated or adapted institutions would incur additional functional problems due to their potential mutual disharmonies and malcoordinations and habitual neglect of the universal orders and societal purposes for their common existence. These problems would intensify the above explained tendency of institutional functional conflation.

4.4 Postcolonial Neotraditionalist Modernity

Korea's fall to Japanese colonialism came as a particularly intense ethnonational shame under the regional historico-civilizational context in which Japan had been regarded as inferior to China and its faithful civilizational subscriber nations, such as Chosun (currently Korea) and Ryukyu (currently Okinawa). During Japan's colonial rule, understandably, the main impetus for Korean anticolonial resistance was supplied by many of the learned Confucian elites from formerly aristocratic families (*yangban*) although even numerous notorious collaborators for colonial rule were also members of such families (Chang, K. 2018). As one of the most fundamental changes made to Korean society, Japan formally reaffirmed the nominal abolition, by the short-lived *Daehanjeguk*, of the feudal status system of Chosun (comprised of *yangban, jungin, sangmin, cheonmin*; or of gentry, middlemen, commoners, slaves), but its position about Confucian culture remained syncretic and flexible in accordance with pragmatic considerations for cost-effective control and exploitation of Koreans (Lee, H. 2011; Rhyu, M. 2005).

Korea's liberation from Japan was instantly accompanied by various dispersed efforts by members of some previously influential Confucian families and traditional communal schools at reinstating Confucian principles in public life and sociopolitical order. While such elite efforts turned out to be largely ineffective, ordinary South Koreans, nonetheless, widely and fervently began to consummate Confucian culture in their private sphere. This phenomenon was contextually coalesced with the new political order of universal democratic citizenship, the new economic order constructed under land reform, and the new system of universal (elementary) public education. That is, as full members of the Republic of Korea – now a nation-state of equally sovereign commoners – virtually all South Koreans tried to assert a dignifying cultural status in tandem with their new citizenship rights in politics, farming, and education. Culturally self-serving aristocratization (*yangbanization*), mainly in family relations and rituals, instantly took place throughout the country, making modern South Korea more Confucian on average than its ancestral society of Chosun (Chang, K. 2018; Jeong, J. 1995). This trend enraged members of many traditional aristocratic families who claimed a supposedly exclusive status of being or remaining Confucian more properly.[24]

Family-based Confucianism, regarded as a socially superior cultural asset, thereby came to constitute the core sociocultural foundation of liberal modernity (in the South Korean version), allowing every citizen to feel equally superior and moral through rigorous participation in (extended) family life. Such cultural self-dignification was practiced often in terms of complex and lavish familial rituals (such as wedding, funeral, ancestral worship, and so forth) – a trend that would seriously worry the developmentalist state in its strenuous effort at minimizing domestic consumption while maximizing industrial investment and economic growth (see Photo 4.1). This phenomenon was *neotraditionalization*, rather than *retraditionalization*, in that Confucianism based upon such cultural egalitarianism directly differs from Confucianism as the core status asset of an aristocratic class (*yangban*) as in Chosun (Chang, K. 2018, ch. 4). As authoritatively explained by Eli Zaretsky (1973), the aristocratic nature of modern (nuclear) family life, as neotraditionalist modernity, is also

63

Photo 4.1 Housewives in the public oath ceremony for abiding by the Standard Rules on Familial Rituals (*gajeonguiryejunchik*) in 1969

Photo source: *Kyunghyang Shinmun*, August 27, 2017

Author's note: The Park Chung-Hee government declared, in 1969, the Standard Rules on Familial Rituals to restrain ordinary citizens' excess practice and consumption in the neotraditional Confucian rituals of ancestor worship, funeral, wedding, etc.

found in the Western context where the Victorian-age family culture was sequentially appropriated by bourgeoisie and proletariat along the transformation of the capitalist production systems and labor regimes. In comparison, the Western case is more a long-term political economic phenomenon, whereas the South Korean case is more an instant sociopolitical phenomenon.[25]

In varieties of neo-Weberian analysis, Confucian modernity has also been a hotly debated issue in regard to the particular nature of South Korean (or East Asian) democracy, capitalism, social security, corporate management, education, religion, and so forth (Kim, K. 2017; Lew, S. 2013). Each of these issues has drawn substantial scholarly research efforts and public attention, but they have a common limit in establishing irrefutably what are genuinely Confucian about the supposed Confucian practices and orders. It may be safe to say that Confucian culture has been applied pragmatically and flexibly in order to manage or solve each of these modern-day tasks, whether successful or not. In so doing, the above-mentioned postcolonial Confucianization of South Koreans' everyday life in family relations and rituals may have helped to establish the epistemological and moral basis for the supposedly Confucian manners and orders in politics, industry, welfare, schooling, and even preaching (see Photo 4.2).[26] It is for this reason that many of the supposedly Confucian-style

Photo 4.2 The opening of Confucianland (Yugyoland) in Andong City

Photo source: *Yonhapews*, July 16, 2015

Author's note: As the hegemonic sociopolitical significance of Confucianism in the national public sphere is no more valid, there have been regionalized efforts at its revitalization in some traditional strongholds of Confucian gentry. For instance, Andong City launched Confucianland (Yugyoland) in 2013 in order to symbolize its traditional status as a key hub of hegemonic Confucian gentry in Chosun.

organizations, institutions, and relationships have openly utilized various terms for private family relations and roles – most familiarly, "company as family," in which *gieopchongsu* (corporate general head, meaning owner-executive) is positioned as grand patriarch in both administrative and cultural senses.[27]

No less significantly, and more systematically, Confucianism has produced various institutionalized effects in a wide range of public matters and civilian concerns, as South Korean families have directly functioned as the main institution and/or actor in them (Chang, K. 2010a). Many well-known (or sensational?) features of South Korean development and modernization – such as excessive education zeal, tenaciously self-reliant welfare, and aggressive corporate conglomeration (*chaebol*) – are institutionally based upon familial relations, interests, and responsibilities. In contrast to "institutionalized individualism" (Beck and Beck-Gernsheim 2002) in Western welfare states, labor markets, lifestyles, and so forth, *institutionalized familialism* (Chang, K. 2010a; Chang et al. 2015) has prevailed as a privately driven but governmentally sanctioned or reinforced paradigm in South Koreans' management of diverse social and economic affairs. Encouragement of and investment in children's education have been regarded as the most honorable (cultural) duty for parents; the strong ethic of filial piety (*hyo*) has long helped delay the public preparation of old-age social security measures (and has thereby caused South Korean elderly to confront the worst level of relative poverty in the industrialized world); the generalized hereditary familial inheritance of conglomerate ownership and management, about which most governments have remained indifferent or tolerant, has involved not only widespread legal and financial irregularities for evading due expenses (taxes) and bypassing fair says of other concerned parties and also frequent conflicts, among heir siblings, about the (culturally?) legitimate order and share of corporate inheritance.

Where social and economic affairs are managed under institutionalized familialism, it is usually Confucian norms, whether historically valid or conveniently asserted, that shape the concrete claims, choices, and actions made by the involved parties. At least according to the perspectives of those directly engaged, education, welfare, corporate governance, and a host of other family-centered affairs do attest to the Confucian nature of South Korean modernity. As a grave consequence, the chronic discrimination against and exploitation of women in various supposedly public affairs have been facilitated and justified by Confucian familial norms shared by their family members, other concerned parties, and, sometimes, disadvantaged women themselves (Chang, K. 2018).

4.5 The Cold War and Free World Modernity

The American contribution to South Korea's political independence (and division from North Korea) was decisive, due not only to its war victory over Japan, but also its conceiving and establishment of a new international political order (namely, Wilsonianism). In practice, the American victory in the Pacific War did not leave the United States in a carefree position about the nations and territories it had liberated or helped liberate. According to the America-envisaged new world of liberal internationalism, such liberated nations had to be transformed or consolidated as suitable constituents of the liberal capitalist order worldwide. This historical requirement would not be achievable by restoring whatever indigenous order and civilization had previously existed in each nation, but by assimilating to the "modern" systems of politics, economy, and society as exemplified by the United States.[28] Modernization, from the very beginning, was defined as such in a particular global historico-political context (Apter 1965).

However, the United States was able to help promote such assimilation, or modernization, in only half of the Korean Peninsula. With an inadvertent – however convenient for the moment – arrangement for managing Korea's postwar social situation, with the Soviet Union's virtually invited engagement in the Northern half of the Peninsula, the United States instantly ended up becoming chiefly responsible for the nation's division between South and North Korea and, ultimately, between capitalism and communism (Cumings 1981). Even for South Korea, furthermore, the American policy of reluctant, minimalistic engagement (except for military campaigns to weed out socialist influences from across the country) and concomitant recycling of many of Japan's colonial institutional, human, and infrastructural resources failed to help establish the solid material and institutional foundations of a new polity in the making (the Republic of Korea), whose fragility would be badly tested by North Korea's invasion for national reunification (Park, M. 1996). While it remains debatable how decisive the role of the Soviet Union was in inducing North Korea into the Korean War (1950–1953), this total civil war simultaneously assumed an automatic quality of the global Cold War between the capitalist and the socialist bloc, which both intensified and would be solidified by it.[29]

The slippage of Wilsonian liberal internationalism into the Cold War's superpower rivalry, as critically triggered by the Korean War (as well as the Soviet invasion and control of Eastern Europe), came to restage South Korea's liberal capitalist transformation from a postcolonial national project to an international political exigency of the Free World. That is, South Korean development and modernization began to assume a group quality defined by the American hegemonic influence over the liberal capitalist regions and countries across the world (Cumings 1997; Kim, D. 1997). The Free World as a whole became the basic unit of liberal capitalist modernity predicated upon the centrality of the American systems of politics, economy, and society. For those nations under America's hegemonic influence (often termed "allies"), the American systems practically became immediate elements of their modernization and development, as suggested by a sort of *Free World citizenship* with which individuals, civil organizations, and business firms in these ally nations have been given

Photo 4.3 The leaders of South and North Korea and the United States at the inter-Korean border

Photo source: *Yonhapnews*, June 30, 2019

Author's note: Many American politicians have underscored South Korea's developmental success as a critical evidence of the supposed superiority of the liberal economic and political system they have promoted in the so-called Free World. Relatedly, they have indicated North Korea's chronic economic crisis as a clear testament to the inevitable pitfall of its socialist system. In fact, North Korea has recently been eager to mobilize South Korean cooperation in its desperate effort to overcome the economic stalemate; however, without giving up its nuclear armament. South Korea's Moon Jae-In government attempted, though unsuccessfully, to persuade North Korea (under Kim Jong-Un) and the US (under Donald Trump) toward a big deal between North Korean nuclear arms and American sanctions, with South Korea's economic compensation for North Korea. The three nations' leaders met at the inter-Korean border in 2019.

preferential access to American education, culture, technology, and commodity market, as well as public aid.[30]

South Korean development and modernization thereafter had to be successful, not only as South Koreans' national goal but also as the Free World's supposed systemic superiority over communism (see Photo 4.3). At the very least, South Korea had to survive as the Free World's strategic politico-military outpost, so the United States began trying to stabilize South Korea politically and socially with various means whenever necessary.[31] Accordingly, the United States kept ensuring the pro-American posture of every South Korean government even when this required tolerating illegitimate power transitions or abuse of democratic citizenship, above all, by military politicians.[32] It even had to tolerate Park Chung-Hee for nearly two decades when he tried to industrialize South Korea in a state-mercantilist manner (see the subsequent subsection) and build up some autonomous military basis (including a suspected nuclear program) (Kim, H. 2004).

South Korea's (conservative) political and military elites welcomed such (re)internationalization of their nation's fate, particularly because of their chronic legitimacy deficit for historical and social reasons. They attempted to keep defining South Korea's situation in terms of an ongoing, if hidden, war with the communists until nowadays; conversely South Korea's political mainstay of conservatism has been defined by state-led anti-communist struggles that, given the long sustained state of truce with North Korea, would necessitate inventing or branding internal leftist elements as alleged spies or collaborators for external enemies.[33] In this context, each of the rightwing state leaders, whether self-appointed militarily or politically elected, had to (or wanted to) go through a *de facto* ratification process with the United States – usually in terms of paying the first official visit to the United States after taking up presidency.[34] In one way, except for Park Chung Hee's developmental contribution, South Korea's political conservatism has been an empty vessel because it has focused so exclusively upon national security while disallowing any potential political influence of industrial elites (*chaebol*) outside its supervision.[35] In South Korea's illiberal liberalism, its illiberal part has been exclusively reserved for various sections of the state's apparatuses for legal and physical coercion, while its liberal part has been largely delegated to business elites.

The dramatic termination of the Cold War at the global level abruptly brought about serious changes to South Korea's status as a Free World client. The neoliberal United States began to perceive South Korea as a recalcitrant and unthankful economic subject and put increasing pressure for its compliance with the new global economic order under which South Korean industries would be structurally enmeshed with America's globalized financial interests (Kong, T. 2000). Such pressure was opportunistically taken by South Korean *chaebol* and finance to quench their thirst for more capital with Western hot money, whereas the incumbent government led by a former democracy fighter, Kim Young-Sam, was determined to show a developmental achievement comparable to that of Park Chung-Hee and thus willingly endorsed unfamiliarly risky financial transactions of South Korean manufacturers and banks. What thereby ensued was not another developmental impetus but an unprecedented national financial meltdown, from which South Korea would be rescued only by accepting the so-called "IMF conditionalities" that were designed to restructure the South Korean economy into a fully (neo)liberalized entity serving the best interests of global financial capitalism (Chang, K. 2019, ch. 3). In a sense, South Korea contributed to completing the Free World in its economic dimension through unreserved neoliberal terms that, however, would subject its ordinary citizens to unbearably painful experiences.

4.6 State-Capitalist Modernity and National Developmentalism

While capitalism arose out of liberal social revolutions or reformations in Europe, its expansion to other parts of the world led to the racist subjugation of peoples and societies therein to militarily organized capitalist interest. Where such subjugated subjects had already experienced indigenously established nation-state rule, capitalist imperialism usually triggered (ethno)nationalist sociopolitical resistance and unintendedly awakened or stimulated local elites about the necessity to build up their own capitalism or turn to socialism as a countermeasure. In this context, capitalism – much like socialism – came to be conceived as a fundamentally collective venture, involving the entire nation (population) and its governing state. A sort of nation-state capitalism began to be envisaged, often with the state assuming the status of bourgeoisie-in-chief (Chang, K. 2019; see Photos 4.4 and 4.5). Japan was exceptional in that it managed to promulgate state capitalism presciently, that is, before or without being conquered by capitalist colonialists from the West. We could say that Bismarck's Germany was another such instance of state capitalism, although it did not require a similar level of prescience given its physical location in Europe.[36]

It was no surprise that Japan's capitalist colonization of Korea immediately kindled Korean elites' aspiration for capitalist national development. This effect was particularly strong owing to Koreans' realization that Japan's overwhelming power had been derived from state-organized capitalist transition (i.e. the Meiji Revolution) (Cumings 1987). But Japan had no interest in making or letting Koreans evolve into autonomous capitalist subjects (Shin, Y. 2001). Moreover, South Korea's immediate postcolonial system of political and economic rule (under Syng-Man Rhee) more closely resembled that of the flatly libertarian United States and failed to meaningfully promote even civilian capitalism.[37] Rhee's economic failure and political betrayal prompted South Korean citizens to oust him, but they soon had to see Park Chung-Hee establish himself into state

Photo 4.4 President Park Geun-Hye at the National Trade Day ceremony in 2015

Photo source: *Republic of Kore Policy Brief*, December 7, 2015

Author's note: Under the militarized state leadership of Park Chung-Hee, economic development was reframed into export-oriented state capitalist industrialization. Each president ever since has assumed, both administratively and symbolically, the status of a grand CEO of collective national(ist) industrial capitalism. The National Day of Export (*suchului nal*) – which was first declared on November 30, 1964 when South Korean export reached a hundred million US dollars for the first time and changed in 1990 to December 5 as the National Day of Trade – would be presided over by each president as the most significant public ritual of such nationalist industrial capitalism, including Park's daughter Park Geun-Hye.

leadership through a military coup. For Park, capitalism was conceived as an indispensable historical instrument for national survival and regeneration, as epitomized by the slogans of *bugukgangbyeong* (rich country, strong army) and *minjokjungheung* (national regeneration).[38] For and through state-led capitalist industrialization (Lim, H. 1986), he turned his political position of state head into a political economic position of bourgeoisie-in-chief for South Korea's state capitalism, often dubbed "Korea, Inc."

Thereafter, national developmentalism, or (ethno)nationalist state capitalism, became the *de facto* hegemonic ideology in politics and society, overriding all other ideologies adopted and promoted in formal politics or civil society (Jeon, J. 1999). For instance, the formal names of political parties, including the one under Park's control (*Minjugonghwadang*, or the Democratic Republican Party),

71

Photo 4.5 President Moon Jae-In addressing at the inauguration of the Presidential Committee on the Fourth Industrial Revolution in 2017

Photo source: *Segye Ilbo*, December 17, 2017

Author's note: Moon Jae-In, while elected into presidency after the political failure of two conservative developmentalist presidents, still had to make himself appealing as a developmentalist state leader. Relatedly, South Korea became in 2017 the world's first national adopter of "the Fourth Industrial Revolution" as an official national developmental paradigm.

were mostly derived from American counterparts, but did not meaningfully reflect or change the prevailing political values and interests centered on collective national developmentalism and its derivative ethos of individual materialism. On the other hand, South Korea's main nominal bourgeoisie, i.e. *chaebol* (industrial business conglomerates), were positioned (and supported) as subordinate instruments for state capitalism and likewise denied any meaningful sociopolitical or ideological position as the key leader class of liberal capitalist modernity in the public arena (Chang, K. 2010a, ch. 7). Apparently, they have felt rather comfortable and even convenient about such ideological or civilizational sidelining and preferred to pursue their interest either through habitual formal dependence on the state or strategically hidden collusion with authoritarian state elites.[39]

Finally, ordinary South Koreans as formal political constituencies of state capitalism, or simply as members of the developmentalist nation, were ideologically exhorted to take on a collective (false?) consciousness as a sort of *bourgeoisie-by-affiliative imagination*.[40] They were tenaciously persuaded and compelled to *imagine national development* as their public duty-cum-right through public propaganda, paragovernmental media coverage, formal education, and so forth. I have elsewhere analyzed this practice as *developmental citizenship* (Chang, K. 2012b). However, this political cultural status has been frontally contradicted by everyday realities of work and livelihood in which most of them have merely remained proletarian subjects abusively exploited by state-backed capitalist employers (Chang, K. 2019, ch. 2).[41] In government interpretations, enduring such exploitation was often considered as a patriotic act for the collective national goods of international industrial competitiveness and rapid capitalist development. Fortunately, or unfortunately, most South Koreans' social identity as proletariat has usually remained flimsy and transitory in accordance with their chronically transient occupational statuses (Choi and Chang 2016), whereas their politico-historical consciousness as abstract developmentalist citizens, once fervently formed under Park Chung-Hee, has been staunchly sustained to date among the currently old-aged and late middle-aged South Koreans.[42]

4.7 Neoliberal Economic Globalism and Cosmopolitan Modernity

Long-sustained rapid economic development enabled South Korea to join the rank of "advanced" or "industrialized" economies, as epitomized by its acceptance into the OECD (Organisation for Economic Co-operation and Development) in 1996. Given this status, the successive global multilateral drives for trade liberalization and integration were posed to South Korea both as an international pressure for economic regulatory conformity and as a national opportunity for further industrial expansion (Ji, J. 2011). The same status also subjected the country to mounting pressure and seduction from earlier developed and thus financially overaccumulated countries for financial liberalization, which would be hastily and haphazardly accommodated by South Korean banks and industries with insatiable thirst for access to more and cheaper loans beyond government control (Kong, T. 2000). Imprudent financial liberalization all of a sudden led the country to a total financial meltdown in 1997. The so-called "IMF conditionalities" for debt renewal paradoxically required South Korea to further strengthen financial and trade liberalization besides usual austerity measures for a debtor regarding labor, welfare, finance, etc. Despite (or due to?) such across-the-board neoliberal prescriptions, many supposedly South Korean industries (whose ownership structures and production locations are now as much global as South Korean) began a sort of second great leap.

Undoubtedly, the key players of South Korean capitalist modernity – that is, mostly export-oriented industrial conglomerates – are now both internally and externally global. Internally global because their ownership structures and technological configurations reflect a wide global spectrum of contributors; externally global because their production sites and commodity markets range across the world – particularly across Asia (Chang, K. 2019, ch. 8). Capitalist late modernity is predicated upon a far-flung globality of economic activities and social relations, and South Korea has certainly become an integral part of it. It was indicated above that the Cold War necessitated a collective or associative unit of liberal capitalist modernity of which South Korea was a critical part. Now, neoliberal globalism has rendered capitalist modernity to assume a world-wide collective or associative attribute. South Korea has been an active facilitator for and critical part of such globalized capitalist modernity.

As in many societies at similar developmental ranks, South Korea's solid status in global capitalist modernity has ironically necessitated a radically wide disarticulation of ordinary citizens in economic and social spheres. These *transformative victims* include industrial workers laid off massively during the "IMF crisis," youth confronted with joblessness under wide overseas relocation of factories and offices, peasants coercively asked to sacrifice themselves to widen export markets for manufactures, and so on (see Chapter 5 below; Chang, K. 2022, ch. 9; see Photo 4.7). These economically victimized groups have ultimately confronted various syndromes of social reproduction crisis (see Chapter 7), including the forced bachelorhood of numerous middle-aged men in villages and urban peripheries. From the early 2000s, in an unprecedented trend, many of them began to marry women from other Asian countries, roughly in the sequences of Korean Chinese (Chaoxianzu) and then Han Chinese women marrying poor South Korean men in urban peripheries and Southeast Asian women (in particular, Vietnamese women) marrying rural South Korean men, many of whom are middle-aged (Chang, K. 2018, ch. 6; see Photo 4.6). Interestingly, such marriage transnationalization triggered sociocultural campaigns for multiculturalism by both civilian advocacy groups and central and local government bodies. A sort of cosmopolitan modernity has been fervently envisioned amid the mass arrival of foreign brides from across Asia and the social and governmental efforts at facilitating their integration with local families and communities while reconfiguring South Korean society as a multicultural or cosmopolitan entity (see Chapter 6 below). Many of the major industrial conglomerates have enthusiastically supported

Photo 4.6 Group wedding of "multicultural couples" in Goesan County, South Korea

Photo source: Goesan County Government, March 9, 2019

Author's note: South Korea's neoliberally caused economic crisis was coped with by a variety of measures for further neoliberal globalization, including the world's most aggressive pursuit of Free Trade deals for strategically supporting export industries (often in exchange for giving away the domestic market for agricultural products). As this policy coincided with the rapid demographic aging of peasants, the socioeconomic decline of village communities kept intensifying, leaving rural bachelors less and less attractive as marriage partners due to worsening material conditions. In a fundamentally unexpected turnabout, rural communities and families embarked on their own sociocultural globalization in aggressivly securing poor brides from other Asian societies, including Vietnam in particular. Many of such international marriages have taken place without satisfactory rituals, so local governments, corporate sponsors, and/or other benefactors frequently organize group weddings for some already married "multicultural" couples.

or partaken in such multiculturalism activities. The cosmopolitan cultural turn of South Korean society is in no doubt a fundamentally useful condition for these globalized business entities. But it is quite ironic that the concrete materiality of the latest multiculturalization of South Korean society has been derived from precisely those who have been economically and socially victimized to such industrial conglomerates' strategic benefits in the world economy and consequently become fairly unattractive as possible husbands to South Korean women.

4.8 Subaltern Liberal Modernity in the Making: Civil Society as (Associative) Subaltern Community

Among the above explained modernities, four of them – i.e. reflexive institutional(ist) modernity, Cold War modernity, state capitalist modernity, and neoliberal global modernity – seem to have exerted, individually and interactively, sustained hegemonic influence on South Korean society and people. These modernities have a crucial common attribute, namely, the state's proactive engagement and support. Perhaps it is their common dependence on the state that has enabled their far-flung societal effects. Conversely, these modernities seem to have rendered South Korea to remain a highly state-centered sociopolitical entity. Those subaltern South Koreans who have been either alienated or subjugated by these modernities broadly constitute a civil society that has a dialectically resistant quality against the nation's state-centered sociopolitical order and economic structure. (Such dialectical quality may be comparable to the colonial dialectical modernity assumed by Koreans as proletariat and civil society during the Japanese colonial reign.) The South Korean state has been subjected to a broadly allied social criticism from those whose activities have been overridden or discriminated by West-oriented institutional modernization in politics, administration, culture, philosophy and religion, education, medicine, as well as economic production, those who have yearned for integrative (ethno)nationalist and/or socialist futures but only suffered McCarthysian suppression, those whose labor and/or life world resources have been aggressively mobilized but unfairly compensated for by state-capitalist industrialization, and those whose economic citizenship has been unjustly deprived or turned unexpectable under violent neoliberal restructuring and globalization.

A civil society, chiefly constituted not by bourgeoisie class but by a series of subaltern citizens adversely affected by reflexive institutionalization, the Cold War order, state capitalist development, and neoliberal globalization, kept erupting forcefully whenever state leadership, along with its power apparatuses and socioeconomic clients, was degenerated into a society-threatening autocracy. April Revolution (1960), Gwangju Uprising (1980), June Revolution (1987), Candlelight Uprising (2008), and Candlelight Revolution

Photo 4.7 "The Candlelight Revolution" (*chotbulhyeokmyeong*)
in Winter 2016

Photo source: *Weekly Dong-A*, November 18, 2016

Author's note: President Park Geun-Hye's revealed responsibilities for her secret crony's administrative interference and corporate extortion triggered nationwide civil protests throughout the winter of 2016–17, ultimately leading to her impeachment. Her degenerated presidency, as Park Chung-Hee's daughter, symbolized multi-layered injustice, from the immediate post-liberation period to the 21st century, prompting nearly all categories of social resistance to be staged side by side.

(2016) were such civil eruptions that fundamentally reshaped the course and structure of South Korea's sociopolitical modernity (see Photo 4.7). Each of these civil eruptions was not identifiable in terms of a specific allegiance to a certain social class, whereas the involved subaltern forces were commonly classifiable only in terms of their dialectical confrontation with the state. South Korea as a nation of "strong state, contentious society" (Koo, H. 1993) may be understood as such. The politically integrating effect of their common confrontations with the state, however, has often nurtured a state-centrism in political reform or modernization among these resistant social actors themselves, inhibiting a sustained organic development of civil society. Too many of them have ended up being scouted into the dominant political parties that suffer from chronic defectiveness in legitimate and/or rational social representation.[43]

In South Korea's twenty-first century, such strength of the state has become decisively liquidated amid the successively manifested inefficacy or derailment of reflexive institutional modernity, McCarthysian rule, state capitalist developmentalism, and neoliberal economic governance. The strong state's slippage has not necessarily implied a hegemonic rise of civil society and its modernization projects, but the latest elected government under Moon Jae-In – seemingly a broad united front of social movements and advocacies with regard to its core policy agendas and appointed key officials – seemingly signifies the potential inception of a new era of subaltern liberal modernity.[44] The wide and complex diversity of subaltern social subjects in such bottom-up liberalism is both the sociopolitical strength and weakness of this only loosely connected constellation of those *transformative victims* (see Chapter 5; Chang, K. 2022) under the previous century modernities. Which side is to be more saliently pronounced will be to a critical extent determined by effective sociopolitical entrepreneurship for weaving them into a new associative civilizational and political economic entity.

4.9 The Clash of (Internal Multiple) Modernities?

Given its internal multiple modernities, South Korea often appears to be a kind of multiplex society subjected to diverse yet coexisting regimes of modernization (or, as suggested in Chapter 2, *modernitization*). Each of these modernities is not uniquely or exclusively Korean because they have been embedded in the global structures and processes of modern social change. In particular, other East Asian nations share many of the above explained multiple modernities. Nevertheless, South Korea is remarkable in the volume of multiplicities of modernities, the dramatic and intense actualization of each modernity, the protracted operation of each modernity, and the highly complicated interactions among such multiple modernities. The last aspect still requires some elaboration. This section discusses various contradictions and contaminations among South Korea's internal multiple modernities by focusing on colonial dialectical modernity, postcolonial reflexive institutional(ist) modernity, and neoliberal economic globalism.

Colonial dialectical modernity's collisions   South Korea's (ethno) nationalist civil society and class identity as colonial dialectical modernity have continued to generate critical impacts on postcolonial politics and society in diverse ways. Among progressive intellectual circles, the question of whether Koreans are "genuinely liberated" has been a continually debated issue, particularly in conjunction with their protracted subjection to tremendous American influence in virtually every aspect of modernity. The American military administration during its occupation period even invited many colonial collaborator Koreans to run public institutions and infrastructures, many of which had been recycled from the Japanese rule (Cumings 1984). However, the thereby sustained (ethno)nationalist ethos was quite difficult, if not altogether impossible, to accommodate in the formal political institutions and procedures of the new liberal republic, reflexively modeled after those of the United States.

Political nationalism was more fervently embraced during Park Chung-Hee's state capitalist rule, which practically nullified normal political procedures and instead tried to complementarily establish a (ethno)nationalist political legitimacy based upon the mercantilist ideology of *bugukgangbyeong* (rich country, strong army). Park did not succeed the colonial dialectical (ethno)nationalism with socialist or liberal orientation, but was able to draw a widely supportive response from ordinary South Koreans through a sort of bourgeois-nationalist agenda and propaganda (as explained above). Another complicated effect of colonial dialectical (ethno)nationalism has been generated against the structural interest of progressive class politics within South Korea's capitalist political economy. By many historically conscious (ethno)nationalists, North Korea has often been considered as a potential partner for national liberation struggles – a position flatly denied by many labor activists and union leaders, who have promoted immediate class justice for South Korean workers while remaining skeptical about the North Korean dictatorship (Park, C. 2016).[45] Nonetheless, the latter's initially successful effort at establishing a formal working-class party with significant recognition and influence would be hijacked by the former through underground tactics, to no one's benefit in the end (Chang, K. 2022, ch. 3).[46]

Postcolonial reflexive institutional(ist) modernity's collisions As indicated above, most liberal social institutions reflexively simulated or adapted from the so-called advanced Western nations have initially suffered varying degrees of inadequate social materiality. A no less crucial dilemma has arisen from the decisive role of the state in establishing what are supposed to be civil society institutions in the originator civilizations – be they market economy, journalism, high education, legal profession, medicine, or a host of other basic elements of a liberal social system (Chang, K. 2019, ch. 2). Both core leaders and rank-and-file members of these liberal social institutions have habitually demanded the state's regulatory and financial support while grossly neglecting to establish their social foundations and legitimacies (Song, H. 2016). Conversely, the defective social materiality of the concerned institutions seems to have induced them to ask for state engagement and support as a quick fix.[47] There have been crucial injuries, in conjunction with the Cold War order and the state capitalist system, to the liberal integrity of reflexive institutions under protracted state engagement and support.

First, the Cold War, as a national-cum-global order, came to reposition liberal institutional modernity from a national project of civilizational (re)construction to an international object of politico-military protection. Paradoxically, the Cold War state's freedom politics began to forfeit civil society's freedom to autonomously debate the goals, measures, and substances of national development and modernization beyond the legal and ideological guidelines of the state about the ideal liberal systems of politics, society, and economy.[48] Any critique from civil society about such state guidelines would easily be identified with or alleged to be a communist/socialist element (potentially linked to North Korea). South Korea's thereby formed illiberal liberalism has been intensifying, not softening, along the course of time as the politico-social forces endowed with related coercive power – in particular, elite members of *gongan* (public security) organs such as prosecution, police, and even MacCarthysian media as a sort of self-appointed ideological police – have been increasingly and firmly established into the national political structure.[49] When the military's developmental autocracy came to abruptly lose its political efficacy amid the nation's democratization and post-developmental transition, they began to occupy most key positions of the mainstream conservative party and helped to protract the domestic Cold War into the twenty-first century.[50]

Second, liberal economic institutions were found to be widely and chronically incompatible with the state capitalist system for national(ist) industrialization and economic development, which in fact arose precisely because liberal institutional modernization had failed to facilitate the critically necessitated national economic transformation. This dilemma led to the rampant dualization of the economic institutional order between on-paper rules and forms and in-practice rules and forms. South Korea's sustained success in state capitalist development tended to strengthen the already prioritized status of informally dominant economic rules and forms – namely, the *chaebol* system of corporate ownership and governance, policy-based market distortion, state-controlled labor relations, and so forth.[51] The destabilizing impacts of both the Cold War order and

80

the state capitalist system on liberal institutional modernity unfail-
ingly vindicate the critical structural risks that arise when reflexive
liberal institutionalization proceeds with pervasive state engagement
and support.

Neoliberal economic globalism's collisions   Neoliberal economic
globalism has been incorporated into South Korean society at a radically rapid pace. Its immediate backgrounds, as openly known both
domestically and internationally, include the corporate and financial
drive for overseas financed maximum expansion since the late 1980s
and the IMF bail-out conditionalities accompanying the consequent
national financial meltdown in 1997 to 1998 (Chang, K. 2019, ch. 3).
However, there have also been less obviously known causes that can
be comprehended only in the particular political economic context of
South Korea's state capitalist development.

First, state capitalist industrialization in South Korea spawned a
deformed institutional and financial order in which *chaebol*'s interest
has been unjustly and sometimes unlawfully realized by sacrificing the
due opportunities, rights, and benefits of other economic participants
and general citizens (Chang, K. 2010a, ch. 7). In this regard, some
activists for domestic economic reform found global (neoliberal)
capital's criticism and reform demand on *chaebol* – as publicized by
global financial media, consultancies, investment banks, as well as
multilateral organizations (such as the World Bank and the IMF) –
strategically compatible with their reform agenda (Chang, H. 2014).
Conversely, global capital also came to find such South Korean
activists useful in inducing the desired reform of *chaebol* to its interest. The two parties' agreement, however, was limited to the issues
of shareholder accountability in *chaebol*-affiliated firms and other
largely liberal regulatory matters.[52]

Second, *chaebol* also found some strategic utility in neoliberal
economic globalization in order to cope with the critical pressure
from South Korean workers and citizens, demanding remedial reform
for their sacrificed interests under state capitalist development. By
reconceiving and repositioning themselves in the (neo)liberal global
economic context, *chaebol* have tried to formulate logics and strategies for fending off domestic sociopolitical pressures for their reform
– namely, global corporate competitiveness, overseas conditions of
labor supplies, overseas environments for corporate investment and
management, and so on. No matter which factors have been the most
decisive, South Korea's neoliberal economic globalism is now a surely
critical part of its multiplex structure of modernities.

Even without mutually affecting or contradicting, or simply by coexisting, internal multiple modernities generate complicated effects on all aspects of people's daily lives, social relations, and institutional activities. Such coexistence of multiple modernities is often embodied in intergenerational differences in society, but even each person, family, organization, local community, or region can be internally subjected to the same condition. That is, multiple modernities may be internal to not only a national society as a whole but also to each of its constituent subunits. At the national level, the social condition of mutual separation, segregation, and/or indifference among multiple modernities, or among their variously embodying subjects (i.e. individuals, families, organizations, communities, and regions), constitutes a structural problem by nature because a national society and its state system are existentially defined in terms of constituent members' mutually accepted relations, duties, and rights whether defined ideologically, morally, or legally. Similar structural problems exist at other collective levels as well. At the individual level, the same condition can lead to a structural impossibility of an organically consistent life, or a civilizational schizophrenia. *Flexibly complex personhood* (as explained in Chapter 2) may be the minimum requirement for each person's sustainable life under internal multiple modernities. Flexible complexity may also be crucially useful to other units including national society itself, but how to achieve it (and how to explain it even when it is achieved) will remain beyond ordinary human intelligence.

4.10 In Perspective: South Korea as Multiplex Theater Society

The internal multiplicity of modernities/modernizations can be documented as to diverse historical manifestations of *modernitization* (see Chapter 2). Since the late nineteenth century, Korean society (then Chosun) and people have been subjected to a series of overpowering international influences and related local upheavals and confrontations. These occurrences were fundamentally different from Koreans' previously experienced wars and conflicts, reflecting mostly the structure and change of regional politico-military relations. In South Korea, as a major historical irony, the internal plurality of modernizations/modernities has been manifested with particular intensity under the political and ideological influence of the Cold War, which helped enthrone a particular political faction into state power against broad local social ideals and interests. Beneath the

82

coerced uniformity of liberal capitalism under the authoritarian Cold War state, paradoxically diverse aspirations for liberation and happiness have nurtured multiple competing axes of modernities/ modernizations. This corresponds to the so-called "second society" phenomenon in many state-socialist countries under Stalinist dictatorship (Hankiss 1988; Suh, J. 1995). Such interactive multiplicity and diversity of modernities in the Cold War context can be understood as an exemplary manifestation of what Therborn (2003: 295) dubs "geo-historical entanglements." That is, the Cold War era may be seen as a world of entangled internal multiple modernities. Most recently, under a multi-faceted globalization defying national particularities and regional barriers, the new century is quickly becoming an era of universalized internal multiple modernities, of which South Korea has again been prominent.

With all such impetuses and forms of modernities permanently extending their lifespan under critically related national exigencies and/or as variously embodied in the identities and interests of different generations, genders, classes, sectors, and/or regions, South Korea has been socially configured and reconfigured as a *multiplex theater society* in which all possible claims of modernities are aggressively and loudly staged side by side and/or one after another. Such staging of multiple modernities has obviously familiar physical manifestations such as mass street demonstrations, resolute strikes and sit-ins, colorful mass parades, aggressive individual picketings, mammoth formal conventions, showily promotional cultural events, large exhibitions, huge placards with slogans, frequent group indoctrination sessions, highlighted socioeconomic statistics, loud media publicities, assertive or flashy personal behaviors, ostentatious familial rituals and symbols, suggestive disciplinary uniforms, very long queues, authoritarian (or authoritative) displays of commands, purposeful collective drinkings, emphatic on-line contents, and so forth. On any day in any year, South Korean society is normally replete with simultaneously staged expressions of multiple rival claims of modernities. South Korea as a society of internal multiple modernities is sustained and reproduced through these socially staged, and often physically spectacular, voices and visions of simultaneously existing and competing forces of postcolonial modernity.[53] This dramatic feature of South Korean society has been adored by global real-time media that frequently cover South Korean affairs as headline news.

The generalized necessity of each modernity's social staging critically reflects, among others, the following three conditions. First, each modernity is mostly a situationally driven reaction or adaptation rather than a socially nested evolution or revolution, so its broad legitimation and effective implementation require constantly repeated social presentation and persuasion to win consent from essential constituencies, not to mention the whole society. For instance, South Korea's state capitalist modernity has been a nationally rational framing of industrial capitalism upon its liberation from Japan's capitalist exploitation, but the initiation and acceleration of state-led capitalist industrialization necessitated a wide range of political pressures and persuasions to virtually all citizens that were loudly propagandized as patriotic obligations rather than systematically explained in techno-scientific terms (Chang, K. 2012b). South Korea's subjection to free world modernity was a seemingly out-of-question path to its postwar economic and politico-military survival, but its McCarthysian socio-political parameters had to be coerced on to South Koreans through a whole array of public propaganda, media manipulation, educational militarization, etc. Ordinary South Koreans' neotraditionalist Confucianism required repeated self-assurance about its cultural and moral validity through hierarchical (sermon-like) conversations and intense rituals about familial services (such as spousal commitment, filial piety, and ancestral worship) that in turn were socially idealized as "traditional" virtues.

Second, and nevertheless, each modernity involves a societal claim – or a societal pretension – about the social institutional, civilizational, and/or political economic order of the whole nation and general population, so its initiation and realization need to be based upon strategically constructed social platforms of communication. For instance, ever since Korea's colonial dialectical modernity in terms of grassroots socialist sentiment and (ethno)nationalist social liberalism was violently frustrated under the American military occupation and during the Korean War, progressive (ethno)nationalist intellectuals and activists have pursued "Koreans' genuine (ethno)national liberation" through high-profile cultural movements, social protests, and political struggles that have constituted the main ideological force in civil society (Koo, H. 1993; Kim, S. 2000). Postcolonial reflexive institutional(ist) modernity rendered the state to declare and reiterate again and again, through innumerable forms, contents, and events of public propaganda and education, that modernization – practically modeled after the Western (American in particular) systems of polity, economy, and society – was a national historical project for which its authoritative leadership should be revered unconditionally.[54]

Third, the very internal multiplicity of modernities spawns a social ecological necessity of accentuated competitive communication and

84

publicization. For instance, South Korean society's late modern project of multiculturalism, as a cosmopolitan self-reinvention amid the mass arrival of foreign brides, has demanded these new citizens should endure repeated staging of their "foreign" bodies with coercively frozen ethnocultural differences, and thereby cooperate in disseminating liberal globalism in the entire society (against its parochial or chauvinist past). Various constituent social groups of civil society as a subaltern liberal community have been engaged in staunch symbolic battles against entrenched and allied forces in polity, economy, and society that have made every street in South Korea an actual or potential stage for liberally promoting new causes of social justice.

In his political anthropological account, Clifford Geertz (1980) described "the theatre state" in the Balinese politics of the nineteenth century as follows:

> It is perhaps most clear in what was, after all, the master image of political life: kingship. The whole of the negara – court life, the traditions that organized it, the extractions that supported it, the privileges that accompanied it – was essentially directed toward defining what power was; and what power was what kings were . . . The driving aim of higher politics was to construct a state by constructing a king. The more consummate the king, the more exemplary the centre. The more exemplary the centre, the more actual the realm.
>
> (Geertz 1980: 124)

In Geertz's view, the Balinese state existed through ritualized spectacles that reminded its political subjects of the particular cultural forces nested in the king's status. In postcolonial South Korea – a society supposedly driven and controlled by forceful state powers – an internal multiplicity of modernities has induced the state and society to complexly interact and coalesce into diverse sociopolitical formations that express their competing forces through a wide variety of socially staged existentialities. In this way, South Korea has become a *multiplex theater society* in which highly diverse claims of modernities are simultaneously staged, however, without a clear clue to civilizational or sociopolitical reconciliation among them.

TRANSFORMATIVE CONTRIBUTORY RIGHTS

Citizen(ship) in Compressed Modernity

5.1 Introduction

Korea (then Chosun) remained one of the longest lasting dynastic states in world history until its subjugation to Japan's colonial invasion in 1905. Koreans lived most of the first half of the twentieth century as Japan's colonial subjects and, in the South of the 38th Parallel, faced a few more years as semi-colonial subjects under America's military occupation. (Capitalist) South Korea's formal independence in 1948 was shortly tarnished by a total civil war with (socialist) North Korea between 1950 and 1953. For South Koreans, however, most of the rest of the second half of the century has been replete with dramatic institutional, developmental, sociopolitical, and ethnonational transformations through which their nation and society would ultimately emerge with fully blown modernity, or *compressed modernity*. South Korea appeared to be entering the heyday of its modernity since the late 1980s, thanks to both rapid economic development and robust political democratization. However, neoliberal globalization – both imposed from outside and embraced from inside – immediately put the country into chilling econosocial crises and transformations that have structurally bipolarized its population and society.

In each of these drastic and fundamental transitions, South Koreans had to confront not only the difficulties inherent in such radical changes but, more critically, the troubles ensuing from the crude institutional conditions for managing them. While both the state and civil society were immature and unstable, with their own survival remaining in question, the internal conditions and international environments required them to embark on, among other changes, rapid institutional and techno-scientific modernization and aggressive economic development. In fact, such transformations were often pursued in order to strategically trounce the sociopolitical dilemmas stemming from the inchoate, dependent, and even illegitimate nature of the state machinery and dominant social order. There have arisen *transformation-oriented state, society, and population for which each transformation becomes an ultimate purpose in itself, the processes and means of the transformations constitute the main sociopolitical order, and the transformation-embedded interests form the core social identity.* While these transformations have usually been circumstantially necessitated or even dictated, the dominance of the transformative order is apparently analogous to what Max Weber (1946) expounded as the means–end reversal under modernity.

In this milieu, a distinct mode of citizenship has been engendered in terms of *transformative contributory rights.* "Contributory rights" is Bryan S. Turner's definition of citizenship – in particular, social rights as compared to individual or human rights – in modern democracies (Turner 2001; Isin and Turner 2007). It is contributory because "effective claims against a society are made possible by the contributions that citizens have made to society typically through work, war, or parenting" (Isin and Turner 2007: 12). Similarly, citizenship as transformative contributory rights can be defined as *effective and/or legitimate claims to national and social resources, opportunities, and/or respects that accrue to a citizen's contributions to the nation's or society's transformative purposes.* As South Korea has been aggressively and precipitously engaged in institutional and techno-scientific modernization, economic development, political democratization, economic and sociocultural globalization, and, mostly recently, ethnonational reformation, its citizens have been exhorted or have exhorted themselves to engage intensely in each of these transformations, and their citizenship, constituted by identities, duties, and rights, has been very much framed and substantiated by the conditions, processes, and outcomes of such transformative engagements (see The Chart of National Education, in Box 5.1, for the state's explicit promulgation of such transformative citizenship). In what follows, I will present a broad citizenship perspective on South Korea's compressed modernity by focusing on its people's transformative contributory rights.

Box 5.1 The Charter of National Education (*gukmingyoyukheonjang*)

We were born into this Land charged with the historic mission to revitalize our nation. This is our moment to establish a self-reliant posture at home and contribute to the common prosperity of mankind globally by rekindling the illustrious spirit of our forefathers. We hereby declare our path forward and set the goals of our education.

With sincerity in our minds and strength in our bodies, we shall engage in scholarship and the arts, develop the innate faculties in each of us and, using the current challenges as stepping stones for speedy progress, cultivate our creative power and pioneering spirit. We shall give foremost consideration to public good and order, place value on efficiency and substance and, inheriting the tradition of mutual assistance rooted in love and respect and faithfulness, inspire a cheerful and warm spirit of cooperation. Realizing that a nation grows through creativity and cooperation and that individual growth is grounded in the prosperity of the nation, we shall do our best to fulfill the responsibility and duty attendant upon our freedom and rights and to raise the national consciousness to participate and serve in building our nation.

The love of country and fellow countrymen, together with the spirit of democracy that resists communism, paves the way for our survival and lays the ground for realizing the ideals of the free world. Looking forward to the glory of a unified homeland for our posterity and, as an industrious people with confidence and pride, let us pledge to make new history with ceaseless effort and the collective wisdom of the whole nation.

December 5, 1968
President Park Chung Hee

Source: *National Archives of Korea* (https://theme.archives.go.kr/next/koreaOfRecord/charterNaEdu.do)

5.2 Institutional and Techno-Scientific Modernization and Educational Citizenship

Upon its colonization of Korea, Japan tried to symbolically justify its imperial rule by building, mostly in Seoul, grandiose public buildings in classic Western style. Seoul's Japan-built Western architectural masterpieces included: the now demolished Chongdokbu (colonial government) complex, the Bank of Chosun (now the Bank of Korea), Seoul Station, Kyungsung Imperial University, etc. In particular, the Chongdokbu complex was erected right before the royal court of Chosun, blocking the entire Gyeongbokgung (the main palace of Chosun dynasty) from Chosun people's view. From or through these buildings, Japan – as a reprocessed Western power – exercised full administrative, financial, spatial, and other control over colonial Korea.[1] After liberation from war-defeated Japan, (South) Koreans had to confront another phase of colonial rule, this time by the directly Western power of the American military occupation authority. However, the above Japan-built Western buildings remained intact physically and functionally. The formal independence of South Korea did not change this situation for most of the latter part of the twentieth century. In fact, South Koreans themselves began to build most of their new buildings and facilities in arguably Western styles and pursue their national reconstruction and development after U.S.-prescribed Western modernity. Obviously, such civilizational dependence was a matter of political inevitability under the hegemonic influence of the U.S., fortified in the Cold War context, but South Koreans did not have much epistemological confusion or moral reluctance about it, either. Their indignation about Japanese colonialism was translated into a national(istic) aspiration for outdoing Japan in (West-set) modernization, and the American engagement and influence only helped to reinforce this collective historical desire (Jeon, J. 1999; Lim, H. 1996). South Koreans were thereby reborn into a zealous student nation of Western modernity and have remained so to date. (The two-millennium history of Korea–China relations had been similarly characterized by the dynastic Korean states' zealous and strategic accommodation of imperial Chinese civilizations, often as an effort to overcome Chinese domination and aggression.)

Postindependence modernization, as modeled after and supported by the U.S., was pursued mainly in two directions: modernization of social and public institutions and modernization of technology and science. Even before independence, the American military occupation authority worked closely with Korean intellectuals in order to establish an effective universal public education system as early as possible (Seth 2002). It even coordinated the launching in 1946 of a comprehensive public university (i.e. Seoul National University) that covered virtually all domains of modernization and served as the standard model for the subsequently established national universities in the main regional centers.[2] Not coincidentally, the U.S.-dependent process of educational institutional modernization became linked to an educationally governed regime of compressed modernity under which the nearly instantaneous formation of various modern (namely, Western) institutions and professions in public, social, and industrial spheres was educationally framed through a sort of short-course-based certification by each academic disciplinary department in the university, mostly at the undergraduate level.[3] It could be said that university educational certificates, sometimes reinforced through corporate, public or professional examinations, thereby constituted a passport to state-driven, West-modeled modernity.

Given the aged ancestral tradition of a meritocratic state rule based upon multi-stage certification of learned knowledge (i.e. *gwageo*), South Koreans did not have much cultural difficulty in accepting such decisive significance of formal education. Instead of challenging the thereby created *hakbeolsahoe* (society ruled by educational backgrounds) morally or politically, South Koreans from all strata have tried to participate in educational competition, usually through excessive educational investment and exhortation for their children (and sometimes siblings). The end results include the world's most intense private spending in education, virtually universalized college education, and so forth (Chang, K. 2010a, ch. 3; Chang, K. 2022, ch. 6; see Table 5.1). In a society where the historical, philosophical and/or moral foundations of the educational curricula and of the civilizational system represented and enforced therein have seldom been debated among general citizenry, parental devotion and sacrifice for children's education have come to constitute a critical part of mass morality – often praised as a "national virtue" by both outside observers and South Koreans themselves.[4] Needless to say, every government has strongly endeavored to provide sufficient educational opportunities for satisfying South Koreans' educational craving.[5]

No less crucially, every government has been highly cautious in organizing and supervising formal education in such a way as to ensure fair and transparent competition in accessing educational opportunities at higher and/or better schools.[6] On the part of institutions of higher learning, their broad failure (or even deliberate

Table 5.1 OECD countries with higher proportions of population aged 25–34 with tertiary education than the OECD average (latest: 2018 or before)

Country	% Population aged 25–34 with tertiary education
Australia	51.39
Belgium	47.40
Canada	61.75
Denmark	44.82
France	46.94
Iceland	47.01
Ireland	56.17
Israel	48.03
Japan	60.73
South Korea	**69.57**
Lithuania	55.58
Luxembourg	54.78
Netherlands	47.60
New Zealand	45.81
Norway	48.21
OECD average	**44.48**
Russia	62.66
Sweden	47.51
Switzerland	51.21
United Kingdom	50.75
United States	49.37

Source: Constructed from "OECD Data: Population with Tertiary Education" (https://data.oecd.org/eduatt/population-with-tertiary-education.htm)

negligence?) to reflectively and critically appraise the historical conditions and civilizational foundations of Western modernity and autonomously proposing civilizational alternatives has been complemented by an excessive pedagogical intensity in replicating and emulating Western ideas, theories, and technologies. That a stunning majority of professors at major South Korean universities hold PhDs from Western – mostly American – universities is thus no surprise.[7] As South Korean students still remain dissatisfied with the effectiveness of their country's higher education in Western or global learning, astonishing numbers of them have advanced to overseas schools for direct access to foreign knowledge.[8]

In most nations today, basic public education is a most universal part of social citizenship, often constitutionally stipulated both as a duty and right of all citizens. What distinguishes South Korea is its educationally framed process of (compressed) institutional and techno-scientific modernization and a concomitant social structure of *hakbeolsahoe*.[9] Where educational credentials have decisively affected individuals' meaningful access to almost all occupational opportunities in various modern sectors, economic, social, and sometimes even political citizenship has been contingently realized through each citizen's formal educational backgrounds and resources (Chang, K. 2022, ch. 6). The state's role in ensuring a fair and clean system of educational competition for accessing higher and better institutions of learning has thereby become a core citizenship policy. Despite the extraordinary public supervision over democratically justifiable educational competition, South Korea has become a society where educationally caused social and economic disparities are incomparably serious.[10] This led each recent government to loudly adopt remedial policies for addressing educationally caused injuries to fair citizenship in social, economic, and other domains.[11] Such policies, however, have been more symbolic than practical because the government's political appeal and moral persuasion have seldom been accompanied by serious incentives and penalties for inducing civilian sectors to systematically rectify educationally caused inequalities, not to mention a major revamping of the country's educational system.

Even decades of South Korea's superb modernization and development have not fundamentally altered the basic parameters of *hakbeolsahoe*. In the new century, perhaps the relative weight of the institutional modernization-linked benefits of formal education has declined as compared to its techno-scientific (hyper)modernization-linked benefits. This trend seems to be reflected or anticipated in the loud slogans of *jeongbohwa* (informationalization), *gisulipguk* (technology-based rise of the nation), *jisikgyeongje* (knowledge economy), *jisikgangguk* (knowledge-strong country), *dunoegangguk* (brain-strong country), and, most recently, *sachasaneophyeokmyeong* (the fourth industrial revolution).[12] However, the neoliberal destabilization of the labor market amid the country's aggressive economic globalization in recent years has ironically intensified young people's competition for educationally certified jobs in medicine, law, teaching, and so forth (Chang, K. 2019, ch. 4). Besides, the increasingly acknowledged necessity of institutional rationalization (as well as techno-scientific upgrading) of the medical, legal, and other professional sectors has led to a strengthening of the formal educational platform for professional expertise – usually in terms of extended education at professional graduate schools.[13] This trend has helped to assimilate many students' college life to that of high-school students because of extreme difficulties in entering such professional graduate schools.

5.3 Economic Transformation and Developmental Citizenship

Institutional and techno-scientific modernization has been far from an easy task for any postcolonial nation, but even its successful accomplishment has been no guarantee of the stable and dignified survival of each nation, especially on the material front. Such was particularly the case with South Korea, which had been colonially exploited, war-destroyed, economically outmoded, demographically overburdened, and even ecologically devastated. In fact, as has been forcefully argued and amply researched by a variety of social scientists, West-modeled liberal economic institutions and practices have frequently turned out to be ineffective in bringing about much needed development in Third World countries (Evans, Rueschemeyer, and Skocpol 1985; Wade 1990; Weiss 1998). Conversely, South Korea's illiberal or statist approach to economic development has often been analyzed as a prime factor for its phenomenal national industrial success (Amsden 1989; Evans 1995; Chang, H. 1994).

South Korea's developmental political economy has been distinguished by the state's active industrial initiative and managerial intervention, *chaebol*'s state-dependent formation and growth, labor's subordinate yet zealous collaboration, and families' aggressive savings and educational investment (Amsden 1989). This combination of unique economic actors and factors has been premised upon a national political supposition that economic development is a collective national agenda, requiring whenever necessary the proactive political and entrepreneurial role of the state for mobilizing, organizing, and disciplining civilian economic actors (such as industrialists, workers, households, etc.) as subjects of *developmental citizenship* (Chang, K. 2012a). Under the circumstances of postcolonial national indignation, inter-Korean confrontation, as well as generalized poverty across society, what may be called *developmental nationalism* became a de facto ruling ideology of which these developmental citizens have served as obvious political constituencies.

A political institutional dilemma arose here in that the successively ruling developmentalist political parties have been unable to formally identify themselves with developmentalism. The ruling developmentalist parties have been officially named in terms of West-derived political ideologies and terminologies such as "liberal," "democratic," "republican," and "justice," or, more recently, in terms of vaguely inclusionary or populist slogans such as "one country," "national forum," "new world," and "Korea." That is, even when authoritarian developmentalist rule was effective, formal politics still had to be justified – or disguised? – with the imperative of (West-modeled) political institutional modernization; whereas, in the democratized and increasingly post-developmental period, it has had rhetorically, though ambiguously, to strengthen its popular (or populist) political basis. On the other hand, the rather autonomously initiated line of developmentalist realpolitik was substantiated mostly in terms of immediate political economic requisites in national development as have been described by institutionalist social scientists as "embedded autonomy" of the state (Evans 1995), "governed interdependence" between the state and business (Weiss 1995), and so forth.

Such instrumentalist politics of the so-called developmental state have fundamental implications for the political nature of developmental citizenship. That is, under developmental citizenship, the collective duties of ordinary citizens for long-term national economic development have been prioritized to their individual rights to immediate material benefits (Chang, K. 2012b). While ordinary citizens' sacrificial economic participation and subordination to authoritarian government and exploitative business have been justified as their citizenship duties for national economic development, the distribution of the resulting material outcomes has rarely embodied a correspondingly collectivist doctrine (Chang, K. 2019).[14] The preferential allocation of national public resources and strategic regulatory support for *chaebol*-affiliated export industries have been justified similarly in terms of national industrial competitiveness as far as they remain, or at least appear, faithful to what may be called *corporate developmental citizenship*. In fact, during Park Chung-Hee's high developmentalist era, *chaebol* were virtually considered as semi-public instruments for national economic development, whose heads had to remain alert even on the president's expectation for acceptable levels of their personal consumption behavior (Chang, K. 2012b).[15] The authoritarian military state habitually and often violently intervened in the conflicting business-labor relations as if they were state-labor relations rather than citizen-versus-citizen relations (Chang, K. 2019, ch. 2). The asymmetrically treated proletariat's discomfort, however, has not necessarily placed them as the most disadvantaged group of citizens under the developmentalist rule. Those who are physically or mentally unfit for, age-wise unready for or suspended from, or socially discouraged or segregated from capitalist production work have had

94

no mainstream citizenship status under the developmentally oriented political rule and its companion state-capitalist economic system (Chang, K. 2012b). Lacking developmental citizenship individually in a social welfare-suppressed nation, the handicapped, youth, elderly, and housewives have had to exist as secondary citizens to date.[16]

The IMF economic crisis of 1997 to 1998 and its neoliberal rescue in terms of radical restructuring of the labor market, aggressive globalization of the production basis, and financial retrenchment of many industries have fundamentally destabilized the social basis and political legitimacy of developmentalist rule. Massive layoffs in the so-called "structural adjustment" terms helped save many nearly bankrupt firms, but their ultimate recovery took the direction of "jobless growth" whether through automation, work outsourcing, or overseas relocation of production (Chang, K. 2019, ch. 4). Given the radical *erosion of developmental citizenship* among rapidly increasing numbers of ordinary South Koreans, the political justification for the state–business developmental alliance has become fundamentally problematic. Nevertheless, *chaebol* and their technocratic patrons continue to insist on the transformative utility of the pro-business policy, often in terms of South Korea's supposedly "sandwiched" position between rapidly catching-up China and still far-ahead industrial leader nations, a supposed current or impending economic crisis, or simply the necessity for still more economic growth (Chang, K. 2012c).

In a great yet transitional political paradox, Lee Myung-Bak, a former industrialist in the Park Chung-Hee era, successfully rallied to South Koreans' despair as disenfranchised developmental citizens during the 2007 presidential election by loudly promising an immediate recovery of developmental citizenship (Chang, K. 2012b). However, his immediate and obvious failure in promised developmental governance led main candidates in the next presidential election in 2012 to make post-developmental pledges such as "the welfare state" and "economic democratization." Interestingly, it was Park Chung-Hee's daughter, Park Geun-Hye, who turned out most successful in the ideologically reframed political race, against all odds associated with her candidacy for the ruling conservative – so far, ultra-developmentalist – party. In her meeting with heads of *chaebol* as president-elect, she resolutely remarked, "I think [your enterprises] have a strong nature of *gukmingieop* (enterprises of national citizens) because there have been innumerable national citizens' backing and sacrifice and lots of state support until their growth into such big enterprises as now" and added, "therefore, I think the managerial

95

purpose of the big enterprises should not remain simply maximization of corporate profits, but they have to pursue co-survival with our community as a whole" (*Financial News*, December 26, 2012). Park's suggestion, while derived from her campaign pledge of "economic democratization," may be summarized as a *transition from corporate developmental citizenship to corporate social citizenship*. While corporate citizenship (or corporate social responsibility) is a global catchword nowadays, largely due to the (often unhealthily) dominant economic position of transnational mega-corporations, South Korea's collectivist national development history seems to present a unique politico-moral platform for corporate citizenship in saving the so-far sacrificed social groups and national community as a whole.

5.4 Democratization and Transformative Political Citizenship

In a great historical paradox, South Korea declared the launching of liberal democracy alongside ferocious crackdowns on its civil society that had been under a strong influence of progressive (ethno) nationalism (Cumings 1981). The constitutionally stipulated liberal democracy was an outcome of South Korea's not-so-voluntary insertion into the U.S.-led global liberal order rather than a revolutionary political accomplishment of an autonomous civil society. In this context, South Koreans acquired democratic political rights, not as active members of a genuine civil society, but as passive subjects of a postcolonial yet dependent nation-state.[17] As such, their political citizenship incurred continual encroachments by state elites, who had installed themselves through access to external influence (i.e. Syngman Rhee) or military power (i.e. Park Chung-Hee). After involuntarily relinquishing democratic political rights during most of the post-Korean War period, South Koreans managed to reinstate them in 1987.[18] This time, however, liberal democracy was (re)established through South Koreans' own stringent political struggles. In fact, their long experience of fighting against the successive dictatorial state powers came to constitute *transformative political citizenship* – namely, their democratic political rights were secured in exchange for their active political contribution to democratization.

In terms of its popular basis, South Korean democratization was a broad social process in which certain generations of the national population were engaged collectively. Ironically, the authoritarian state's success in rapid national economic development led to the quick formation of an urban middle class and the explosive growth of students at advanced institutions of learning (i.e. colleges and universities) (Kim, S. 2000; Han, S. 2009). Given their strong intellectual and moral desire for democratic political rights (Choi, J. 2002), these two groups became active agencies of transformative political citizenship. Besides, since the laboring class understood their asymmetrical or discriminated developmental citizenship very much as an outcome of pro-capitalist state dictatorship, they developed a strong instrumentalist desire for political as well as industrial democracy. Not coincidentally, many student activists strategically turned themselves into industrial workers – they were called *hakchul*, meaning "from academia"– and helped to socially organize and politically mobilize the working class from within (Koo, H. 2001). In this way, South Korean democratization was propelled through a strong class-alliance framework.[19] Consequently, in June 1987, South Korea's activist students and intellectuals, along with civilian opposition politicians, effectively rallied against the military junta's attempt to extend its political power indefinitely. Organized workers and urban citizens instantaneously joined them in demanding an immediate restoring of democratic political procedures.

Each of the historic struggles for democratization against the successive autocrats (i.e. Syngman Rhee, Park Chung-Hee, Chun Doo-Hwan, and, arguably, Park Geun-Hye) not only resulted in civil society's political (re)activation and/or democratic political reform but also critically helped form the main political class to take charge of running representative democracy. Paradoxically, there has developed a major political line that tries to practically capitalize on this apparently regressive trend, by strategically (re)arousing the anti-dictatorial political emotions of middle-class citizens, urban youth, and so on. This group of "movementist" (*undonggwon*) politicians – reminiscent of Maoist cultural politics in China – has tried to fixate politics in a permanent struggle against deep-rooted and even recently regenerated authoritarian forces.[20] Arguably, they have tried to reactivate transformative political citizenship among the general public; but, as revealed repeatedly in terms of disappointing election outcomes, their cause does not seem to have persuaded a majority of South Koreans effectively. Instead, they are sometimes suspected or criticized for an intellectual elitism by which the former activists' self-centered political cause is arrogantly and arbitrarily imposed as grassroots citizens' permanent political duty.[21] However, from their perspective, democratization – as compared to the state-dominated processes of institutional and techno-scientific modernization and economic development – has been a civil society-centered project, and democracy should imply civil society's permanent control over the state. Unfortunately, or inevitably, this position has justified democracy activists' aggressive self-appointment into state offices, particularly during the Roh Moo-Hyun presidency – and, a decade later, during the current Moon Jae-In presidency.[22]

The relative robustness of contemporary South Korean democracy is politico-culturally embedded in the broad popular experience of democratization movements.[23] However, this collective historical asset has not necessarily assured an evolutionary political transition into substantively effective democratic governance, as exemplified by the rise and sustenance of the social democratic systems in Europe. In reality, the post-military state leaders elected by democratically conscious citizens have ended up anachronistically mimicking or complementing the aged developmentalist rule, while frequently relying on neoliberal ideas and policies (Yoon, S. 2008). In a great irony, the resulting economic and social catastrophes – including the 1997 to 1998 economic crisis – have induced increasing numbers of South Koreans to develop the so-called "Park Chung-Hee nostalgia" in regard to economically effective political governance. While the supposedly progressive political parties and governments failed to initiate an effective policy transition to the much-propagated welfare state, the deceased Park Chung-Hee was able to make his outright mimicker (i.e. Lee Myung-Bak) and his daughter (Park Geun-Hye) *democratically* elected into presidency.

"Democracy after democratization" – as opposed to the political institutionalist position of Choi Jang-Jip (2002), who wrote an influential book under this title – has therefore involved a lengthy societal struggle against entrenched statist forces and interests. In no surprise, this struggle has been an arduous uphill battle, in part because many former participants and activists in democracy movements now have a double-identity as liberal democratic citizen and statist developmental citizen, occupying a lion's share of economic opportunities (Lee, C. 2019). When "movementist" politicians tried to warn against the possible election of Park Chung-Hee's apparent political heirs into state leadership supposedly as an automatic political crisis, a majority of ordinary South Koreans seem to have disagreed. Whether the corruptions scandals of Lee Myung-Bak and Park Geun-Hye have fundamentally changed such disagreement between self-centered liberal politicians and ordinary materialist citizens remains a key question in South Korean politics. In sum, South Koreans' transformative political citizenship has been critically tarnished by its failure in meaningful substantive evolution.

5.5 Globalization and Neoliberal versus Cosmopolitan Citizenship

After achieving institutional and techno-scientific modernization, economic development, and democratization, all at globally sensational speeds and/or levels, still transformation-thirsty South Koreans embarked on another major transformative project from the early 1990s – namely, globalization or *segyehwa*, an ad hoc Korean expression of globalization coined during the Kim Young-Sam presidency. In a sense, the country's earlier transformations of modernization, development, and democratization also constituted globalization in that the pressures, impetuses, directions, resources, knowledge, and models for such transformations all involved transnational influences and relations. Its more proactive globalization since the early 1990s may be understood as a critically heightened and widened stage of institutional, techno-scientific, economic, sociocultural, and political transformations. However, as its globalization did not begin of its own making but was, in many aspects, necessitated by the political economic context of West-led neoliberal globalization, the concerned transformations have embodied various neoliberal tendencies (Chang, K. 2019, ch. 3).[24]

If neoliberalization has implied intensification and/or reinstatement of liberal principles and structures in the West and their peripheries, the same has been the case in South Korea where earlier institutional, techno-scientific, economic, sociocultural, and political transformations had taken place basically in the liberal (and often statist liberal?) context. In this milieu, the so-called "global standards" became the catchword for aligning the country's legal, economic, social, and cultural institutions with the unfettered global capitalist system; technological development and scientific research in corporate and academic organizations have been encouraged and sometimes compelled to aspire for global-level free economic ventures and joint ventures; corporate globalization in terms of both transnationalized production and marketing and accommodation of global financial interests has become a core strategy for sustaining and strengthening national economic strength; South Korean democracy, both at the nation-state and civil society level, has felt increasingly pressured to emulate Western democracies in advocating and supporting liberal communitarian goals in the global arena, through developmental and social aid, human rights advocacy, global ecological commitment, and so forth (Kim, T. 2019). Besides, as unprecedented and surprising

99

developments, South Korea has aggressively outsourced foreign human resources for its domestic industrial production (i.e. foreign workers with non-renewable contract, mostly in labor-intensive sectors) and social reproduction (i.e. foreign brides, mostly in rural and poor urban families). Ostensibly, these trends have added up to make South Korea a leader country in globalization, particularly in the Asian context.[25]

To the extent that South Korea's recent globalization drive represents a heightened and widened stage of its transformative modernity, the relevance and importance of citizenship as *transformative contributory rights* remain unabated. Again, despite occasional complaints about the terms and processes of free-trade agreement, corporate takeover by foreign capital, and so forth, surprisingly rare controversies and objections have been pronounced on the basic tenet of globalization itself.[26] Instead, South Korean people and institutions at all levels have competed fiercely against one another in preparing and investing for globalization, often with loud demands for state support.[27] Interestingly, but logically, this competition has been more symbiotic than mutually upsetting because each participant has found that the others' globalization efforts help stabilize the nation's commitment to globalization and thereby strengthen the prospect for satisfactorily benefitting from her/his own investment in globalization.[28] In this instrumentalist way, globalization has become an almost undisputed national and societal agenda, and South Koreans' citizenship duties and rights have accordingly been readjusted, albeit without an overarching supervisory public authority.

South Korea's instrumentalist globalization – or, in effect, globalization without globalist philosophy such as cosmopolitanism – is somewhat reminiscent of its century-ago doctrine of *dongdoseogi* (Eastern spirit, Western technology, which in practice led to Westernization without Western ideology or philosophy). However, this instrumentalism as a potential manifestation of South Koreans' self-centered nationalism, corporate capitalism, and even familialism tends to directly contradict the legitimacy, if any, of their rapidly expanding global interests, influences, and relations. Living in an exceptional nation that has proudly built up this much of global stake, influence, and prestige without having any previous history of imperialism, South Koreans have grown increasingly uncomfortable about the apparent inconsistency between their global material positions and parochial ideational conditions.[29]

This inconsistency gradually turned from a cultural and philosophical shame into an ethical and political liability as massive numbers

100

of foreign workers and brides from across Asia began to arrive as the country's invited new members (Seol, D. 2014; Kim, N. 2012; Kim, H. 2012, 2014). While all individual counterparts of transnational liaison in industrial work (i.e. foreign workers and their South Korean employers, mostly in sweatshop industries) and in marriage (i.e. foreign brides and their South Korean spouses, mostly in rural and peripheral urban areas) have had legitimately pragmatic reasons for entering such relationships, the South Korean counterparts' instrumentalism immediately gets translated into extremely abusive and alienating practices in work and life toward these invited citizens (Seol, D. 2014; Kim, H. 2012, 2014). These unfortunate practices, however, should not be easily regarded as a manifestation of any racist prejudice because they used to be imposed on South Koreans as well. In a crucial aspect, globalization – mostly Asianization – of the labor and marriage markets is a strategic attempt to *reinstate South Korea's past conditions of work and marriage through foreign bodies* (Chank, K. 2022). Besides, many of these cruel South Koreans themselves, as disadvantaged small industrialists and shopkeepers and alienated peasants, have had long experiences of sacrifice under South Korea's ruthlessly bipolarizing political economy and are now trying to complement their disadvantages by mobilizing human resources from overseas. In an epochal turnaround, however, the dire miseries of foreign workers and brides began to awaken South Koreans about the categorically immediate necessity of a cosmopolitan value system. Through a sort of *reflexively reflective* process – that is, by drawing on other countries' experiences and countermeasures under similar situations – South Korean civil society proposed an active social and governmental pursuit of *multiculturalism*. The government immediately echoed this proposal, however, without relinquishing its steadfast pro-business developmentalist stand. The result has been the so-called "multicultural family" policy that is applicable only to foreign brides and their children – that is, excluding foreign workers (Yoon, I. 2008; see Chapter 6).

This policy indirectly notifies foreign workers that they should work (or get exploited) as non-citizens and that they will never be allowed South Korean citizenship or the social services and benefits it carries (Seol, D. 2014).[30] By contrast, given that foreign brides are here to stay permanently, help South Koreans form and maintain family, and procreate future generations of South Koreans, their ethnic backgrounds and cultural resources are supposed to be respected and protected, and their difficulties in language, family norms, human relations, and a host of other matters should be monitored and eased (*Danuri* 2013). Their increasing presence – and that of their children – is now taken even to be a critical asset for desirable cosmopolitan reconfiguring of the Korean nation and society, constituting a sort of *transformative cultural citizenship*. In fact, the fervent campaigns, services, and supports for "multicultural families" by nearly all national and local public institutions, diverse civil society actors, business firms in various sectors, schools at all levels, and virtually all types of media – despite the still apparently uneven proportions of foreign brides who actually receive such benefits (Kim et al. 2010) – suggest that South Korean society-at-large is now trying to reinvent itself as an ostensibly cosmopolitan entity by utilizing as a handy platform the increasing presence of foreign brides with highly diverse national, racial, and cultural backgrounds (see Chapter 6).

Concurrent with the heavy influx of foreign workers and brides, there have been sustained outflows and circulations of native South Koreans into virtually all corners of the globe. Some have simply accompanied their employers, but much more have been exploring global opportunities in work, education, and/or citizenship (for themselves or sometimes for their born and unborn children).[31] Given their aggressively globalizing country's strong prospect for sustained development on the one hand and its structural instabilities and vulnerabilities on the other hand, many of the latter are trying to strategically multinationalize their identities, resources, and opportunities instead of fully uprooting themselves from the country (Lee, K. 2008; Kim, H. 2006). Such flexible and adaptive behavior is very much analogous to that of rapidly transnationalizing South Korean business and now constitutes a generic part of (much neoliberalized) South Korean citizenship. On the other hand, according to Kong Suk-Ki (2012), South Korean civil society is now endeavoring hard in order to transnationalize or cosmopolitanize their purposes and activities. A *cosmopatriotic civil society* (cf. Jurriens and de Kloet 2007) appears to be in the making, though very gradually, with increasing participation of South Korean citizens, NGOs, and public institutions.

5.6 National Reconfiguration and Compatriotic Citizenship

By the early 2010s, South Korea's sustained acceptance of foreign brides (and foreign contractual workers) and its fervent support campaigns for "multicultural families" do not merely appear as some pragmatic practice and related face-saving gesture. Even intellectual and communal criticisms against the rigid discrimination against temporary guest workers in such campaigns are gradually but seriously heard.[32] A rather fundamental transformation has been hinted at about the way South Koreans perceive and even define their nation (Lee, S. 2008; Kim, H. 2006). This is also detected by various concurrent social trends involving diverse compatriotic groups of ethnic Koreans.

Korea's turbulent political history and complex international relations have made the Koreans one of the world's most widely dispersed nations, constituting sizable ethnic minority populations across Eurasia (i.e. China, Japan, Russia, and Central Asia) and, more recently, in Western nations in North America and Oceania (i.e. the United States, Canada, Australia, and New Zealand).[33] Even the native seventy million population on the Korean Peninsula is politically divided between South and North by a roughly two-to-one ratio. Until the early 1990s, despite the South Korean government's both propagandic and covert efforts to elicit exclusive political support for it over the North Korean regime, South Koreans' contact and relationship with these diverse compatriots (except those in the United States, Canada, Australia, and New Zealand) had been largely restricted by the rigid bilateral political relationship between South Korea and each of its compatriots' residential countries. Ironically or understandably, after South Korea normalized diplomatic relationship with most of the (formerly) communist states, the political effort to win over overseas compatriots to its side has notably abated.

However, South Korea's sudden globalization drive, especially after the national financial crisis, has induced various governmental, corporate, and civilian actors to explore active practical relationships with overseas compatriotic Koreans residing mainly in East and Central Asia and North America. The Korean diaspora, estimated to be more than seven million across the world, has thereby become a strategic human platform for South Korea's socioeconomic globalization. Partly for this purpose, the Chinese experience of actively utilizing the global *huashang* (Chinese business) network has been emulated in terms of *segyehansangdaehoe* (the World Korean Business Convention). A series of proactive campaigns and policies for bringing them into strategic economic and social relationship with various domestic and overseas South Korean counterparts – closely reminiscent of post-Mao China's outreach for overseas Chinese business – have thereafter been deployed.[34] On the other hand, many Koreans from China and Central Asia have assumed a sort of proletarian denizenship by entering the South Korean labor market on a long-term basis.

In sum, from around the mid 1990s, the South Korean government and industries began to rediscover overseas Koreans as new economic resources in human, managerial, and financial terms. These efforts have been finely (or hierarchically) tuned to the basic economic nature of the relationship between South Korea and each of the overseas Koreans' residential countries (Lee, C. 2014; Seol, D. 2014). That is, Koreans from advanced capitalist economies, with relatively rich financial and technological resources, have been offered preferential conditions for working with or living in South Korea. However, even those from China, Central Asia, and Russia have eagerly been approached as valuable resources for the country's global takeoff, in particular, serving as middlemen between transnational South Korean firms and local workers, consumers and officers, and offering useful and affordable service labor by coming to South Korea.[35] In this way, overseas Koreans in the globe's diverse regions have instantly become a tightly integral part of the aggressively globalizing South Korean economy and society.

In quite an interesting contrast, while North Korean defectors/refugees began to enter South Korea in rapidly increasing numbers (particularly since the North Korean economic crisis of the 1990s), both political interest and public enthusiasm about them have drastically dwindled.[36] The inter-Korean summit in 2000 ultimately helped accelerate this process because the post-summit sociopolitical environment has been all about reality issues such as financial costs of national reunification, risk of military diversion of South-to-North Korean humanitarian aid, chronic human rights violation in North Korea, and so forth. The only group of North Koreans that used to receive sustained attention was roughly forty-eight thousand North Korean workers employed by South Korean companies in the inter-Korean industrial complex in Kaesong (i.e. the Kaesong Industrial Region) in the period between 2004 and 2006. Nowadays, many North Korean defectors/refugees openly express great disappointment and dissatisfaction at the gradually decreasing special benefits from the South Korean government and at ordinary South Koreans' increasing indifference to them (Yoon, I. 2012). Some of them even decide to return to North Korea while many others opt to migrate to third countries using their newly acquired South Korean passport. On the other hand, given the policy primacy and resourcefulness of multicultural affairs, even North Korean defectors/refugees are sometimes offered protections and benefits as multicultural citizens. Actually, this practice tends to anger some newly arrived North Koreans, who are strongly imbued with the ethnohistorical identity supposedly combining both Koreas.

All these tendencies concerning foreign workers and brides, overseas Koreans, and North Korean defectors/refugees seem to insinuate a fundamental transition in the epistemological basis of South Korean (ethno)nationalism – namely, from historically reinforced *bio-cultural identity* to pragmatically reconfigured *performative communal identity*. In the new century, even the (ethnic) nation has become a basically transformative subject or project. National citizenship as ethnosocial boundary and identity on the one hand and as national duties and rights on the other hand is constantly being reconfigured. In this process, the individual and relative status of each compatriotic or migrant group toward national citizenship has been significantly reshaping in accordance with their respective functional, and sometimes cultural, fit for South Korea's global takeoff.

5.7 Prospect: Transformation into Post-Transformative Society?

Making of "a society that can be sustained even without economic growth" is a must. The present has become an era that cannot endure the lack of growth or change, but it is necessary to create a society that remains fine without development.

(Karatani Kojin, in a new year interview with
Kyunghyang Shinmun, January 7, 2013)

Although the above advice by Karatani Kojin, a globally distinguished progressive liberal intellectual of Japan, is not necessarily confined to South Korea, its appeal may be particularly strong among those South Koreans who have opposed and criticized their country's extremely hasty, obsessive, and often unphilosophic pursuit of continual national and societal transformations and various problematic costs and consequences accompanying such transformations. However, the above-suggested change into post-transformative society constitutes still another transformation, which may be much more challenging than any of the previous ones because of the now built-in transformative order of contemporary South Korean society.

Since the mid-twentieth century, postcolonial and war-devastated South Korea has kept impressing the world and even its own people by aggressively and precipitously carrying out institutional and techno-scientific modernization, economic development, political democratization, economic and sociocultural globalization, and, mostly recently, ethnonational reformation. While each of these transformations is rather a generic experience in postcolonial societies, South Korea's impulsively proactive pursuit of them has induced the country to become a fixatedly transformative social entity. From this transformative modernity have arisen a transformation-oriented state, society, and population for which each transformation becomes an ultimate purpose in itself, the processes and means of the transformations constitute the main sociopolitical order, and the transformation-embedded interests form the core social identity. Relatedly, a distinct mode of citizenship has arisen in terms of transformative contributory rights – namely, effective and/or legitimate claims to national and social resources, opportunities, and/or respects that accrue to each citizen's contributions to the nation's or society's transformative purposes.

By the early twenty-first century, it has painfully turned out that the citizenship regime of transformative contributory rights, despite its apparent effectiveness in generating and accelerating successive societal and national transformations, has a fatal problem of structurally and precipitously engendering *transformative victims*, in numbers and extents that are no less conspicuous than those for transformative beneficiaries. These victims have been not only inherent in the substantive nature of each transformation (e.g. traditionalists and nativists in West-dependent modernization, peasants in capitalist industrialization, local interests and communal agencies in neoliberal globalization, and so forth) but also embedded in the impulsive, excessive, and violent manners of pursuing the transformations (i.e. students in cramming educational institutions, workers controlled and even tortured by the authoritarian developmental state, women abused at home and work under patriarchalized capitalism, foreign workers and brides maltreated respectively by opportunistic employers and in-laws, and so forth). The sacrifices and injuries made by these transformative victims have often been euphemistically considered as part of their transformative citizenship that should be accepted in conjunction with the supposed rain-checks for future benefits – as exemplified by the slogans of "growth first, distribution later," "save the economy first," and so forth.

Since such rain-checks have been delayed unduly and sometimes indefinitely, many of these victims have tried to autonomously reconstitute their citizenship by reducing or avoiding duties (e.g. shirking military conscription, resisting taxes, avoiding or minimizing procreation, refusing (underpaid) employment, and so on), transnationalizing their practical and/or legal belonging (e.g. pursuing overseas education and work, seeking (hidden) dual citizenship, and so on), and sometimes removing their sheer physical existence (i.e. committing

106

suicide at one of the world's highest rates) (Chang, K. 2018, 2019). Do these, often desperate, reactions of transformative victims clearly and coherently indicate that they will sociopolitically support and practically contribute to a post-transformative transformation? Or do they still wish that the current societal and national transformations should continue until the moment when they can participate from more prepared or advantaged positions or when the delayed rain-checks for their earlier transformative contributions finally arrive?

— 6 —

COMPLEX-CULTURALISM VS. MULTICULTURALISM

6.1 Introduction

Until the eve of the twenty-first century, South Korea (and North Korea) consciously and proudly remained a supposedly homogeneous ethnic nation. Such ethnonational homogeneity has even served a strong moral foundation for the supreme political goal of inter-Korean (re)unification. However, it took only several years afterwards for South Korea all of a sudden to declare itself to be (or to become) a "multicultural" society. It was as if South Korean institutions and citizens of all backgrounds resolutely decided to do a much delayed homework in the modern (and late modern) age. This suddenness in South Korea's cultural self-reinvention has much to do with the no less sudden growth of transnational marriages, mostly between underclass Korean men and foreign brides from poorer Asian countries (Kim, H. 2012, 2014).

While international marriage had been quite rare for South Koreans up until the late 1990s, this trend was suddenly turned around from the very beginning of the twenty-first century. In its desperate effort to overcome the post-IMF crisis developmental impasse, the South Korean government decided to aggressively outreach compatriotic Koreans overseas for financial and human resources. Accordingly, Chaoxianzu (Korean Chinese) began to inundate the South Korean labor market through circular or long-term visits. Ultimately, many Chaoxianzu women entered even the South Korean marriage market in urban peripheries, and also played an intermediary role for many Hanzu (the main Chinese ethnicity) women's marriage with South Koreans. Such accidental transnationalization in urban marriage was succeeded by a more inventively aggressive trend in rural "forced" bachelors' marriage with Southeast Asian, particularly Vietnamese, women. Rural bachelors' communally organized (and commercially aided) international marriages became a nation-wide trend from the mid 2000s (Chang, K. 2018, ch. 6).

This unprecedented trend led civilian experts and advocates to proactively urge the South Korean government for various public assistances, which would be formally consolidated as the "multicultural family support policy" (*Danuri* 2020). Such officialization of the public support for internationally married families was in turn interpreted by civil actors and local media as tantamount to declaring the nation as an (aspirational) multicultural society (Yoon, I. 2008, 2016). This could not but be a highly interesting ideational conversion because South Koreans used to proudly identify themselves as a supposedly homogeneous ethnic nation with distinct culture and history. How can the current national zeal for multiculturalism be explained against this seemingly contradictory background? Does the multiculturalism drive signal a fundamental departure from the country's probable monocultural (?) past? How can pre-multicultural South Koreans be characterized in cultural or even civilizational terms?

The current chapter addresses these questions by focusing on the structural characteristics of the supposedly pre-multicultural cultural system of South Korea and its extension or conversion in the showily multicultural present day. (The sociodemographic dimension of South Korea's marriage transnationalization is more systematically discussed in Chapter 9 of this book.) A key thesis here is that South Korea's postcolonial (and postwar) modernization and development required a highly complex cultural system that was both externally liberal, if not fully cosmopolitan, and internally neotraditional. When it had become obviously necessitated, by the late nineteenth century, for East Asian countries to convert to Western systems of politics, economy and technology as a last resort for national survival or revival, each of them openly promulgated the strategic guideline of "Eastern spirit, Western instrument" – i.e. *dongdoseogi* in Korea, *zhongtixiyong* in China, and *wakonyousai* in Japan (Yoon, S. 2017). Instead of observing this guideline strictly, each country turned pragmatic in accommodating Western thoughts and cultures for the sake of material and sociopolitical utilities, while flexibly reprocessing indigenous traditions for practical usages. This tendency has been particularly pertinent in South Korea, where institutional and cultural modernity has been established under both the strong external influence of the United States and the postcolonial neotraditionalism based upon socially generalized Confucian norms.[1] Under what can be conceptualized as *complex culturalism*, South Korean institutions and citizens have instrumentally, selectively, and flexibly incorporated into themselves various historical and civilizational sources of culture in order to expediently consolidate the postcolonial sociopolitical order and then to maximize socioeconomic development.[2]

This complex cultural system used to be embodied in the South Korean nation or population as a seemingly homogeneous racial entity. The legal acceptance and physical integration of rapidly increasing numbers of foreign brides into South Korean society, or the accompanying governmental and civil drive for multiculturalism, implies neither that South Korea used to be culturally isolated nor that it only now wishes to convert into a multicultural or cosmopolitan entity. If any, the unexpected mass presence of "multicultural brides" seems to have further reinforced complex culturalism by enabling South Korean citizens and institutions to conveniently interpret that their open accommodation and active support for the marriage migrants help make their cultural complexity a more self-contained civilizational property. That is, the recent multiculturalism drive does not seem to have lessened or diluted but rather to have fortified the South Korean ethos (or subjectivity?) of self-centered globalism.

6.2 Complex Culturalism:
The Cultural Platform of Compressed Modernity

The global popularity of various genres of South Korean popular culture – dubbed "the Korean wave" initially in China and now globally – has been puzzling analysts, media, and sometimes audiences themselves across the world (Chua, B. 2012; Joo, J. 2011; Shim, D. 2006; Kim, Y. 2013; Lie, J. 2012). Many analysts have attempted to decode the contents and styles of South Korea's popular cultural products as a cultural manifestation of compressed modernity.[3] The Koreanness in South Korean cinemas, television dramas, "K-pop" songs, and other genres of popular culture has been found and enjoyed in terms of the dynamic complexity of South Koreans' life experiences and emotions about extremely diverse civilizational elements, whether indigenously Korean, Asian, Western, or global, or whether traditional, modern, or late/postmodern (Ryoo, W. 2008; see Photo 6.1). The Korean wave offers a crucial implication in analyzing the South Korean cultural system in general. The dynamic complexity of South Koreans' sociocultural life is the theoretical essence of what I propose as complex culturalism below. (Relatedly, as evidenced

110

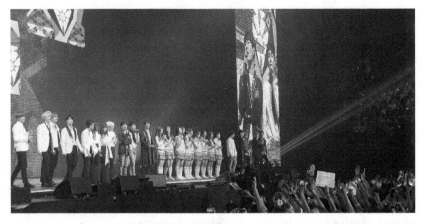

Photo 6.1 The "KCON 2016 France", June 2, 2016

Photo source: The Republic of Korea Ministry of Culture, Sports, and Tourism, June 3, 2016

Author's note: The Koreanness of South Korea's globally adored popular culture has not been actively specified by those cultural, corporate, and administrative agencies that promote the so-called "Korean wave". Innumerable dramas, movies, and K-pops produced and performed by South Koreans have been enjoyed by highly varied audiences across the world in respectively diverse manners and feelings. The remarkable substantive, aesthetic, and technological complexities of South Korean popular culture seem to have enabled any society's audience to find or develop interesting links to their own imaginations, aspirations, and/or experiences. The "KCON 2016 France" in June 2016 in this photo, along with many similar annual occasions across the world, attracted a passionate audience from across Europe fully packing the event's arena.

by their global prominence, South Korean popular culture genres seem to have been much more successful in grasping at and thereby profiting from such distinct national realities than the country's West-dependent academic social sciences.)

As postcolonial South Korea's modernization was heavily con-trolled and influenced by still another hegemonic foreign power – i.e. the United States – its cultural reconstruction closely reflected the American cultural system both in the pluralist contents and liberal patterns (Kim, H. 2013; Lee, B. 2015). Under the American military occupation governance, in fact, postcolonial South Korea underwent a political process of illiberal liberalization, whereas the Korean War experience intensified this process in the Cold War context. Despite the political assault on the leftist forces and ideas, civilian life in the post-Korean War period was openly inundated by diverse forms and contents of Western culture (Kim, C. 2014). As the politico-ideological

111

dependence of the South Korean state on the United States implied a lack or deficiency of self-propelled ideology and philosophy, its direct rule was highly limited in the civilian cultural sphere. Conversely, civilian forces found in culture a sociopolitical space for counteracting the authoritarian political rules of the successive undemocratic state leaderships (Song, E. 2011). Even the state's quasi-McCarthysian raids over civilians ended up fortifying civil society as an exclusively legitimate agency of ideological discourses and cultural imaginations (Koo, H. 1993; Kim, S. 2000). As compared to the externally dependent and ideologically biased state, civil society began to assert the status of a cultural agency of compressed modernity that proactively and flexibly accommodates, on the one hand, indigenously Korean, Asian, Western, and global elements and, on the other hand, traditional, modern, and late/post-modern elements.

Once the modernization drive was set in full motion, South Korean institutions and citizens began to appropriate Western culture more frontally and intensely. Where modernization was conceived in terms of civilizational and material catching-up with the West, Western culture (as well as Western knowledge and technology) became both the goal and method of modernization. Public education, on the basis of widely West-dependent formal curricula, was upheld as the central instrument for Westernization-as-modernization (Seth 2002; Chang, K. 2010a, ch. 3; Chang, K. 2022, ch. 6). Other institutions followed suit for both their own institutional modernization and contribution to national modernization and development; however, their appropriation of Western culture was more syncretistic and/or peripatetic, in accordance with particular institutional necessities and interests. In the modernization regime of *reverse-engineering the West* promptly, social institutions and their cultural resources arose and evolved in a mutually compartmentalized manner, producing a wide-ranged yet discrepantly diverse cultural platform for the general social system (Kim, M. 2010; see Chapter 4 above).

The highly conflictual relations between the state and civil society and between social classes that arose from the very beginning of the Republic of Korea and got intensified along the course of modernization and development induced most South Koreans to frame their lives through highly family-centered values and efforts (Chang, K. 2010a, 2018). They have strategically mobilized family relations and resources for competitive social pursuits (such as education, business, and so forth), but such pragmatic familialism itself would constitute a core moral value because it implies mutual sacrifices among family members. As familial endeavors have been geared to privately maximize social gains, family life has embodied all social values and interests as routine concerns – a common feature analyzed as *accidental pluralism* in my earlier work (Chang, K. 2010a, ch. 2). Besides, their daily exposure to Western family values and lifestyles through media-based cultural consumption and common postcolonial aspiration, now without caste differences, for neotraditionalized (or *yangbanized*) family life, rendered South Korean families to become a complex receptacle for varieties of family values and norms, ranging from past to present and from East to West.

Individually, South Koreans have had to develop a cultural person-hood that is extremely complex yet highly flexible. Their personal lives have been situated and managed in the national, institutional, and familial contexts that are all full of striking cultural diversities and transitions. After embodying indigenously Korean, Asian, Western, and global characteristics on the one hand and traditional, modern, and late/postmodern characteristics on the other hand, South Koreans need to skillfully select and practice certain cultural attributes that are deemed appropriate and/or effective in each concerned situation (Chang, K. 2016a). While this *flexibly complex personhood* chronically overburdens South Korean individuals, it also enriches their lives with all the benefits and pleasures attached to each cultural attribute.

South Korea's dynamic complexity in culture, or complex culturalism, encompasses various systemic features that reflect the above-explained global, national, institutional, familial, and individual conditions and processes of cultural life. Above all, there is an instrumentalist openness to plural – external as well as internal – sources of culture, but such instrumentality brings on peripatetic, syncretistic, and/or contingent approaches to cultural appropriation (Kang, M. 1999). Second, reflecting the sociopolitical and/or institutional orders behind, cultural plurality is routinely confined by the mutually compartmentalized and/or hierarchical structural relationships among diverse sources of culture (Kim, J. 2019). Third and similarly, under the West-dependent regime of national development and modernization, the international order of political, economic, and cultural hierarchies is internalized in terms of the hierarchical patterns of international cultural accommodation, often at the cost of self-Orientalism (Kim, M. 2018). Fourth and relatedly, external cultural openness and dependency induce a sort of reactive cultural indigenization whose effect reinforces the tenet of postcolonial neotraditionalism under both democratic sociocultural and authoritarian political motives (Chang, K. 2018). Fifth, under the lack or indeterminacy of a paradigmatic modern regime of national or societal culture, simulative consumption (cf. Baudrillard 1994) of maximum varieties of foreign (mostly Western) culture constitutes a surrogate cultural self, for whom cultural appreciation and praxis routinely remain superficial, ambivalent, and/or reified (Kang, M. 1999). Sixth, at the individual and the family levels, cultural pluralism is often organized sequentially according to varying stages of individual life courses and family life cycles – that is, individuals and families systematically change guiding cultural values and norms so that Western/modern culture gradually gives way to (indigenously) Korean/traditional culture along the passage of a lifetime (Chang, K. 2010a, ch. 2).

These systemic features of complex culturalism should be carefully considered in order to understand South Korea's recent multiculturalism drive against the precise historico-social context that has governed and continues to govern cultural life in this society. In triggering, managing, and usurping multiculturalism in South Korea – and in any other societies – the grammatical features of the cultural system matter much more critically than its substantive contents. In the following, it will be shown that the unexpected mass presence of "multicultural brides" has reinforced complex culturalism by enabling South Korean citizens and institutions to conveniently interpret that their open accommodation and active support for the marriage migrants help make their cultural complexity a more self-contained civilizational property. Therefore, the recent multiculturalism drive, however improvised it may appear, has not lessened or diluted but rather fortified the South Korean ethos of self-embodied globalism.

6.3 Ad Hoc Multiculturalism under Reproductive Globalization

Beneath South Korea's unprecedentedly rapid industrialization and urbanization, its villages have formed and maintained a socioecological museum-like setting of traditional peasant life, of which the meager livelihood and antiquated lifestyle have become a subject of both social pity and cultural romanticism.[4] The country's industrialization and urbanization have been a heavily age-selective process in which an overwhelming majority of rural youth and young adults have ended up working, studying, and/or living in various types of urban places. The remaining middle/old-age peasants have been "aging" in rural areas under the permanently frozen economic institutional

114

and cultural conditions of familial peasantry. Many middle and late-middle-age bachelors, without having been able to find spouses locally with a willingness to accept patriarchal peasant life, have had to live with elderly parents in unprecedentedly deformed family structures (Chang, K. 2018, ch. 6). But, all of a sudden, many of them have recently found foreign brides from many poor Asian countries as a convenient human resource for rural socioeconomic maintenance.

Native South Koreans' international marriage had been extremely rare until the end of the twentieth century, but the country's aggressive globalization policy, particularly since the 1997–1998 national financial crisis, abruptly turned the situation around. This globalization policy involved, among others, active socioeconomic integration with China, under which Chaoxianzu (Korean Chinese) began to assert an increasingly transnational status in terms of circular and long-term visits to South Korea. As an apparently unexpected consequence of this trend, numerous Chaoxianzu women ended up entering the highly hierarchical South Korean marriage market by marrying poor South Korean men in urban peripheries in the early 2000s. At the same time, many Hanzu (the main Chinese ethnicity) women began to be introduced to similar South Korean men for marriage.

Before long, such transnational developments in the urban marriage market were more inventively accommodated in rural communities in order to secure foreign brides for desperate peasant bachelors with no hope for finding Korean spouses (see Table 6.1). Much like the slightly earlier Taiwanese experience (Wang and Tien 2009; Kung, I. 2009; Kojima 2009), young girls from poor Southeast Asian families – in particular from Vietnamese rural families – were approached. Frequently, commercial matchmaking arrangements were utilized. The idea of arranging rural bachelors to marry Southeast Asian women, as communally organized (and commercially aided) efforts, sprang in the mid 2000s and became a nation-wide zeal shortly (Yoon, I. 2008, 2016). Many villages have seen a third to a half of villagers' recent marriages taking place with foreign brides (Kim et al. 2010).

In a great paradox of South Korea's (late) modernization, villages with virtually frozen traditional socioeconomic characteristics have come to spearhead a sort of cosmopolitanization by accommodating foreign brides from across Asia as new members of local families. A long list of difficulties and contradictions in marriage and family life ensued immediately, prompting both governmental and civilian efforts to help facilitate foreign brides' local and familial adaptation. As villagers' worry about local men's protracted bachelorhood was met with both local and national governmental concern about

115

Table 6.1 Accumulated marriage migrants and other naturalizers by country origin and manners of linking with Korean spouses as of 2018 (n=280,020)

Country origin	%	Number	Manners of linking with Korean spouses among those with spouses (n = 205,887)					
			Family, relative introduction	Friend, colleague introduction	Matchmaking agency	Religious institution	By self	Other
Chinese	19.3	54,070	17.2	39.2	10.3	0.9	32.0	0.4
Korean Chinese	31.1	87,003	30.1	36.6	3.3	0.6	29.2	0.1
Japanese	4.2	11,734	3.5	21.7	0.5	36.6	36.8	1.0
Taiwanese/Hong Kong	1.7	4,700	8.5	35.8	0.8	2.0	51.1	1.9
Vietnamese	23.4	65,490	18.2	23.7	50.9	0.3	6.9	0.1
Philippino	6.2	17,451	15.5	31.2	23.7	12.3	17.1	0.1
Thai	1.3	3,516	11.6	30.0	5.7	7.3	44.9	0.5
Cambodian	2.6	7,199	22.8	19.2	52.3	0.9	4.7	0.0
Other Southeast Asian	0.5	1,500	12.6	26.8	13.9	3.7	41.6	1.4
South Asian	1.2	3,448	12.9	22.1	22.5	3.2	39.1	0.3
Mongolian	1.1	3,077	12.8	33.4	14.6	3.1	35.6	0.6
Russian/Central Asian	2.1	5,904	14.0	31.9	18.5	3.3	31.5	0.7
Ameri/Euro/Ocean	4.7	13,252	7.5	36.6	1.2	4.3	49.4	1.0
Other	0.6	1,676	5.1	25.3	0.1	3.6	64.0	1.9
All with spouses			19.0	31.5	21.1	3.5	24.6	0.3

Note: Among 280,020 persons included, marriage migrants were 238,567 (85.2%) and other naturalizers were 41,453 (14.8%); whereas women were 231,474 (82.7%) and men were 48,546 (17.3%).

Source: Constructed from data in *The National Survey Study of the Actual Conditions of Multicultural Families*, pp. 63–64 and pp. 70–71.

rural demographic extinction, the globalization – or Asianization (Chang, K. 2014) – of rural marriages was soon ratified as a *de facto* state policy through various official assistances and programs for promoting international marriage and easing intercultural marital life. Under the urge of civilian experts and activists, the national government ultimately decided to brand such assistances and programs as the "multicultural family support policy." This official(ized) policy, in turn, was interpreted by civil actors and media as tantamount to declaring South Korea to be (or to become) a multicultural society. Nearly all sections, institutions, and localities of South Korean society began to participate in various activities, events, and programs for assisting "multicultural brides" and promoting a sort of multicultural consciousness (Yoon, I. 2008).

Governmental and civilian fervors for multicultural causes have been mutually escalating in a country that used to be marred by chronic ideological conflicts ever since the controversial postcolonial political independence in 1948 (Im and Park 2012; Yoon, I. 2008). While its unprecedented success in state-led capitalist industrialization since the mid 1960s briefly helped to cement the state–society ideological rift through what may be called *developmental nationalism* (Jeon, J. 1999; Kim, D. 2010), the no less rapid neoliberal restructuring of the national economy since the late 1990s has critically undermined the social efficacy of such mercantilist ideology. Under this context, multiculturalism has arisen as a rare and dear national agenda that even defies the notorious bipartisan politico-ideological rivalry in national politics. The successive administrations under Roh Moo-Hyun, Lee Myung-Bak, Park Geun-Hye, and Moon Jae-In, despite their wide ideological differences, all have emphasized the public importance of multiculturalism and allocated substantial resources for its practical promotion (*Danuri* 2020). Within civil society, even the severely politicized and mutually conflictual media all have concurred on the desirability and urgency of a multicultural reconstruction of South Korean society, even offering special programs and reports that are implicitly designed to promote multiculturalism.[5] Major business enterprises, most unions, activist NGOs of all sorts, schools in all areas, and diverse voluntary associations have seemingly competed against each other in promoting variously defined multicultural causes (Yoon, I. 2008; Im and Park 2012).

In a widely known secret, the actual benefits delivered to foreign brides in villages by public and civilian multiculturalism programs have been rather limited (Kim, H. 2012), but a critical hidden (and more crucial) effect has consisted in the fact that such programs often serve as an expedient platform for enabling South Korean citizens and institutions to develop or assume a multicultural attribute among other cosmopolitan virtues. As materially cosmopolitanized subjects under one of the most aggressively globalizing national political economies, they have found the mass arrival of foreign brides from across Asia to be a rather opportune development to themselves from a sort of self-serving sociocultural perspective. That is, they now feel like asserting that they finally exist in a (contemporarily desirable) multicultural society thanks to these Asian brides.[6] South Koreans' widespread feeling of sociogeographic isolation, with all their fervent complex culturalism in postcolonial modernization and development, has been conveniently attenuated under the sudden mass arrival of Asian brides and the public and civilian campaigns for accommodating them as *cosmopolitan others*.

Such epistemological utility induces that the foreign brides are often expected or even practically asked to preserve and display their home-country cultural characteristics permanently. Local governments and communities, diverse civilian social organizations, and business enterprises have promoted various types of "multiculturalism" events and activities in mutually escalating manners. On such occasions, as a widespread practice, they are staged, paraded, and, of course, photographed, so that their presence can help South Koreans feel cosmopolitanized in one way or another (Chu, B. 2011; *Wando Times*, January 9, 2013). Usually dressed in home-country costumes and expected to exhibit home-country culture (in cooking, singing, etc.), they inevitably end up feeling more differentiated from than integrated with native South Koreans (Yoon, I. 2016). Such segregative staging of racially embodied cultural foreignness is an improvised condition for multiculturalizing native South Koreans' life world. On returning home, paradoxically, most foreign brides have to play the role of a (neo)traditional Korean housewife, which has been flatly denied by so many South Korean women.

6.4 Borrowed Docility: Re(/neo)traditionalization through Foreign Bodies, Particularistic Multiculturalism, and Complex Culturalism

Through their marriage-related immigration status, a kind of *transnational reproductive citizenship* is conferred upon Asian brides, as they are practically obliged to fulfill various familial duties of social reproduction such as homemaking, childbearing and childrearing, and elderly care, often in addition to farm work and other income-earning activities (Chang, K. 2022, ch. 8; Turner 2014). At the private level, however, multiculturalism often grinds down to linguistic and cultural impossibilities of effective and harmonious everyday interactions between foreign brides and their Korean spouses, in-laws, and neighbors (Kim, H. 2012, 2014). In a great paradox, such interactive difficulties are cemented by the unidirectional authoritarian desire of patriarchal Korean families for reinstating the supposedly traditional norms and practices of social reproduction through yet-innocent (or not-yet-modernized) foreign bodies (Chang, K. 2022, ch. 8).

In South Korean villages, traditional culture has extended its lifespan through a very much late modern social condition, namely, hyperaging (Chang, K. 2018, ch. 6). With most young individuals moving out, many villages maintain their demographic basis mainly thanks to the constantly elongated lifespan of elderly persons, and concomitantly remain a traditional cultural entity. In both farm production and household maintenance, such traditionality used to be sustained by patriarchal family relations between generations and genders (Kim, J. 1994; Chang, K. 2018, ch. 3). The exodus of young people – in particular, young women – inevitably began to destabilize family-centered farm production and household maintenance. In a catch-22 situation, the traditionality of villages has been instrumentally threatened by the very demographic condition for it – that is, highly aged villagers can sustain traditional village culture only for the duration of their remaining short lifespans. Under this context, the transnationalization of rural marriages is an ironic effort to mobilize foreign (female) bodies for sustaining the traditional arrangements for rural household maintenance and farm production (Chang, K. 2018, ch. 6). In still another irony, as indicated above, the central and local governments as well as various civilian institutions and supporters have approached these marriage immigrants (serving as transnational human resources for South Korea's traditional rural livelihood and work) in the showy frame of multiculturalism.

Not coincidentally, a majority of foreign brides has moved from rural communities across Asia (Kim et al. 2010). Their rural backgrounds, on the one hand, may reflect poverty to be overcome through marriage migration and, on the other hand, can offer sociocultural familiarity with extended family relations common in South Korean villages (Kim, H. 2014). This is a hidden dimension of the transnational cultural interactions that have been engendered by South Korean rural bachelors' marriage with foreign brides from diverse rural areas of Asia. The civil and governmental characterization of

119

these interactions as multiculturalization falls short of revealing this potential sociocultural commonness between foreign brides' families of origin and their families-in-law. Virtually, none of innumerable events and campaigns touting foreign brides as South Korea's valuably new multicultural subjects acknowledge or indicate that their welcome of sociocultural qualities, utilized for social reproduction labor in South Korean families, are a sort of *borrowed docility* for coping with the disappearance of docile Korean women from villages (Kim and Kim 2008).[7] It is suggestive that many rural families have expressed low preference, as possible brides, for Chaoxianzu and Hanzu women, who are, originally or recently, more likely to have urban backgrounds (Kim, H. 2012).

In a great contradiction, South Korea's multiculturalism drive has borne a fundamentally *particularistic nature* in that it rigidly divides between foreign brides and foreign guest-workers as formal subjects for public social services of the multiculturalization policy (Chang, K. 2013). Foreign guest-workers from across Asia, who were first allowed into South Korea in the early 1990s and began to fill significant shares of wage labor in low-end manufacturing, construction, and farming and fishery sectors since the 2000s, have been frustrated not only by the exploitative terms of their production labor but also by their *official exclusion* from the multiculturalism policy (Seol, D. 2014). The official term for this policy – namely, "the multicultural family support policy"– clearly specifies that only those migrants forming families in South Korea are qualified as its policy constituencies, whereas marriage with a South Korean citizen is virtually the only way of family formation in this society. A critical ramification of foreign guest-workers' formal exclusion from the multiculturalism policy is the permanent legal denial of their right to settle down in South Korea or to invite and live with their families therein (Seol, D. 2014). This policy-line is contradictory to South Korea's eager subscription to the multiculturalism canon of Western Europe and North America because the latter's multicultural transitions were significantly necessitated by the permanent settling of many foreign guest-workers.

The rigid confinement of the multiculturalism policy to marriage migrants is necessitated not by any inherently cultural differentiation between foreign brides and foreign guest-workers, but by a practical material consideration about the basic nature of foreign brides' social reproduction labor. Spousal union, childbirth and childrearing, and care-giving for elderly all require the long-term, if not necessarily permanent, physical presence of participating subjects. This is why legalized marriage has been a virtually universal institution worldwide. (Europeans' increasing avoidance of legalized marriage does not imply a general liquidation or disappearance of long-term associations and commitments between participants in familial unions.) From this perspective, South Korea's multiculturalism policy constitutes – or, is hoped to constitute – a sort of long-term naturalization regime for those migrants who need to reside in the country permanently.

The particularistic quality of South Korea's showy multiculturalism should not be simply taken as a structural limit to the country's cosmopolitan status but more as a strategic platform for a sort of *managed* cosmopolitanism or cosmopolitanization. As indicated above, the unforeseen mass arrival of "multicultural brides" has reinforced South Koreans' complex culturalism by allowing ordinary citizens and various institutions to conveniently, if not opportunistically, interpret that their open accommodation and active support for the marriage migrants help make their cultural complexity a more self-contained civilizational property. Neither the legal acceptance and physical integration of rapidly increasing foreign brides into South Korean society nor the concomitant governmental and civil drive for multiculturalism implies that this society used to be culturally isolated and only now wishes to convert into a multicultural or cosmopolitan entity. In sum, the recent multiculturalism drive does not seem to have lessened or diluted but rather to have fortified the South Korean ethos (or subjectivity?) of self-centered globalism.

6.5 Discussion: Cloakroom Cosmopolitization

The name "cloakroom community" grasps well some of their characteristic traits . . . It is the evening performance that brought them all here – different as their interests and pastimes during the day could have been. Before entering the auditorium they all leave the coats or anoraks they wore in the streets in the playhouse cloakroom . . . During the performance all eyes are on the stage; so is everybody's attention. Mirth and sadness, laughter and silence, rounds of applause, shouts of approval and gasps of surprise are synchronized – as if carefully scripted and directed. After the last fall of the curtain, however, the spectators collect their belongings from the cloakroom and, when putting their street clothes on once more, return to their ordinary mundane and different roles, a few moments later again dissolving in the variegated crowd filling the city streets from which they emerged a few hours earlier.

(Bauman 2000: 200)

121

Cloakroom communities need a spectacle which appeals to similar interests dormant in otherwise disparate individuals and so bring them all together for a stretch of time when other interests – those which divide them instead of uniting – are temporarily laid aside, put on a slow burner or silenced altogether. Spectacles as the occasion for the brief existence of a cloakroom community do not fuse and blend individual concerns into "group interest"; by being added up, the concerns in question do not acquire a new quality, and the illusion of sharing which the spectacle may generate would not last much longer than the excitement of the performance.

(Bauman 2000: 200)

Whether the contemporary globalization is to transform the world into a meaningful cosmopolitan community in the end is perhaps the most essential question for humanity as a social entity in the coming decades. For the time being, evidence abounds in showing that cosmopolitan social associations and formations often take the nature of what Bauman wittily dubs "cloakroom community." That is, we seem to live in an era of cloakroom cosmopolitan communities. While globalization – especially in its neoliberal economic form – has accentuated socioeconomic inequalities and disparities across (as well as within) the national borders, it has simultaneously accelerated transnational sociocultural encounters and interactions among the thereby dissimilated humans and their communities. It is no surprise that multiculturalism has recently drawn keen social attention and strong political emphasis in various countries and world regions. As vividly illustrated in the South Korean episode, the recent aspiration of increasing numbers of societies for reinventing or reinforcing themselves as a multicultural entity often halts at proliferating cloakroom cosmopolitan communities of various sorts.

The literally explosive growth of transnational marriages between Korean men and mostly Asian women seemingly signals that South Korea has entered a genuinely new epoch of cosmopolitan existence and change. This basically new-century phenomenon has drastically reconfigured diverse corners and peripheries of South Korea into manifestly multi-ethnic entities. The national and local governments have been quick in initiating a comprehensive policy of "multicultural family support"; whereas various civil groups, media, and even business corporations have echoed the governmental drive with their own multiculturalism initiatives. Curiously, such seemingly cosmopolitan moves have been subjected to deep criticism from critical intellectuals and advocates, from segregated foreign guest-workers, and from many foreign brides themselves. Above all, many foreign brides and their

122

children, along with their Korean advocates, have even asked South Korea to "stop calling [them] multicultural" because they often feel alienated and even embarrassed under the governmental and social approaches to multiculturalism.[8] As the notion of "multicultural" has frequently been abused to segregatively denote marriage migrants and their mixed-blood children, there is an increasing antipathy among these "multicultural" subjects and their sympathizers against the arbitrary linguistic order of discriminatory multiculturalism under which native Koreans can simply remain Korean while social multiculturalization is supposed to reflect the mere physical presence of "multicultural" brides and children. They recurrently find themselves being staged as what Bauman above dubs "spectacles" for the sake of native South Koreans' multicultural or cosmopolitan desires and feelings.

South Korean institutions and citizens, as agencies of complex culturalism, have instrumentally, selectively, and flexibly accommodated and utilized diverse historical and civilizational sources of culture in their effort to expediently consolidate the postcolonial sociopolitical order and then to maximize socioeconomic development. Such complex cultural systems used to be embodied in the ethnic nation or population as a supposedly homogeneous racial entity. Neither the legal acceptance and physical integration of rapidly increasing foreign brides into South Korean society nor the accompanying governmental and civil drive for multiculturalism testifies that this society used to be culturally isolated or that it only now aspires to turn into a multicultural or cosmopolitan entity. The unforeseen wide presence of "multicultural brides" appears to have further fortified South Koreans' complex culturalism by inducing a convenient interpretation that their open accommodation and active support for the marriage migrants help make their cultural complexity a more self-contained civilizational property.

However, the more their multiculturalism as part of their self-centered globalism is framed through "cloakroom" communal experiences, the more the Asian marriage migrants will remain differentiated, if not discriminated. What nevertheless remains to be seen is if the foreign brides themselves could or would ultimately accommodate South Korean culture (and even South Koreans' self-centered globalism) and thus sustain the nation's cultural status quo, or if they would permanently be asked or forced to preserve and display their home-country cultural characteristics as an indispensable condition for native South Koreans' still elementary multicultural experiences and feelings. In the meantime, their hidden commonness

123

with South Korean women as docile subjects of social reproduction labor will be utilized or necessitated as an essential condition for their practical integration with South Korean rural families-in-law.

— 7 —

PRODUCTIVE MAXIMIZATION, REPRODUCTIVE MELTDOWN

7.1 Introduction

The condensed capitalist economic development in South Korea and other East Asian societies has been accompanied by the astonishing trends of social withdrawal and displacement (Lie, J. 1998) – namely, epidemic suicide, extremely low fertility, widespread postponement, denial and breakage of marriage, pervasive poverty of elderly and youth, excessive rural exodus, rampant dismissal and withdrawal from industrial work, and radical cultural and normative self-isolation (particularly among youth), etc. For such trends, both in scholarly and public discourses, the conservative ideologies, policies, and actions of the oligarchic political, administrative, and industrial leaders of the region's developmental political economies are often criticized in relation to the deficient and defective welfare programs, the generalized pro-business socioeconomic policies, the systematized exploitation of labor and women, and so forth. While largely agreeing to such criticisms, I propose to probe further the disturbing social trends from a social systemic perspective on the relationship between economic production and social reproduction as a critical aspect of the region's compressed modernity.[1]

Social reproduction involves preparation and maintenance of everyday livelihood, preparation of social and occupational participation, courtship and marriage, procreation and rearing of children, care-giving for spouses and parents, and a range of other, mostly family-based activities that are deemed indispensable for the maintenance and enhancement of human and social conditions (Laslett and Brenner 1989).[2] To simplify, social reproduction is the entire range of individual, familial, communal, corporate, and administrative

125

activities for generating and managing human life (population) and labor (class). Social reproduction enables these action units to accomplish the securing, maintenance, and improvement of constitutive members essential for their immediate as well as long-term survival and development. Among others, the growth/reduction of population, the quantitative/qualitative change of labor force, and the securing and recruitment of constitutive members are the essential collective outcomes of social reproduction activities. While capitalism is often defined in terms of the organizational principles in the production system, social reproduction has to be managed effectively and stably in order to achieve the smooth and sustained development of capitalist firms and local and national economies. Sociologically, diverse lines of modernity involve correspondingly diverse regimes of social reproduction. As argued in this chapter, theoretical and analytical attention to social reproduction (and its relationship with economic production) is particularly crucial under the condition of compressed modernity.

In East Asia – particularly in South Korea – compressed modernity is to a critical extent the process and outcome of the developmental(ist) political economy that has been forcefully initiated from above (i.e. by the state) and actively propelled from below (i.e. by ordinary citizens). East Asians framed modernity in a fundamentally developmentalist or productionist manner, so modernization principally became the politico-social project of achieving time-condensed economic development and thereby joining the world rank of "advanced nations"(*seonjinguk*).[3] Such purposeful approach to modernity in terms of condensed national development has been substantiated by various policies, actions, and attitudes that are designed to maximize economic production and, not coincidentally, to systematically sacrifice the conditions and resources of social reproduction.[4] To take a simple example, South Korean workers have been forced to labor for far more hours annually than most of their counterparts in other societies, however only by chronically skipping enough sleep.[5] In fact, sleeplessness is no less problematic among South Korea's future laborers – namely, students who cannot go to bed until well after midnight due to study burdens. Across the country, in another serious example, rampant ecological predation by industries, developers, and local governments – often in some supposed developmental(ist) alliance – has subjected innumerable rural and urban communities to critically hazardous conditions of human livelihood or social reproduction. The list of no less serious examples is nearly inexhaustible.

The developmental outcomes of such productionist political economy (i.e. new or modern types of industries, (urban) spaces, family forms and relations, lifestyles, etc.) in turn would justify various social ramifications of sacrificed social reproduction (i.e. demise of subsistence economic sectors, socially gainful laboring processes, culturally autonomous families and communities, ecologically embedded lifestyles, etc.).[6] After decades of successful economic development, this asymmetrical approach to economic production and social reproduction seems to have critically lost its instrumentality. In spite of their enviable façade covered with hyper-advanced industries, physical infrastructures, services, and lifestyles, the civilizational and even economic progress of East Asian societies is now crucially impeded by the disenfranchisement, shrinkage and/or demise of those classes, spaces, communities, cultures, and wisdoms that have been treated practically as *disposables* (unworthy of social reproduction) under the narrowly focused developmental political economies.

This chapter purports to look into the factors, processes, and nature of South Korea's social reproduction crisis from a social systemic perspective on the relationship between economic production and social reproduction under compressed modernity. Specifically, the class (labor) dimensions of South Korea's social reproduction crisis will be discussed in the current chapter, whereas most of its demographic dimensions will later be touched on in Chapter 9. I will systematically appraise the asymmetrical relationship between economic production and social reproduction as a key structural factor for both the country's compressed capitalist development and instantly concomitant crisis in social reproduction of class members of farming villages and urban industries and neighborhoods.

7.2 Varieties of Productionist Systems and Reproductive Crises

It should be noted that the systemic crisis in social reproduction is not limited to productionist capitalist political economy. In fact, a much more formalistic regime of asymmetrical relationship between economic production and social reproduction used to govern a great mass of modern states under Stalinist socialism. Productionism was a national political manifestation of Marxist materialism in which the class primacy of producers (i.e. laborers) was transposed into the statist rule of mobilizational economic development. State economic planning served as a formalized or bureaucratized framework for

maximizing economic production, with its emphasis on heavy industrialization automating the minimization of people's consumption
(mostly for social reproduction activities) (Kornai 1992). On top of
economic productionism (or economic bias against social reproduction), Marxist materialism also spawned a hostile politico-cultural
approach to social reproduction in general. The revolutionary social
transformation, or socialist system transition, supposedly required
a complete break to feudal and/or capitalist elements in the economy and society, so that social reproduction (conceived in terms
of social relations of production) became a critical area of direct
state intervention. The Stalinist solution for this social transformation was to completely subdue social reproduction to the industrial
production system, as symbolized by the formalistic reconfiguration
of the social statuses and mutual relationships of socialist citizens in
terms of ranks and functions in the state-controlled production units.[7]
Through these economic and social arrangements, most state-socialist
countries initially achieved astonishingly rapid economic growth and
social transformation. However, such productionist development
was unsustainable precisely due to the structured limit of its social
reproduction basis. When the Stalinist economic systems came to an
abrupt halt, not only was national economic production arrested, but
also people were totally devoid of self-supporting capacities due to
their subjection for decades to state intervention against autonomous
social reproduction. In one of the twentieth century's greatest para-
doxes, such crisis was experienced more seriously by more developed
state-socialist countries.

Ironically, or conversely, post-socialist transition has been most
successful both in economic and social terms in those countries where
the earlier socialist transformation of the economy and society had
been most retarded because their underdeveloped status had required
them to maintain in varying degrees the traditional and/or indigenous
social framework for economic production and social protection.
The prominent examples include China and Vietnam. In particular, China's People's Communes (renmingongshe) were no less local
communitarian than state-socialist because natural village members
– frequently including common-family-name kin members – worked
together for largely subsistence-oriented agricultural production,
relying often on traditional social norms and relations.[8] In embarking
on post-socialist reform, the Deng Xiaoping leadership went further
to reinstate family-based rural production and social protection and,
concomitantly, strengthened familial autonomy in social reproduction
(Chang, K. 1992). The immediate economic outcome in privatized

128

agricultural production (as stimulated by drastic upward adjustments in state procurement prices for crops) was astonishing, but even this became dwarfed by the totally unexpected explosive growth of rural industrial and tertiary sectors which were autonomously initiated by rural people as familial or communal ventures. Not surprisingly, Chinese villagers' economic success was immediately accompanied and buttressed by their intensified desire for social reproduction – in particular, having more sons, even against the state's stringent birth control policy.[9]

In China's capitalist neighbors in East Asia, diametrically opposite trends in social reproduction have been observed these days. The sequential achievement of compressed capitalist industrialization and economic development by Japan, Taiwan, and South Korea has paradoxically been accompanied by the failure and/or avoidance by individuals, families, communities, and corporations to sufficiently reproduce and maintain constitutive members of families, communities, industries, and, ultimately, nations (national populations). Like in many other aspects, South Korea appears particularly extreme in such trends. In South Korea, the productionist state's biased approach to social reproduction has been framed through what is explained below as *developmental liberalism* in social policy – that is, the developmental state's social policy liberalism (Chang, K. 2018, 2019). This approach has induced and intensified such practices by citizens and firms as to maximize economic production by purposely sacrificing social reproduction.

As compared to the late or "catch-up" industrialization of state socialist countries, that of capitalist developing countries has been a much less programmatic, or even "peripatetic," experience.[10] The formation, operation, and transformation of the developmental political regimes or governance systems that have successfully orchestrated late but condensed capitalist development have drawn intense and zealous scholarship in political economy, political science, and comparative sociology. These studies have collectively shown that, while not sustained or framed by any deductively acquired schemes for developmental governance, many of the successful national cases of late capitalist development have been ruled by what is often called "the developmental state." Unfortunately, in researching various developmental states which, as implied above, are overwhelmingly productionist, these studies themselves often remain productionist and fail to pay sufficient attention to social reproduction and to its structural relationship with economic production as crucial components of developmental(ist) political economies. That is, the stance and impact of the developmental state on social reproduction still need to be scrutinized as a nearly fresh subject. This subject, in turn, has to be approached in conjunction with the broad issue of the general social policy orientations of the developmental states.

In South Korea – or in capitalist East Asia in general – the state's active developmental pursuit of catch-up industrialization and condensed economic growth has been backed up by what can be characterized as *developmental liberalism* in its social policy front (Chang, K. 2019). State policies regarding, among others, labor, welfare, and education have been generally considered conservative and/or liberal in terms of both spending levels and institutional configurations, but the state's developmental proactivism has frequently effected a systematic harnessing and/or sacrificing of social policy and grassroots livelihood for the sake of maximum economic growth. In this milieu, the South Korean state has been *developmentally liberal* in social policy.

The main concern of the developmental state has no doubt been rapid industrialization and economic growth, but social policy has not been delegated to a different political body. The developmental state itself has also been accountable to the basically liberal doctrine of social policy partially coated with culturalist ideologies (in particular, Confucian familialism) and, more recently, covered up with the (Continental Europe-style) conservative programs of social insurance (Chang, K. 2019, ch. 4). We thus need to document any systematic relationship between economic developmental goals and liberal social policies, both of which are attributes of the developmental state. That is, there is a pressing academic as well as practical need for more systematic analysis of the structural relationship between economic developmentalism and social policies and practices, instead of dwelling on a supposed zero-sum relationship between them. Particularly with respect to the suppressing or sacrificing of social policy concerns, the motivations, conditions, manners, and outcomes of such actions should be systematically documented in order to explore any possibility that they are *developmentally liberal*, as opposed to being *liberally liberal* as has been the case in the United States and, to lesser extents, other settler colony societies.[11]

As to social reproduction, the developmental liberal state has shown several traits as follows:[12] (1) as revealed in regard to the abrupt demise of family farming and labor-intensive manufacturing, the public necessity of supporting social reproduction of labor in those sectors excluded from the state's developmental priorities has been bluntly denied in order to enable the maximum mobilization of public and private resources into sequentially selected strategic industries (dubbed "the leading sectors"); (2) the responsibility and expenses for social reproduction have been attributed to workers and their families as much as possible, and even the infrequent public assistance for social reproduction has usually taken the form of repayable finance, instead of social wage; (3) as revealed with regard to housing, health care, and education, the market-commoditization of basic social reproduction goods are practically endorsed and, not infrequently, even encouraged tacitly, and, in conjunction, various types of *social reproduction loans* have been devised and provided for these matters; (4) as revealed particularly in the area of public education, the nature and contents of social reproduction have been arbitrarily manipulated in order to justify and facilitate economic productionism or the developmentalist political economy in general. With these traits combined, developmental liberalism can be seen as a social policy regime that functions in order to systematically reinforce the asymmetrical relationship between economic production and social reproduction and thereby intensifies the productionist nature of compressed modernity.

Such passive or conservative stance of the developmental liberal state toward social reproduction has inevitably imposed serious economic and social burdens on the everyday livelihood and family relations of its citizens, which in turn constitute a serious factor for social discontent and political upheaval. In particular, the interfamilial differentials in social and economic resources can be translated into different likelihoods of successful social reproduction and thereby systematically amplify unequal conditions in social and economic competition. However, most South Koreans used to do their best in social reproduction as familial responsibilities, in a great part thanks to the broad improvement in their income levels amid rapid economic growth. More critically, instead of resisting the developmental (liberal) dogma of the state, most of them have tried to *manage their family relations and personal lives developmentally* and thereby have actively adapted to the conservative political economic order.[13] For instance, their intensity in educational investment for children has been nearly unparalleled across the world, the financial support for the economic activities of their children and siblings has often been taken for granted, and their prompt withdrawal from the declining industries such as farming has been linked to the exploration and undertaking of newly promising industries by their siblings and children (Chang, K. 2010a; also see Chapter 8 below). By contrast, their concern and preparation for the long-term stabilization of social

131

reproduction have been as deficient as those of the developmental liberal state. In the worst example, the almost generalized and protracted indifference to the preparation of old-age security by both South Korean workers and their developmental liberal state has led to the widespread poverty and personal desperation among aged people – as infallibly evidenced by the world's highest level of elderly suicide in this country.[14] In sum, the developmental state and *developmental families* have colluded with each other in maintaining a social reproduction system full of speculative or gambling characteristics. While private families may not allocate a fundamental value to macro-level developmentalism and behave accordingly, they nevertheless function as the most basic unit of the developmental systemic order by internalizing such macroeconomic order into their microsocial space of everyday life and by reacting very sensitively and adaptively to the accompanying material opportunity structures.[15]

As indicated above, the class (labor) dimensions of South Korea's social reproduction crisis will be discussed in the following sections; whereas most of its demographic dimensions will later be touched on in Chapter 9. Under the extremely rapid industrial restructuring narrowly focused upon a few strategic sectors and the indiscriminate trade liberalization for assisting the export-based growth of such strategic sectors, conventional industries such as agriculture and simple manufacturing have instantly been abandoned one by one. As a consequence, an overwhelming majority of the population that used to be engaged in these sectors became subjected to a fundamental crisis in their economic management and social reproduction, and this in turn began to aggravate the instability of the macroeconomic and social conditions. In the following, I will systematically appraise the asymmetrical relationship between economic production and social reproduction as the key structural factor for both the country's compressed capitalist development and instantly concomitant crisis in the social reproduction of class members of farming villages and urban industries and neighborhoods.

7.3 Dissolution of the Farm Family Reproduction Cycle

The traditional family-based peasantry, which organically integrates both farm production and social reproduction on the basis of the patriarchal familial organization (Chayanov 1986), had survived into modernity as the most universal microsocial system not only in South Korea but also through the entire human history. After a half century of industrial capitalism, however, South Korea is now faced with the potential extinction of familial peasantry, as evidenced by the fact that its proportion of the peasant population is now one of the lowest in the world, with a great majority of them being elderly persons left behind by their city-dwelling children. The fundamental collapse in the social reproduction of peasant families is demonstrated more systematically by the distribution of farm households across the different stages of the family reproduction cycle (Chang, K. 2018, ch. 6). That is, among the remaining farm households, only a small minority are in the stages of familial formation and expansion, whereas other farm households are in the stage of familial reduction or dissolution. Therefore, there is a fundamental limitation for peasant families to function as the basic unit of economic production and social reproduction in rural South Korea.

This trend of the extinction of peasant families has been induced mainly by the fact that peasants themselves have pursued, as a familial developmental strategy, the education and employment of their children and/or siblings in urban areas wherein most of the handsome economic opportunities accompanying industrial capitalism have been found.[16] In this way, *most of peasant families have virtually functioned as the social reproduction organizations for the urban economy*. However, peasants' adaptive behavior as such has also reflected a kind of defeatism amid their structural subordination to the "acyclic" or "rush-forward" capitalist industrialization promoted jointly by the developmental state and its client business community. Instead of rising up collectively as a social class, most peasants have surrendered themselves individually to the developmental state that, on the one hand, has refused or failed to acknowledge the complex set of economic, social, cultural, and ecological values embedded in agriculture, peasant, and village and, on the other hand, has not bothered to hide the presumption that farming cannot but be sacrificed, particularly in the latest era of global free trade, to accomplish the maximum growth of export-oriented capitalist industries.

Such individualized surrender by rural citizens has been particularly prevalent among young women, who have tried to cast off the social pressure from the patriarchal production-cum-reproduction system of peasant households (Kim, J. 1994). As detailed in Chapters 6 and 9, this in turn has brought about a marriage crisis to rural bachelors. In the social policy front, the (developmental liberal) national state does not seem to have felt a serious necessity to make much public investment and support for the social reproduction of rural population and localities that have supposedly lost strategic developmental values.[17]

133

If anything, the recently reinstated local autonomous governments are trying hard, despite their fundamental budgetary limitations, to stabilize the social reproduction of rural population for the sake of their own politico-administrative survival. Most recently, the neoliberal globalization drive of the state and its industrial partners has explicitly intensified the agriculture-sacrificing nature of the economic development policy – as exemplified by the almost indiscriminate pursuit of FTAs with agricultural exporter countries such as the United States, Chile, Australia, Canada, Vietnam, and so forth.[18] Ironically, as detailed in Chapters 6 and 9, in another aspect of this globalization process, international marriages have rapidly increased for the remaining peasant bachelors as their last resort in social reproduction (Kim, H. 2012, 2014). Those rural elderly without any willing successor in farming, if they are aged 65 years or older and have farmed for at least five years, are now encouraged to participate in the farmland pension (*nongjiyeongeum*) program that provides monthly income in exchange for mortgaged farmland (https://www.fbo.or.kr/contents/Contents.do?menuId=0400100010).

7.4 Industrial Working Life History and Social Reproduction

The rush-forward economic development strategy has also disrupted the social reproduction system of a majority of urban proletarian families. As has been debunked by now, lifetime employment has been an exceptional privilege confined to fairly limited scopes and numbers of workers in South Korean industries, whereas the working life histories of most other workers have been filled with frequent interruptions and sectoral complexities (Choi and Chang 2016). In the early industrialization period, the corporate requisite of cheap labor-based export competitiveness did not allow industrial labor to become an ideal career even to industrial workers themselves (Koo, H. 2001). The industrial structural upscaling led by a handful of export-centered industrial conglomerates (called *chaebol*) in the later stages of development has been less "the social evolution of the producer classes' community based upon the employees' improved skill levels than the business restructuring and/or expansion based upon technological outsourcing" (Kong, T. 2012).

In this process, a staggering proportion of industrial workers have been laid off during their companies' technological transition and factory automation. Furthermore, since the national financial crisis in 1997 to 1998 regulated by the International Monetary Fund (popularly dubbed, among South Koreans, "the IMF crisis"), many companies have refused regular employment to a majority of new employees often regardless of their skill levels (Chang, K. 2019, ch. 4). Moreover, the labor policy that has been fundamentally subordinated to the business-centered industrial policy has not focused upon the human capital improvement of the existing employees, unless demanded otherwise by export-oriented *chaebol*. Tat Yan Kong (2020) offers a highly suggestive warning that, unlike Germany or Japan, South Korea may not be able to leap into a socially advanced economy as long as it adheres to the industrial system in which industrial development is not systematically embodied into the workers' human capital.

Such structurally frequent interruptions in most industrial workers' employment histories, as combined with their suppressed wage levels, kept presenting a serious obstacle to the stable fulfillment of their role as family provider. More fundamentally, in a situation where industrial workers cannot perceive their jobs as the human embodiment of national economic development, there is no social reproduction of industrial labor sustained by the workers' intention to hand their jobs down to the next generations in families.[19] In quite an interesting paradox, union members of a globally successful auto manufacturer, Hyundai Motors, once demanded that their regular employment status should be inherited by their children as a corporate guarantee (*Kyunghyang Shinmun*, April 14, 2011). This incident, as heavily publicized by media, dealt a critical blow to the already damaged social reputation of large corporate unions, which comprise the main body of the nation's organized labor.

7.5 Urban Poor Families:
Women under Old and New Social Risks

It was pointed out earlier that the peasant family is a social system for organically combining economic production and social reproduction. Such complex functionality is also found in the individual wives of urban poor families. Although women's lifelong employment, especially among the high education-based professional occupations, is rapidly increasing as a new social trend, the long-term, albeit frequently interrupted, economic participation of married women has been a class-wide phenomenon among the urban poor. Many middle-aged employed women from this class have contributed to the social reproduction and income maintenance of their families through the so-called "M-curve" working-life path, consisting of premarital employment, post-marital temporary retirement for childbirth and childrearing, and middle-age reemployment (Chang, K. 2010a, ch. 5). Under a strong trend of intra-class marriages, however, their spouses have been distributed mostly in unstable and low-income occupations, while their own jobs have been concentrated in menial service jobs.[20] This implies that their dual income has rarely enabled them to climb the class hierarchy within their own lifetime, or to see their children achieving serious intergenerational mobility, particularly through privately financed educational competition. Since the "IMF economic crisis," such class immobility has been pretty much fixated, as believed by a majority of contemporary South Koreans.[21]

While the lives of urban poor housewives have always required combative commitment, they have recently been exposed to the so-called "new social risks" and, as a result, have to go through aggravated personal burdens and pains (Yoon, H. 2008).[22] Above all, under South Korea's compressed population aging, the rapid elongation of the lifespans of their already old parents(-in-law) has necessitated urban poor housewives to take up a sort of *third shift* as the main caregivers for the aged familial dependants – on top of "the first shift" of wage labor and "the second shift" of household management (cf. Hochschild 1990). These elderly people, after living through middle age plagued with overwork and excess financial contribution for family, have often been inflicted by multiple chronic diseases and are seldom prepared with sufficient stable financial resources for old age. More recently, the postindustrial-cum-neoliberal economic hazards in terms of adult children's failure in employment and concomitant demand for further education and husbands' chronic occupational instabilities have helped worsen these women's multiple shift lives.[23] As detailed in Chapter 9, grown-up children's increasingly unstable employment status and the resultant rapid increases in late marriage, non-marriage, and divorce imply that middle- and old-aged women nowadays cannot expect easily a leisurely and fruitful life based upon the timely transfer of their familial roles to the next generation family members (*Chosunilbo*, January 14, 2011). Most of these women, hoping that their daughters should not live like themselves, would not frontally object their hiatus from marriage under a confession, "I don't want to live like you, Mother!" (KimGoh, Y. 2013). The continual thinning of the stable middle class implies that such intergenerationally shared pessimism about marriage is constantly increasing.

7.6 Debt-Sustained Livelihood:
Financialization of Social Reproduction

In past agrarian societies, if the distorted structure of land ownership deprived peasants of opportunities for normal economic activities and forced them into poverty, many of them had to rely on landowners' usuries and, in the end, dispose of their means of agricultural production and social reproduction (such as livestock, farmlands, household goods, and houses). Some of them even had to sell their children and wives. This meant that their individual and familial lives were ruined through a process describable as *financialization of poverty* (Chang, K. 2019, ch. 5).[24] In the twenty-first century's South Korea, the explosive increase in household debts, over which even the conservative administrations have kept expressing serious concerns time and again, also attests to the widespread financialization of poverty, accompanying the chronic structural crisis in ordinary South Koreans' work and livelihood. The excessive burden of debt repayment has been driving rapidly increasing numbers of individuals and families into horrible experiences of persecution and ultimately into such ruinous incidents as family dissolution and suicide. Many such suicides have been preceded by desperate parents' killing of little children before removing their own lives under an assumption that their children would be subjected to extreme misery if left behind without parental material protection (Lee, H. 2012).

The average debt–income ratio for South Korean households has already exceeded that for the notoriously indebted American households. The radical economic restructuring in the post-IMF crisis period, focused on the quick revival and enhanced competitiveness of the key export industries of *chaebol*, resulted in the wholesale sacrifice of agriculture and labor-intensive light industries, as well as the overseas transfer of industrial production (and jobs), for the sake of maximum economic opportunities and profits of industrial enterprises (Chang, K. 2019, ch. 4). Those South Koreans deprived of their opportunities for economic activities in this process have had to supplement their lost wages or business incomes by disposal of household properties, financial support and loan guarantee among kin members, consumer lending, and so forth. In conjunction with this social trend, the government has endorsed and sometimes even encouraged, arguably in a new area of its developmental industrial policy, the rapid establishment of various new financial service commodities and the aggressive business expansion of financial industries of various types (Chang, K. 2016). In particular, the credit card-based cash loans and housing mortgage loans began to increase explosively from the turn of the century.

As the minimum material resources for familial or individual social reproduction are often secured by financial services instead of production activities, this is tantamount to *financialization of social reproduction*. Under the excessive pressure of debt repayment, even if they resume economic activities against various difficulties, they cannot exercise normal bargaining power against their employers or business counterparts and thus become subjected to abnormally disadvantageous terms in their economic activities (Chang, K. 2016b). There are frequent cases where creditors, abusing their rights, demand economic activities that are virtually slave labor.[25] Some creditors have even coerced debtors to agree to human organ transactions (*Minjushinmun* 2011). In this way, financial indebtedness has become another defining basis for class status in the production system.

As the debtor status has become common among the general population, the successive governments have attempted to design and provide various forms of financial rescue programs (Chang, K. 2016b).[26] As shown by the state-backed introduction and expansion of various new commercial loan programs for education, housing, and so forth, a *de facto* financial service system for all dimensions of social reproduction has been in the making. However, given the developmental liberal government's near inaction on the rapid inflation of college tuitions, virtual protection of speculative profits earned through housing and land transactions, and other instances of excusing economic distortions in the supply of social reproduction goods, it is hard to tell whether the government-designed and/ or encouraged commercial loan programs for easing poor people's access to social reproduction goods constitute, in effect, a genuine social policy or a disguised new industrial policy. (The current Moon Jae-In government has broadly inherited these socially targeted loan programs while being flatly unable to curb the trend of household debt bloating.)

7.7 Conclusion and Prospect: After Condensed Social Divestures

In South Korea (and other East Asian societies), modernity was conceived in a fundamentally developmentalist or productionist manner, so modernization principally became the politico-social project of achieving time-condensed economic development and thereby becoming an "advanced nation" – *seonjinguk* in Korean – as swiftly as possible. Such purposeful approach to condensed national development has necessitated various policies, actions, and attitudes for maximizing economic production and, not unrelatedly, systematically sacrificing the conditions and resources of social reproduction. Under such asymmetrical approach to economic production and social reproduction, South Korea's condensed national development has caused an inescapable decline or demise of subsistence economic sectors, socially gainful laboring processes, culturally autonomous families and communities, ecologically embedded lifestyles, and so on. With all the nation's hyper-advanced industries, physical infrastructures, services, and lifestyles, its civilizational and even economic progress is now increasingly impeded by the disenfranchisement and demise of those classes, generations, communities, cultures, and wisdoms that have been treated practically as *disposables* – unworthy of social reproduction support – under the narrowly focused developmental political economy.

The above overview of South Korea's various crisis tendencies in social reproduction associated with industrial and class restructuring, as well as those associated with demographic transformations as explained in Chapter 9, leads to a conclusion that its compressed modernity is the amalgamation of both condensed (economic) achievements and condensed (social) divestitures. The miraculous economic accumulation in the hands of mammoth industrial conglomerates has structurally required the radically abrupt and expansive divestitures in the agrarian, proletarian, demographic, cultural, and ecological foundations and components of the Korean civilization. While the long-term sustainability of the mega-industrial South Korean economy itself is a subject for serious disputes, the twenty-first century in this country should be lived or managed increasingly without stable agrarian life, gainful industrial work, secure household livelihood, sufficient demographic replacement, predictable life courses, and dependable national political economy and life world. Under such comprehensive and swift social divestitures, the post-compressed modern condition in this society is likely to be characterized by *radical liquidity* (cf. Bauman 2000) in the personal, social, cultural, demographic, as well as economic configurations of human life.

— 8 —

SOCIAL INSTITUTIONAL DEFICITS AND INFRASTRUCTURAL FAMILIALISM

8.1 Introduction:
Infrastructural Familialism, from Above and from Below

This chapter presents a broad analysis of the macro-structural significance of familial norms, relations, and resources that have served as a
key social infrastructural condition of compressed modernity in South
Korea. In a fundamentally family-dependent way, South Koreans
have managed their modern history and made various internationally
envious achievements. The compressed nature of their modernity is
structurally enmeshed with various social infrastructural utilities of
families. A careful understanding of the sociocultural characteristics,
organizational structures, and resource endowments of Korean families is thus indispensable in explaining not only the detailed aspects of
everyday personal life but also, as comprehensively explained in my
earlier work (Chang, K. 2010a), the macro-structural conditions and
changes in the social, economic, and even political domains.

This feature of South Korean society has been derived not just from
its traditional – say, neo-Confucian – heritage of family-centered life,
but more critically from the processes and manners by which South
Koreans have coped with various modern sociocultural, political, and
economic forces. When colonial economic exploitation and political
abuse of grassroots were rampant, when a total civil war denied any
certainties in social relations and economic activities, and where postwar ruling elites were unreliable and only authoritarian in managing
civil life, most South Koreans felt and regarded their own family
as the only reliable source of protection and survival.[1] However,
even after the state managed to effectively govern national economic
development and social institutional modernization, South Koreans'

reliance on familial norms, relations, and resources has remained unabated. In fact, the familialized nature of South Korean modernity has kept intensifying, albeit in continually refashioning modes, as the state and its allied social actors have found and consciously tapped various strategic utilities from ordinary people's eager effort to sustain their family-centered/devoted lives.[2]

When the postcolonial state embarked on modernization and development since the late 1940s, its primarily bureaucratic and propagandic approach, clumsily coated with locally alien West-reflexive concepts and goals, fell far short of making its citizenry meaningfully persuaded about its top-down causes. Most crucially, the situationally improvised liberal state's lack of adequate financial resources and basic social institutional apparatuses for systematically incorporating its citizenry in national development and social modernization resulted in a chronic instability in social governance. While the South Korean state was barely enabled to function in the immediate post-Korean War period under the American foreign aid and institutional-legal advices, grassroots citizens, most of whom being peasants who were tilling equally redistributed, yet commonly limited farmland, were basically left to themselves in reorganizing their material livelihood and communal order according to certain locally remembered and reinvented norms centered on familial relations and duties (Jeong, J. 1995).

Nonetheless, and indeed miraculously, the country came to assume full velocity in sociopolitical and economic transformations from the 1960s. While "the authoritarian bureaucratic state" since Park Chung-Hee's reign has been much accredited with South Korea's globally recognized success in development and modernization, it has been critically dependent upon grassroots citizens' familial norms, relations, and resources in pursuing every national goal. This has been evident, as explained subsequently in this chapter, concerning nearly all major features and conditions of South Korean development and modernization, including early Lewisian industrialization based upon stable supplies of rural migrant labor, universalization of high-level public education enabling constant improvements in human capital, and sustained common ethic for familial support and care buffering the chronically defective public welfare.[3]

In this national historical experience, familialism is not just a private characteristic or value of certain individuals or groups of individuals. The South Korean state itself has been familialist in organizing and leading its (familialist) citizenry. Like most other states in the modern world, it does reflect, consciously and formally, individual citizens' private values about family relations, goals, and duties in its legal codes and social policy principles for dealing with both civilian and governmental affairs.[4] But the state's own practically driven familialist stance is not reducible to such private family values, but represents a distinct line of technocratic deliberation that I propose to conceptualize as *infrastructural familialism*. In what follows, I will show that the South Korean state has found and used various *social infrastructural utilities* of its citizens' familial norms, relations, and resources, in pursuing national development and modernization under extremely difficult financial and social institutional conditions. Conversely, the state's such utilitarian familialism has made individual citizens realize that their developmental and sociopolitical participation in national life is systematically facilitated through familial allegiance and cooperation. *Infrastructural familialism has been upheld both from above and from below.*

8.2 Family and Modernity: Academic Debates and Historical Realities

The social relations, demographic structure, norm and ideology, and other elements in the Korean family have been studied in sociology and related disciplines under the heavy influence of American functionalism. South Korean sociologists used to find this theory quite useful in interpreting the transformation of family structure and relations in the process of rapid urbanization and industrialization.[5] It is necessary to examine briefly the functionalist explanation of modern family change and point out its theoretical and empirical limitations with regard to South Korean society. This is because the thesis of infrastructural familialism is a line of neo-functionalist argument with a keen emphasis on diverse historical and social institutional conditions of family life and social change.

Functionalism of modern family change consists mainly of two theoretical elements. First, the weakening of the supposedly archaic familial organization and culture has been regarded as a precondition, as well as an outcome, of socioeconomic modernization centered on industrialization. For instance, Goode (1963) presented his functionalist proposition that the change of family patterns – above all, family nucleation – is a functional imperative of industrialism. Under this generalized supposition on the minimal, though universal, family in modern industrial society, family research has been directed to such areas as morphological studies of family forms and family life

142

cycles. The second theoretical element of functionalism is the subjective intimate domain assigned to family. While the role of family is supposedly minimized in the larger social arena of economic and political relations, the continuing universality or primacy of family has been theoretically justified in terms of its functions in emotional support and spiritual regeneration. By playing a central role in the preservation of the private domain as well as in the reproduction and socialization of children, family is supposed to function as a key "pattern maintenance" mechanism in the Parsonian social system (Parsons and Smelser 1956). The modern family is theorized to be an affectionate and romantic entity that is safeguarded against hostile and alienating forces of industrial capitalism. Accepting these theoretical parameters, a new branch of sociological studies began to delve into the emotional processes in the modern family (see Shorter 1988).

While these lines of family research have produced abundant knowledge on many narrowly defined issues, the classic sociological goal of understanding family as an aspect, determinant, and consequence of long-term macrosocial change has been unduly neglected. This lacuna is particularly problematic in societies like South Korea, where modern history has been made in a fundamentally family-dependent way. In such societies, not only the detailed aspects of everyday personal life but also the macro-structural changes in socio-political order and economic development have closely reflected the sociocultural characteristics, organizational structures, and resource endowments of local families. Much innovation is thus needed both in empirical and theoretical research, in order to present a correct picture of the macro-structural as well as personal conditions of family life and its converse societal influences on national development and modernization.

Fortunately, relevant theoretical and empirical insights can be drawn from outside the conventional domain of family sociology. As early as in the 1980s, in particular, many innovative historical, anthropological and political economic approaches were deployed as to the structural positions and utilities of grassroots families in the modernization and development of various world regions and societies. For instance, from the "putting people first" perspective, abundant research outcomes were produced on the roles and experiences of grassroots families in the processes of economic (under) development and social change in Third World societies (e.g. Safa 1982). Some perceptive scholars were able to grasp at the familial foundations of capitalism in East Asia (e.g. Redding 1990). Even

143

concerning European and North American societies, many sociohistorical studies presented revealing findings on the active roles and efforts of grassroots families in adapting to and even shaping the process of industrial revolution (e.g. Hareven 1982). Relatedly, class conflict was analyzed in terms of the abuse and struggle of proletarian families in Western societies (Humphries 1982) and peasant families in Third World societies (Meillassoux 1981).

Even a sketch perusal of South Korea's recent historical and social conditions easily generates ample testaments to social phenomena that can be explained by applying or comparing these studies on family and modern social change in various structural perspectives. For instance, when full-scale industrialization began since the early 1960s, it was (rural) families, along with other groupings with similar social characteristics, from which migrant workers and peddlers, early industrial entrepreneurs, and other actors of capitalist industrialism eked out the initial resources for economic success (Chang, K. 2010a, ch. 6). Even in the mainstream industrial economy, the family-centered structure of ownership and management in major business conglomerates, *chaebol*, is a key feature of South Korean capitalism (Kang, M. 1996; Chang, K. 2010a, ch. 7). Noneconomic spheres are not excluded from such practical, if not clearly ideological, primacy of family.

While this social feature is no less a modern invention than an inherited tradition, pre-modern Korea (Chosun in particular) was similarly family-centered in social order, politics, and economy. The neo-Confucian ideology, formally codified into the principles of political rule and social relations, governed Chosun society by rendering family to play a central role in social control and protection, political rule, and economic production (Choe, H. 1991). A comprehensive set of norms, customs, and laws prescribed the attitudinal and behavioral details of such family-centered life. Even the state–society relations were described as a type of pseudo-familial bondage, and individuals' loyalty to the state – royal authority – was carefully interpreted as an extended expression of filial piety to their own parents. While the fall of Chosun under Japanese colonialism and the postcolonial division (from North Korea) and liberal capitalist transition of South Korea liquidated Confucianism as a ruling sociopolitical ideology, there occurred a highly interesting universalization of Confucian familial relations, norms, and rituals among all citizens ever since their liberation from Japan (Chang, K. 2018, ch. 3). Such neotraditional cultural homogenization of ordinary South Koreans was matched with their equalized social and political citizenships (in terms of land reform and

144

representative democracy respectively), which were derived by and large from South Korea's accommodation of American systems and advices (Park, T. 2008). Grassroots South Koreans, an overwhelming majority of whom being smallholder peasants, began to organize their material livelihood and social order according to this tripod endowment of political, economic, and sociocultural equalities (or uniformities).

The postcolonial state in South Korea was, in form, liberal democratic, but it was governing a population of highly complex systemic and civilizational characteristics. Given the inchoate state's acute institutional, social, and financial limitations, the nation's present and future were critically predicated upon an effective mobilization of civilians' efforts and resources into the urgent public goals of development and modernization. In this respect, the needy state carefully endeavored to accommodate its familialist citizens' aspirations and resources as a sort of social infrastructure for strategic national purposes such as labor-intensive early industrialization, education-based human capital upscaling, social support and protection for deprived and/or enfeebled citizens, and so forth. The broadly family-reliant regime of social and economic policy thereby arose and has remained largely effective to date. This policy line made most South Koreans comfortably enfranchised into key national purposes, albeit under the condition of family-based voluntary provisions of human efforts and financial resources. At the same time, in a historical phenomenon comparable to the unintended ethical effect of Calvinist Protestantism for capitalist development in Western Europe (as argued by Max Weber), grassroots South Korean families' sociocultural characteristics – in particular, neotraditional Confucian norms and relations – began to take on a sort of *unintended societal significance* as an indispensable infrastructural resource for the nation's modernization and development.[6]

8.3 Late Capitalist Industrialization and Its Familial Parameters

Modern economic development in most postcolonial societies has been equated with industrialization, namely, the rise of manufacturing industry and its replacement of agriculture as the concerned society's economic core. Industrialization, in turn, has generally been considered as a historical process in which the family's socioeconomic institutional primacy, as generally based upon agriculture, declines and is ultimately replaced by special economic organizations designed for mechanized production of industrial goods. However, South Korea's industrialization – and even its postindustrial transition – cannot be properly understood by this simplistic explanation. Families have constantly sustained and even renewed their socioeconomic institutional significance, for instance, through (1) the nation's postcolonial socioeconomic stabilization based upon the universally reinstated familial agriculture (i.e. land reform), (2) its swift Lewisian industrialization since the 1960s with sustained supplies of dependable industrial labor from rural families, and (3) its radical progression into capital-intensive sectors and abrupt postindustrial transition, both socially buffered by widespread familial self-employment. As explained in the subsequent sections of this chapter, such modern – and even late modern! – economic functions of families are coalesced with their additional critical functions in social welfare, education, and so forth.

Above all, South Korea's family-based peasantry has performed various indispensable functions for rapid capitalist economic development. Family farming in East Asia has historically shown the world's highest-level productivity per unit land, for which the social viability and organizational efficiency of the familial work organization are most responsible (Kim, S. 1998).[7] South Korea's land reform, carried out in the late 1940s and the early 1950s, reinstated family farming nationwide after decades of distortion and destruction under the Japanese colonial rule. Afterwards, most of the nation's already burdensome yet rapidly growing population had to be socioeconomically absorbed in the agricultural enterprises of rural families on the basis of familial moral relations of mutual support.[8] The socioeconomic rationality behind the institutional universality of familial agricultural production in populous nations (Georgescu-Roegen 1960; Chayanov 1986) has been particularly relevant in this postcolonial, war-torn society. The socioeconomic *carrying capacity* of the family-based peasantry needs to be fully recognized as a critical precondition for socially sustainable economic development. As explained below, this is also a crucial prerequisite for effective (labor-intensive) industrialization.

In conventional sociological understanding, industrialization has been considered as a process of achieving a modern industrial economic system and securing its social institutional and technological conditions. In the historical reality of late developing societies like South Korea, however, the most decisive phase of economic development has consisted in the initial socioeconomic transition period,

146

during which massive and rapid rural-to-urban transfers of labor have taken place. This possibility was systematically explained by W. Arthur Lewis (1954) as "economic development with unlimited supplies of labour" (from rural families). When a *Lewisian industrialization* was launched in South Korea from the early 1960s, rural families took on another historical function – that of bearing various *social transition costs of industrialization*. The rapid accumulation of industrial capital cannot be meaningfully explained without considering the social transition costs of industrialization borne by individual peasant families. The Lewisian idea of basing industrial development on the lengthy abundant supply of cheap labor of good quality presupposes that various costs accruing to the formation and rural-to-urban transfer of labor should be borne by individual peasant families in the spirit of familial assistance and support (Kim, H. 1992). These costs include – besides the initial parental efforts for raising children into serviceable labor – moving expenses, housing rents, fees for schooling and/or vocational training, seed money for peddling, direct food supplies, and so on (Chang, K. 2010a, ch. 6). The rural familial bearing of such costs renders the so-called "demographic dividend" to be conveniently reaped by industrial capital without the state's direct social contributions. In fact, the notion of *dividend* in "demographic dividend" becomes problematic if its socioeconomic results are not justly allocated to the families of migrant workers as the direct demographic contributors.[9] The state did not have any significant social programs to ease such familial burdens, and industrial capital did not have any serious intention to reimburse them. Relatedly, the South Korean government once estimated that there had been a net outflow of capital from rural to urban areas, even during the critical period of unprecedentedly rapid industrialization and relative decline of agriculture since the early 1960s.[10]

The economic importance of familial production and labor support has not been limited to the peasant population. Much of the heavy population in poor urban neighborhoods has been absorbed in the so-called informal sectors, of which familial self-employment is quite common (KFSRG 1992). The urban economy in South Korea has long been characterized by an extremely high proportion of self-employed persons, which is a result of both economic developmental success and failure (Choi and Chang, K. 2106; Kim, D. 2015). As of 2017, for instance, the proportion of self-employees among all employed population was 25.4% in South Korea, ranked at 5th among all OECD member countries, as compared to 6.3% in the United States, 8.3% in Canada, 9.8% in Sweden, 10.2% in Germany, 10.4% in

Japan, 11.6% in France, 15.4% in the United Kingdom, and 23.2% in Italy (OECD 2019). South Korea's later economic development has been propelled by incessant and abrupt industrial restructuring into heavy capital-intensive sectors, ICT sectors, and so forth. Each part of such industrial restructuring, when successful, has inevitably ramified the systematic economic deletion of workers in the thereby deserted industries, a majority of whom would end up entering self-employment of various sorts (Choi and Chang 2016). The financially triggered national economic crisis in the late 1990s (i.e. the so-called "IMF economic crisis") radicalized the nation's already excessive industrial restructuring and concomitant labor reshuffling (Chang, K. 2019, ch. 4). In most industries, corporate survival supposedly necessitated massive layoffs and pay-cuts, to which even organized labor agreed, albeit reluctantly. An equally drastic economic recovery did not meaningfully restore the damaged industrial employment system, but was based upon an aggressive transnationalization of industrial production into neighboring demographic giants such as China, Vietnam, and so forth. The combined number of local workers employed in South Korean manufacturing companies in China and Vietnam now roughly equals that of all domestic industrial workers within South Korea! (Chang, K. 2019, ch. 8). A majority of those domestic workers permanently disenfranchised from mainstream industries in this process have flocked to all sorts of self-employed familial business.[11] Beneath South Korea's glaring performance in high-end global industries, familial solidarity and sacrifice have become a key organizational basis for economic survival among the largest group of economic citizens.

Another, highly unique economic function of family has been found in the ownership and management structure of large industrial firms affiliated with the South Korean business conglomerates, called *chaebol*. One of the core social characteristics of these conglomerates and their corporate affiliates is their almost universal dependence on the kinship and marriage network in maintaining the control structure of ownership and management (Kong, J. 1990; Cho, D. 1991; Kang, M. 1996). Family-based control mechanisms of corporate ownership and management are not non-existent in other capitalist economies, but those found in South Korea are certainly unique and, in turn, responsible for the particular organizational structure and economic behavior of the concerned companies. In most of the *chaebol*-affiliated firms, a crucial part of the highest-level managers, not to mention the largest stock-holders, belong to a same kin group, often called *chongsu gajok* (general head's family) (Cho, D. 1991;

Kang, M. 1996). That is, a *chaebol*-affiliated company's top management is dominated by the members of the *chongsu* family and/or their in-laws, and business interests stop where the *chongsu*'s family line stops.[12] When a *chongsu* family breaks up due to familial dispute or in the process of intergeneration succession, new – and not always friendly – units of *chaebol* are established. There are a whole bunch of other examples in which certain "family matters" of the *chaebol* community become crucial business affairs and, due to their dominant national economic positions, even turn into national economic concerns. Ownership-management separation is only exceptionally observed in this context. The state, whether developmental or regulatory, does not formally ratify *chaebol*'s such familialized business structure and practice, but its strategic utilization of *chaebol* in certain directions of capitalist industrialization has kept engendering an implicit endorsement effect (Chang, K. 2012b). Also, when a major labor dispute arises in a *chaebol*-affiliated firm, workers' resistance is often mobilized toward the unfailing target of the *chongsu* person or his/her family members, whereas the role of pure employee executives are taken less than seriously. There develops a sort of *chongsu* family-versus-proletariat class struggle, which clearly deviates from the Western experience of labor-capital sociopolitical compromise as persuasively explained by Ralph Dahrendorf (1959).

8.4 Familial Self-Welfare instead of the Welfare State

In a not-so-hidden aspect of South Korea's rapid economic development, the protracted strategy of "growth first, distribution later" (*seonseongjang, hubunbae*) has left the country with an extremely underfinanced and ill-organized system of social welfare.[13] This general development strategy was occasionally reconsidered – for instance, in the late 1980s under the "democratic welfare state" slogan of the Roh Tae-Woo government and in the early 2010s under the welfare state campaigns of next presidential hopefuls – but political reversions to developmentalist governance were rather customary after short-lived propagandic suggestions of progressive social welfare. In this political economic context, family has remained the only universal institution for civil welfare, with familial self-support serving as the only universal mechanism for relief from poverty, illness, handicap and other welfare needs (Chang, K. 2018). Culturally, there has been a tenacious ideological resistance on the part of both the state and society to the conception that familial support and protection are not just the moral behavior of each family but also the political responsibility of the state (Chang, K. 1997). Most, if gradually decreasing, Koreans, imbued with the neo-Confucian ideology through national history and personal life, came to believe that many of the apparent and increasing problems in such familial self-welfare could have been prevented if the tradition of strong familial solidarity and personal sacrifice had been better preserved. Under this conservative understanding, various social problems that threaten stable family life used to induce society-wide moral condemnations of the individuals in the troubled families, instead of prompting governmental or communitarian efforts to help relieve the troubles collectively (Chang, K. 1997).

In its actual administrative practice, more fundamentally, the developmentalist state has done everything to redefine social policy – or, for that matter, social citizenship – in terms of private responsibilities for mutual support and protection.[14] Above all, the openly touted policy principle of "familial protection first, social welfare later" (seongajeongboho, husahoebokji) has remained mostly intact to date. Families have accordingly been summoned so as to meet various public necessities in social welfare. The developmental state in South Korea has coincided with the early modern liberal states in the West in articulating various social problems accompanying industrial capitalism as private responsibilities of individuals and families, and in morally regimenting them for cultivation of certain qualities and attitudes suitable for industrial work and life (cf. Donzelot 1979).[15] In so doing, the South Korean state used to be equipped with a distinct advantage of its developmentalist appeal to culturally conservative and socioeconomically motivated citizens.[16]

As a specific form of such policy line, there emerged a unique model of "family welfare" (gajokbokji), as distinguished from the conventional family policy affairs in the West. Family welfare came to be considered as a core element of the supposedly Korean-style welfare state in the making. An official in charge of governmental welfare affairs once pointed out, "since the family is the basic component of the state and society, sound family welfare shall result in social stability and help to achieve the welfare state" (Chung, D. 1991: 38). There have been three ways of understanding family welfare in South Korea: family as the target, mechanism, or provider of social welfare. Family welfare in the first sense is not basically different from the Western European conception, whereas family welfare in the last sense is nothing other than a technocratic reiteration of the conservative, anti-welfarist ideology. By contrast, family welfare in the second sense may imply a unique strategy of pursuing social policy – for

150

instance, elderly care through family as a culturally embedded social policy in South Korea (and other East Asian Societies).[17] While family welfare in official policy statements, in spirit, seems to have referred to the option of supporting the elderly, children, handicapped and other needy persons through the social institutional framework of family relations, the continuing undercommitment of the state to social welfare, in reality, has made it a mere euphemism for familial self-support. These governmental practices unmistakably indicate the social infrastructural indispensability of family in maintaining the developmentally framed passive welfare policy – or *developmental liberalism* as the developmental state's social policy paradigm (Chang, K. 2019).

To the extent that South Korean citizens concurred with state leaders on the urgency of national economic development and thereby became a sort of developmental citizenry (Chang, K. 2012), the state's minimal commitment to social policy and the concomitant private shouldering of various welfare needs were nothing deplorable.[18] As indicated above, South Koreans have largely maintained Confucian values and norms in private life under which mutual support duties have been heavily emphasized among members of (extended as well as nuclear) families and other nepotistic groups (Chang, K. 1997, 2018; Kim, D. 2002).[19] Above all, filial support for aged parents and meritorious upbringing of children used to be universally upheld as "Korean virtues." The socially conservative developmental state could not wish for more when its citizens voluntarily relieved it of the grave burdens of protecting elderly livelihood and health and covering educational expenses for youth. Since the late 1990s, however, a growing impracticality of the family-dependent system of care and support has become evident amid the massive structural disenfranchisement of familial breadwinners from the mainstream industrial economy. Relatedly, rapidly increasing numbers and proportions of young women have begun to explore alternative individual life courses that are based upon the now generalized participation in the labor market and the carefully calculated acceptance, or avoidance, of marriage and procreation.[20] Familial self-welfare, not because it is now normatively rejected but because its practical realization is increasingly difficult, tends to induce young South Koreans to *refrain responsibly* from "unprepared" marriage and parenthood (Chang and Song 2010).

8.5 Educationalized Modernization and Family-Sustained Public Education

South Korea's postcolonial modernization has been a fundamentally *educationalized* project, so its educational development has assumed a particular significance to both the state and ordinary citizenry.[21] As explained in Chapter 4, the postcolonial nation's West-reflexive institutional(ist) modernization was based upon legal declarations in form, but the substantiation and operation of the thereby installed public and social institutions required an intensive absorption of Western knowledge through public education at various levels. In later years, the nation's industrial take-off and sustained economic growth had to be critically buttressed by the active obtainment and rapid accumulation of scientific and technological knowledge from Western societies, both through domestic education (with West-oriented curricula) and studying abroad. Both institutional modernization and industrial development, as they were heavily predicated upon the formal utilization of Western knowledge through public education, prompted South Korea to become a heavily educationalized social system. South Korea's broadly sustained success in these national goals has made governmental and civilian educational investment amply rewarded. In particular, highly dissimilar rewards accruing to individuals' diverse levels and areas of public education have induced virtually all South Koreans to engage in familially driven pursuits of educational credentials (Chang, K. 2010a, ch. 3; Chang, K. 2022, ch. 6). Both parents and student children have felt exceptionally strong moral and/or pragmatic obligations in dealing with public education as familial commitment.

South Korea has thereby become a society with many of the world's top records in educational affairs. Its population boasts the world's highest level of tertiary education completion (that is, academic degrees at the college level and above).[22] South Korean students are only behind Chinese and Indian students in enrollment at American universities, while South Korea's total population is less than 4 percent of those of China and India, respectively (SEVIS 2020). The average amount and proportion of private citizens' – mostly parents' – spending in public education, even when expenses for private tutors and cram lesson institutions are excluded, are consistently among the world's highest.[23] South Korean colleges and universities used to charge the world's second most expensive tuitions (after American counterparts), until many neoliberalized European universities began to require high tuitions. The highest rate of South Korean elderly's relative poverty among all OECD countries has been most significantly caused by their exhaustion of household savings for children's college education (Kim, C. 2017). In return for such (parental) spending, South Korean youth study the world's longest hours, particularly for their college entrance exams.[24] In many of the most authoritative international competitions, South Korean secondary school students' performance in math and science is rivaled only by those from a few East Asian and Nordic countries. Educationally determined stratifications in occupational access, wage income, social prestige, and even marriage prospect, are incomparably intense (Park, K. 2014; Park, M. 1991).[25] Accordingly, study pressure and stress are the most critical causes of parent–child conflict. Indeed, South Korean youth's suicide at one of the world's highest rates is most frequently caused by their desperation in educational competition (usually in conjunction with parental pressure and expectation) (Hwang, Y. 2013; Lee, Noh, and Lee 2012).

In a word, South Koreans' globally distinct educational achievements (and related pathological problems) are far from a direct governmental accomplishment. Most of the public educational expenses have been directly borne by its citizens (as enthusiastically devoted parents), whereas an overwhelming majority of schools at all levels of public education are "private" (*sarip*) institutions operating according to the same rules, curricula, and nominal financial subsidies as are taken by "public" (*gongrip*) ones. In fact, many of such private schools have attempted, and have been administratively allowed to attempt, to manage their programs and facilities as *de facto* profit-seeking ventures, which has been far from difficult under the almost guaranteed popular demand of privately paid public education at all levels.[26] It should also be indicated that the sustained ample supply of qualified teachers in primary and secondary public education has been programmatically enabled by the externally learned college/university system of formally specialized education in pedagogy and the huge flocking of (mostly parent-financed) eager and smart aspirants in the concerned tertiary education programs (Kim, B. 2009).[27]

The state's role has not been minimal or insignificant altogether in this remarkable episode of national educational progress. Duly acknowledging both public education's supreme significance in national modernization and development and its chronic financial and social institutional limitations, the South Korean government has effectively tried to harness ordinary citizens' universal aspiration for own and/or children's best educational opportunities, as a kind of sociocultural infrastructure. In so doing, every government has found a crucial political significance in its regulatory and supervisory functions for allocating access to public education most fairly and broadly. The transparent administering of school entrance exams and even school term exams (that are often counted toward next-level school entrance exams) have been considered as a key issue in the national government's education policy (Chang, K. 2022, ch. 6).[28] Various proposals and experiments for specialized and/or innovative public education, particularly at secondary levels, have usually been rejected or interrupted due to the apparently political consideration of maintaining a completely flat national ground in educational provision and competition.[29] The state has normally been conscious that special school selection rules and in-effect gated schools that may privilege any elite class will incur intense popular antipathy among educationally devoted South Korean parents and children. While disputable, this (over)cautious policy line has been regarded as a supposedly progressive one by both ordinary citizenry and the self-admittedly progressive politicians (who continue to enjoy comfortable victory in the general elections for regional educational governance). Public education has been regulated in a very similar way to physical infrastructures and public utilities (such as roads, bridges, piped water, electricity, etc.) in assuring fair access, often through quite mechanical procedures and rigid rules. This has been considered as the most essential condition for preserving grassroots citizens' family-mediated educational commitment, in which the state itself has found an indispensable social infrastructural utility.

8.6 Conclusion and Prospect:
Family as Overloaded Social Infrastructure

Various types of state proactivism in the otherwise liberal capitalist nations have been revealed, theorized, and/or prescribed by heterodox social scientists across the world. South Korea has been internationally hailed as an exemplary case of the so-called *developmental state* by numerous top-notch scholars. In addition, so many domestic scholars have analyzed and evaluated South Korea in terms of its characteristics and qualifications as a candidate or yet defective *welfare state*, or as an East Asian type of (developmental) welfare state. More recently, the *social investment state*, more in the education-focused British neoliberal version than in the European refashioned social democratic version, was once strongly advocated by the South Korean government and some pragmatic civil activists.[30]

In South Korea's historical and social realities, there seem to have existed interestingly corresponding forms of familial proactivism in the nation's remarkable economic, sociocultural, and even political transformations. The preceding discussion in this chapter, as well as my earlier work (Chang, K. 2010a), on industrial, social, and educational advancement in South Korea strongly suggests that its families have been functioning simultaneously as *developmental family, welfare family*, and *social investment family* in effect. Many of the South Korean state's actualized and/or aspired tasks in national economic and social development have been organized, complemented, substituted, or even financed by grassroots citizens' familial efforts and resources. The state's approach to its citizens' familial proactivism is not predicated upon any cultural or religious subscription to a certain line of family ideology, but has remained flexibly inclusionary in consideration of a wide variety of coexisting family ideologies in South Korean families. While the state's own practically driven familialist stance is not reducible to a certain (private) family ideology, it does represent a distinct line of technocratic deliberation conceptualizable as *infrastructural familialism*. This can help explain many parts of the nation's "unique" social conditions that have been left as a realm of culturalist description.

The early twenty-first century of South Korea seems to be marked by drastic declines in its citizens' familial proactivism and accompanying difficulties for the state in relying on their familial norms, relations, and resources to solve various socioeconomic problems. Broadly speaking, South Koreans are now beset with two sets of unprecedented socioeconomic troubles, namely, the so-called "new social risks" ensuing from the nation's sociodemographic maturation and the neoliberal predicaments in employment and livelihood since the "IMF economic crisis" (as part of the Asian financial crisis). With these two sets of problems combined, South Korea has become a structurally bifurcated society in which a large majority of its citizens are now disenfranchised from the mainstream economy, while being confronted with continually worsening risks in employment, income, housing, health, and so forth. It is these new structural conditions that make rapidly increasing numbers and proportions of grassroots families incapable of servicing social infrastructural utilities for the state's socioeconomic policy efforts. On the one hand, they have been stripped of financial and other material resources for such roles; on the other hand, they have become organizationally and/or normatively

155

weakened (or restructured) and thus relinquish many of the previously taken-for-granted socioeconomic functions.[31] In particular, to those young generations who now have to consider marriage and childbirth, their prospect or willingness to build a developmental, welfare, and/ or social investment family is much weaker than that of their parent generations. On the other hand, most of them would still hope for the state to remain an effective developmental state and to become both a serious welfare state and a strong social investment state. Without social infrastructural families being earnestly maintained and sufficiently reproduced, the late modern or post-developmental state's public work in economic, social, and educational affairs will be much more burdensome and difficult than in any previous period.

— 9 —

THE DEMOGRAPHIC
CONFIGURATION OF
COMPRESSED MODERNITY

9.1 Demographic Parameters of
Compressed Capitalist Development

South Korean development was initiated mainly through a Lewisian path of capitalist industrialization with "unlimited supply of labour" (Lewis 1954), which existed mostly in rural areas. The social, economic, and even ecological devastations caused to peasant life under Japanese colonial aggression and the Korean War did not uproot Korean peasantry from its millennia-long agrarian basis. The American military occupation authority attempted to stabilize postcolonial South Korea's social, economic, and political conditions mainly through restoring the basic parameters of familial agricultural production and social reproduction – namely, the implementation of a relatively thorough land reform. Despite initial reluctance on the part of its conservative Korean ally, land reform was implemented as a fundamental scheme for reenfranchising South Korea's predominantly agrarian population through a sort of universal social citizenship to egalitarian peasant life. The civil war with North Korea had an interesting acceleration effect on land reform in South Korea (Ki, K. 2012).[1]

The organizational and economic robustness of family farming, which had enabled a few dynastic states on the Korean peninsula to last hundreds of years respectively, was clearly vindicated again. Despite political corruption and lax economic governance during the Syngman Rhee dictatorship, peasant families enabled the country's predominantly agricultural economy to gradually stabilize through sustained increases in agricultural productivity (Cho and Oh 2003). With their material and social conditions of livelihood also stabilized,

157

South Koreans' postwar desire for procreation was further intensified, leading to sustained fertility hikes (Kwon, T. 1977, 2003), with the highest recorded TFR (total fertility rate) of 6.33 in 1960. Along with the extension of life expectancy, accompanying rapid improvement in public health programs and individual health conditions, the South Korean baby boom made the national population swell to such a point that the socioeconomic carrying capacity of the country's agrarian economy was made to appear increasingly limited. A sort of egalitarian poverty characterized grassroots livelihood in agrarian South Korea into the 1960s, whereas the rapidly industrializing North Korea began to emerge as a model case of socialist postcolonial development (Brun and Hersh 1976).

Park Chung-Hee's military junta, which took over state leadership after coercively thwarting the liberal political government elected after Syngman Rhee's downfall, came to forge a political line of authoritarian developmental governance. The Park government appointed itself as a sort of state bourgeoisie, which envisioned and pursued rapid capitalist industrialization by effectively organizing the national economy as a quasi-corporate entity, and actively participating in the capitalist world economy mainly through the cheap and abundant labor-based production and export of low-end industrial consumer goods (Amsden 1989). South Korean labor was also of good quality, thanks to the effectively institutionalized universal public education system in which civilian participation and cooperation were exceptionally active (Seth 2002). The supply of cheap, abundant, and good-quality industrial labor was shouldered by increasingly "overpopulated" villages and thus involved massive sustained rural-to-urban migration. As this developmental strategy was met with various opportune economic and political conditions of the world – often systematically channeled through the Cold War foreign policy of the United States – South Korea was almost instantly enfranchised into the global capitalist division of labor under which its population kept transforming into constantly upgraded industrial labor. Accordingly, the share of agricultural employment (in percent) changed from 63.0 in 1963, to 50.4 in 1970, 34.0 in 1980, 17.9 in 1990, and 10.9 in 2000, 6.7 in 2010, and 5.0 in 2019 (e-Narajipyo 2020a).[2]

Within two decades of state-led export-oriented industrialization fueled by rural-to-urban migrant labor, South Korea turned itself into a predominantly urban-based industrial society, accompanied by such typical demographic characteristics of industrial modernity as low fertility, extended life expectancy, nuclear family, late marriage, and so forth (Kwon, T. 2003). South Korean transformation was literally history-making both in economic and demographic terms. This double transformation was no coincidence. While the initial industrial takeoff was enabled mainly on the basis of abundant human resources mostly from rural villages, the success of swift capitalist industrialization itself triggered demographic transformations at no less swift paces. The sustained velocity in industrialization and economic growth facilitated explosive growth both in regional and national metropolises and in strategically developed industrial cities throughout the country. South Koreans' almost instantaneous clustering into these urban spaces as wage workers, professionals, entrepreneurs of various scales, students and job trainees, and current or prospective spouses of urban residents and migrants came to constitute an episode of *compressed urbanization* unprecedented in human history – namely, the country became over 70 percent urban by the late 1980s, while it had been rural in the same degree merely three decades before (Cho, M. 2003). This process of industrialization-cum-urbanization-cum-proletarianization led to radical transitions in the basic parameters of individual and familial life.

Above all, in accordance with Caldwell's (1982) prediction, urban-based South Koreans began to realize that their intergenerational relationship with children was increasingly burdened with downward duties of care and education, and even their aspiration for intergenerational class mobility was manifested in a *parsimoniously patriarchal* manner – namely, producing and heavily investing in one or two sons while avoiding or minimizing daughters.[3] Even most rural residents behaved similarly because their aspiration for intergenerational class mobility was similarly premised upon children's urban socioeconomic opportunities (Chang, K. 2010a, ch. 6). A barely replacement-level fertility (e.g. TFR of 2.23 in 1985) with a skewed sex ratio was thereby arrived at by the mid 1980s. Mortality change was also drastic and reflected the patriarchal socioeconomic order in an interesting way – that is, the male-centered industrial economy on the so-called extensive growth path led to South Korean men's chronic exposure to overwork, fatigue, injury, and illness and ultimately a sustained gender gap in the increase of life expectancy (*e-Narajipyo* 2020b). Marriage remained universal despite a gradual rise in the average age-at-(first) marriage; whereas social and familial aversion to divorce kept its rates minimal (Choi, S. 2020).

These demographic attributes seemed to enter a sort of "stable" period just as the South Korean economy was enjoying sustained growth until the early 1990s.[4] However, the abrupt neoliberal globalization as well as built-in technological/sectoral restructuring of the South Korean economy soon began to put adverse pressure on the hitherto almost fully employed labor force.[5] The national financial meltdown in 1997 to 1998, whoever its most fundamental culprits in and out of South Korea were, drove the national economy as well as a majority of major industries and banks into a corner from which an immediate escape was conceivable only through across-the-board dismissal of employees (Chang, K. 2019, ch. 3). After laying off millions of workers, the fast recovering South Korean economy has incorporated blatantly neoliberal industrial institutions and labor practices in virtually all sectors. "Non-regular" employment became an almost universal norm in the post-crisis labor market, destabilizing the socioeconomic status of new entrants – mostly youth – structurally and chronically.[6] Due to the male-centered or patriarchal nature of the South Korean economy, this trend of semi-proletarianization, or precariatization (Shin, K. 2013; Lee et al. 2017), has ironically effected a downward equalization of men and women in socioeconomic conditions. As young people's lack of stable wage income has been matched with excessively inflated prices for urban housing, there has been an unchecked expansion of slapdash suburban bed towns surrounding several mega-cities.

Stripped of the current and/or prospective status of stable work, grassroots South Koreans have profoundly altered demographic behaviors such as marriage, divorce, fertility, and so forth (Chang and Song 2010). Marriage has been continually delayed or shunned by a majority of young people. Divorce, both in legal and practical terms, has increased to such an explosive level as seemingly rivals the U.S. and the U.K. The national population census of 2000 showed crude divorce rate at its peak of 2.5 per 1000 people, and the following years have so far sustained similarly high levels of divorce (www.kosis.kr). Mainly due to such marriage-related difficulties, the nation's (total) fertility rate plunged to a "lowest-low" level, sometimes competing against East Asian city-states, Hong Kong and Singapore (Kim, B. 2009).[7] The TFR (total fertility rate) has kept renewing its lowest level, e.g. 1.05 in 2017, 0.98 in 2018, 0.92 in 2019, and 0.84 in 2020 (KSO 2020; see Figure 9.1). Domestic and international projections repeatedly remind South Koreans that their national population could be halved within the current century.[8]

As the radically reduced fertility has been matched with a sustained increase in life expectancy, South Korea has become one of the fastest aging societies in the world. The percentage of those aged 65+ changed from 3.3 in 1970 to 3.9 in 1980, 5.0 in 1990, 7.3 in 2000,

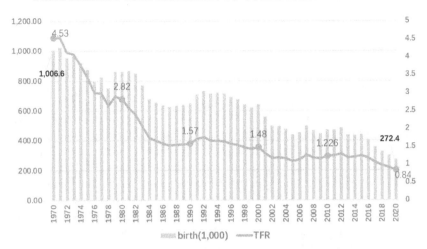

Figure 9.1 The trend of total fertility rate (TFR) in South Korea

Source: Created by the author based upon fertility data in *e-Narajipyo* (2020c), "The Trends in Birth and Death" (http://www.index.go.kr/potal/main/ EachDtlPageDetail.do?idx_cd=1011#quick_05)

11.3 in 2010, and 15.5 in 2019; life expectancy at birth changed from 61.93 in 1970 to 65.69 in 1980, 71.28 in 1990, 76.02 in 2000, 80.79 in 2010, and 82.7 in 2017 (KOSIS, June 28, 2020). An interesting feature of South Korea's *compressed population aging* is that nearly a half of the currently aged population are rural elders who have remained in rural townships and villages after sending away their children to cities (Chang, K. 2019, ch. 6). Thus, most villages have become predominantly aged communities. Whether residing in rural or urban areas, most South Korean elders' extension of life expectancy has not been materially prepared for by satisfactory public and individual means. Almost generalized poverty and problematically high morbidity have marred the otherwise blessed period of South Korean elders' extended life, which is often arbitrarily terminated by suicide.[9] Even more shocking are spousal or familial killing called *ganbyeongsalin* (killing by illness caregiver) and suicide by illness caregiver called *ganbyeongjasal*, the frequencies of which have led local media to devise such special terms.[10] South Korean media have kept sensationalizing this unfortunate situation by referring to "the developed world's highest rate of elderly poverty," "the world's highest rate of elderly suicide," and so forth.

161

9.2 Compressed Demographic Transitions

Half a century of radical sociodemographic changes have transformed South Korea from a society known for very high fertility, universal marriage, rare divorce, etc. into one of "lowest-low" fertility, widespread singlehood, rampant divorce, etc. The country's *compressed* sociodemographic changes under a socially complex developmental context present several significant historical and/or theoretical implications, including among others (1) spatial demographic imbalances due to intergenerationally divided urban migration, (2) fertility decline with alternating gender asymmetry, (3) demographic individualization under sustained normative familialism, (4) constant realignment between individual life course and family life cycle, and (5) socioeconomically discrete two-stage population aging.

Double (Developmental and Demographic) Rural–Urban Divide

South Korean industrialization has been an age-selective process in which an overwhelming majority of rural youth and young adults have ended up working, studying, and/or living in various types of urban places. The remaining middle/old-age peasants have been "aging" in rural areas under the permanently frozen economic institutional and cultural conditions of familial peasantry. They have thereby formed and maintained a socioecological museum-like setting of traditional peasant life, in which meager livelihood and antiquated lifestyle have become the subjects of both social pity and cultural romanticism. Such conditions of rural life have been by and large a consequence of both protective and exclusionary state policies. The constitutional principle of "tillers should own land" (*gyeongjayujeon*) for maintaining rural socioeconomic stability through standardized family farming has remained intact, but the statist drive for urban-centered capitalist industrialization has effected various degenerative economic and social tendencies in rural areas – including the behavior of *indirect exit* by which rural people have diverted most of their material, human, and psychic resources to urban areas through city-bound/based children and siblings and have thereby led their own rural livelihood in a sociopolitically docile manner (see Chang, K. 2010a, ch. 6).

In terms of sociodemographic structure, South Korean villages have become assimilated with Western retirement towns like in Florida – an age/generation structure of no further social reproduction – but

162

the former's future is likely to diverge from the latter because of a chronic paucity of new entrants migrating from other areas. More systematically, the family life cycle composition of South Korea's rural population shows an accelerated thinning of families at formative and expansion stages (Chang, K. 2018, ch. 6). Unable to find spouses accepting of patriarchal peasant life, many middle and late-middle-age bachelors have had to live with elderly parents in unprecedentedly deformed family structures, but many of them have recently found foreign brides from poor Asian countries as a convenient human resource for rural social, if not economic, maintenance (Kim, H. 2012, 2014). In recent years, one out of ten marriages in South Korea has been international; whereas in many villages as much as one third or more of marriages has been with practically(?) imported brides, leading to an unforeseen social setting of cosmopolitan or multicultural reconstruction (see Chapter 6).

(Gender-Selective) Fertility Decline under Double-Patriarchal Capitalist Industrialization

As one of the socially striking features of South Korean industrialization, the so-called *housewifization* of native and migrant urban women took place almost simultaneously with their massive proletarianization (i.e. participation in industrial or urban wage labor) since the mid 1960s (Choi and Chang 2004; Chang, K. 2010a, ch. 5). Most village-originated "factory girls" opted to marry in the "marriage-proper age period" (*gyeolhonjeokryeonggi*), leaving industrial work before or upon marriage and frequently returning to the labor market in middle age to make up for their husbands' meager and/or unstable income in meeting children's educational cost, aged parents' livelihood, and so forth. This age-wise "M-shape" economic participation by women was induced by a politico-economically reinforced cultural norm that women's happiness is supposed to consist in subordinate fulfillment of patriarchally defined duties of procreation and homemaking.

In social institutional essence, there used to be a patriarchal alliance between South Korea's capitalist industrial economy and private families under which the male domination of the former used to be systematically buttressed by the latter's gender-segregating demographic and social behaviors. South Koreans' (in)famous "son preference" manifested itself in terms of bloated sex ratio at birth, asymmetrical investment in sons' education, son-biased inheritance of familial financial and social capital, etc. In a sense, the distorted sex ratio at birth should be seen more as an outcome of female-centered

163

fertility decline – or avoidance of daughters as brutally evidenced by rampant abortion of female fetuses (Park and Cho 1995). The so-called "first fertility transition" between the mid 1960s and the mid 1980s thereby occurred in a fundamentally gender-selective manner. However, a brief stabilization of fertility between the mid 1980s and the mid 1990s did not eradicate but intensified such strategic but controversial and illegal procreative behavior. The sex ratio at birth reached 111.7 in 1986, and remained above 110 until 1996, except in 1987 (KOSIS, each year). In 1990, 1993, and 1994, it was even above 115. Living in the heyday of popularly based industrial development, South Koreans seemed to be quite confident about a men-centered future for their national economy and family structure.

Such optimism turned out to be flatly unfounded from the late 1990s. The 1997 to 1998 national financial crisis and the accompanying radical neoliberal restructuring required a majority of South Koreans to abruptly confront a post-developmental or even postindustrial era without any meaningful preparation of public or private safety net (Chang, K. 2019, ch. 4). The phenomenal recovery and growth of the now deeply globalized industrial conglomerates (*chaebol*) have ironically necessitated and caused widespread economic disenfranchisement of current and prospective laborers, with immediate damages concentrated on male economic prerogatives.[11] Such unprecedented and unfamiliar economic distress foisted on contemporary South Koreans instantly triggered the "second fertility transition," under which South Korean fertility became "lowest-low," competing against Taiwan, Hong Kong, and Singapore whose fertility has been additionally subjected to unique political and socio-ecological pressures.[12] In another paradox, the latest fertility cutback has produced a corrective effect on South Koreans' gender-biased demographic behavior – that is, the average sex ratio at birth has recently recovered its "natural" level (Chang, K. 2018, ch. 4). As the patriarchal developmental prospect for sons has fundamentally crumbled amid the nation's jobless economic growth, South Koreans have rapidly veered to the "romantic" value of having daughters. It is highly interesting to note that South Koreans have maintained particularly high levels of gender-specific preference (as opposed to gender indifference) in fertility (Eun, K. 2013). Their propensity to find a strategic procreative reason in conjunction with their children's gender has not lessened in spite of the apparent demise of patriarchal demographic culture. Familialism is changing in content, not disappearing.

Risk-Aversive Individualization, Marriage Crisis, and Second Fertility Transition

Since the mid 1990s, the trends among the young generation to indefinitely postpone or give up marriage, to have no or a minimum number of children in marriage, and to choose separation or divorce without hesitation, have been strengthening rapidly. South Korea's fertility at one of the world's lowest levels is systematically linked to its extremely high divorce rate and rapidly rising age of first marriage (Byun et al. 2010; Chang, K. 2018). Behind these trends lies a rapid growth in the number of young people who feel extremely burdened about the formation and maintenance of familial relationships for social reproduction and even feel doubtful about the practicality of social reproduction itself. These trends, however, do not necessarily attest to young people's abandonment of familialism or sociocultural changes toward individualistic life. Instead, they can be understood as *individualization without individualism* (Chang and Song 2010) because familialism still remains strong even among the young population as shown by their general willingness to get married and to have children in marriage. Since the "IMF economic crisis," however, the devastating impacts of economic turbulence and social instabilities on the material conditions of family-centered social reproduction have made most young women and men extremely cautious about marriage and procreation from the perspective of *risk aversion* (Chin, M. 2013). (On the other hand, thanks to the democratization of family order and gender relations and women's expanding job opportunities in tertiary sectors, more and more young women seek active social participation and resist individually the social pressure for marriage and procreation.) As familial relationships are more than ever prone to function as transmitters of social risks rather than of social resources, the motivation for securing the partner (spouse) and successors (children) for family-based social reproduction has been undermined more seriously than ever.[13]

While familialism now serves only to deter (materially unprepared-for) marriage and fertility, this normative dilemma has not been relieved by any significant compensatory ideational development – for instance, as is now widespread across Western Europe, women's individualistic or autonomous procreation for the sake of maternity itself (Chang, K. 2018, ch. 4). Apparently, the traditional era of familial(ist) fertility has critically subsided, but a new era of individual(ist) fertility is not yet clearly in sight.[14] The aggregate consequences of such a motivational crisis – namely, marriage reduction, fertility decline, and aged demographic structure – cannot but cause serious destabilizing effects on the maintenance of the macro social and economic systems. Paradoxically, the pronatal policy discourses of the developmental liberal state, by highlighting the prospect for related social and economic crises incautiously, are suspected to have aggravated the familial risk concerns of young South Koreans.

Disembedding and Reembedding Between Individual Life Course and Family Life Cycle

The severely deteriorating material conditions among young people, who face chronic structural difficulties in economic participation, not only discourage their own marriage and fertility but also cause social and economic distress across all generations by prolonging their dependence on parents indefinitely. As increasing numbers of children, who are "adults" by the conventional age standards, keep relying on their middle-aged or aged parents for housing, livelihood, and education and thereby extend their dependent status within their parents' nuclear family – instead of forming their own nuclear family by marriage and procreation – this can be seen as a rapid increase in *extended nuclear families*.[15] Furthermore, even when these young people get married, their dependence on middle-aged or aged parents for housing, childcare, and livelihood often continues and thereby reverses the hitherto common direction of family support relations in the traditional stem family – that is, a sort of *reverse stem families* are on a rapid increase.

These trends attest to fundamental changes in the systemic relationship between family life cycle and individual life course (Chang, K. 2018, ch. 2). Whereas strong parental authority used to be exercised on children's individual life courses (concerning the timing and/or nature of material independence, marriage, fertility, etc.) as an effort to smoothly complete the parents' own family life cycles, more and more parents nowadays find it extremely difficult to exercise such authority to un(der)employed and often indefinitely schooling children. Thus, many parents have ended up reflecting their children's revised life courses into their own family life cycles, producing new family forms, such as extended nuclear family and reverse stem family (as indicated above). However, in spite of the materially caused increase in such (adult) children-centered family forms, the social norm for children's separation in life from parents upon marriage has been strengthening (Yoo, S. 1996). For both children and parents, the stem family norm of old parents' livelihood dependence on cohabiting adult children

166

is no more in effect, whereas marriage and procreation are now understood as the development and management of children's own individual life.

Actually, such gaps between family norms and family forms are nothing new. During the swift industrialization and urbanization in the 1960s and 1970s, rapidly increasing numbers of children from rural families began to live in independent nuclear families on the basis of new economic and social opportunities in urban areas, but most of them upheld quite long and strong stem family-type *normative* relationships with their village-remaining parents.[16] They maintained what may be called *in-effect stem families*. Under this circumstance, children's marriage was not only taken for granted but also had to reflect closely parents' preference or opinion with regard to marriage time, mate selection, etc.; married children's procreation was also culturally mandatory and often reflected parents' gender and number preferences; and divorce was unthinkable, in consideration of parents' foreseeable embarrassment or anger (Park and Cho 1995).

The historic shift from the order of the normative stem family–material nuclear family to the order of the normative nuclear family–material extended nuclear family/reverse stem family has only taken the period of a generation, manifesting compressed modernity in a highly interesting way. The crucial problem is that this transition is a reflection of temporary private measures to smooth over the familial mishaps caused under the cumulatively devastating impacts of developmental liberalism, economic crises, and radical neoliberal restructuring, rather than a result of sociocultural evolution or systemic adaptation of a new era. The spread of extended nuclear families and reverse stem families implies the indefinite postponement or even cessation of the intergenerational succession of the family-based social reproduction system (Chang, K. 2018). Consequently, middle-aged and aged South Korean women have become, in an international social survey, the "world's unhappiest" group because they have collectively lost their traditional right to a leisurely and fruitful life conditioned upon a timely transfer of their roles to the next generation.[17]

From Developmental to Empty Aging

In a not-too-rare social tragedy, an illness-stricken old couple committed suicide together, feeling sorry for the hardship of their son's family in taking care of them earnestly and indefinitely (*Kyunghyang Shinmun*, May 9, 2011). On the other hand, sadly, some old people have to appeal to the law to win a sustenance allowance from impious children, who are forgetful of their parents' earlier devoted support for them.[18] Although there are many old people who enjoy active and fruitful – or "productive"– later life in the process of *compressed population aging* (Chang, K. 2009, ch. 4), a near majority of South Korea's aged population lead a spartan life, experiencing the OECD's highest level of relative poverty in everyday life.[19] According to 2009–2011 data from OECD, the relative poverty rate (i.e. the percentage of those whose income after taxes and transfers is less than half of the national median income) among South Koreans aged 66 to 75 was 45.6, as compared to the average of 11.3 among all OECD member countries (*Dong-A Ilbo*, May 16, 2013). The average disposable income for the same age group in South Korea was only 62 percent of the national average, as compared to 90 percent for all OECD member countries. Moreover, given the extreme intragenerational economic inequalities among the elderly population, the above numbers severely underrate the actual conditions of poverty for most elderly persons. According to an estimate in 2013 (by Korea Invest and Securities Co. Ltd.), the richest 10 percent of those aged 50 or over own 49 percent of the net wealth (*Edaily*, July 6, 2013). Relatedly, the GINI coefficient of the gross income among those aged 65 or over has been much higher than among the younger population. For the former, it changed from 0.393 in 2006 to 0.410 in 2007, 0.408 in 2008, 0.402 in 2009, 0.419 in 2010; for the latter, it changed from 0.288 in 2006 to 0.292 in 2007, 0.295 in 2008, 0.290 in 2009, 0.284 in 2010 (Seok, S. 2013). Such economic hardships and inequalities in turn have driven South Korean elderly to commit suicide at the world's highest level (Chang, K. 2018, ch. 5).

Rapid population aging is not a new social phenomenon exclusive to the twenty-first century. That is, along with numerous other countries, South Korea had already experienced a sustained rapid rise in life expectancy in the twentieth century. For instance, according to a historical life table in part constructed from demographic data of the Japanese colonial government (by Koo Ja-Heung), the average lifespan was 33.7 in 1927, 37.4 in 1933, 45.0 in 1942, 52.4 in 1957, 62.3 in 1971, 66.2 in 1981, 71.7 in 1991, and 75.5 in 1999 (*Dong-A Science*, September 11, 2001).[20] According to the official data of the South Korean government, average life expectancy was 52.4 in 1960, 63.2 in 1970, 65.8 in 1980, 71.6 in 1990, and 75.9 in 2000, and 80.8 in 2010. During the early industrialization period (i.e. the 1960s to the 1980s) alone, South Koreans' average lifespan increased by nearly twenty years. The rapidly increased (relatively) old population at

168

that time, however, was able to enjoy most of their extended lifespan either as the main subject of rapid urbanization, industrialization, and economic development or as the continuing social basis of traditional peasantry. In particular, thanks to the newly engendered economic and social activities then, they went through highly *productive* early aging. *Epistemologically, their aging status was rarely acknowledged as such.*

However, a majority of the same cohort of aged people has thereafter gone through another stage of population aging – that is, *second population aging* – without being too productive, due to ill health and poverty (Park, K. 2003). Their older-age poverty has been caused by their failure to make adequate material preparation for later years while economically active. Such failure, in turn, reflects the fact that they have spent most of their meager income – often coerced by the developmentalist state in terms of administratively suppressed levels of industrial wage and agricultural procurement income – for downward familial investment (including, above all, children's education). In this context, many elderly persons have endured poor livelihood by proudly reminding themselves of their devotion to "send their children to college." A more crucial problem here is that even the state, from its developmental liberal position, has indeterminately postponed systematic public preparation for their older age, often under the historically unrealizable and unrealized slogan of "growth first, distribution later" (Chang, K. 2010a, ch. 4). As many elders' lives need to be accommodated in their children's livelihood, confusion, conflict, and agony abound in their relationship with the supporting children. To make matters worse, because the economic status of the elders' children has become extremely unstable since the "IMF economic crisis" and because their children's children – i.e. their grandchildren – now suffer from widespread structural difficulties in employment, their stable material dependence on children cannot but be a very limited class-specific experience.

Most crucially, in urban areas, their later years cannot be absorbed into the mainstream production system, due to the forceful trend of deindustrialization and globalization, and their lack of secure regular income inhibits not only stable individual livelihood but also decent social participation as "consumer citizens" (like many pensioners in the United States and Japan). A majority of urban elders are now confronted with a socioeconomic process of what may be called *empty aging* or even *nude aging*, in which only their geriatric characteristics and problems are highlighted in media coverage, scholarly discussion, and policy debate. An interesting contrast exists in rural areas where

169

nearly a half of South Korea's old population reside. The aging population tends to define the basic nature of contemporary village society under the sustained tapering of younger population (Chang, K. 2018, ch. 5). Paradoxically, the lifespan of their traditional way of rural work and life has been elongated due to the (late)-modern trend of their extended biological survival. In fact, given that the extension of human lifespan has commonly taken place in societies at various development levels and that neoliberal globalization has preempted possibilities of aging people's mainstream or innovative socioeconomic participation, *frozen aging* (i.e. growing older in practically frozen conditions of work and life) appears to be a rapidly universalizing phenomenon. Such frozen conditions of rural work and life, however, are destined to melt into mere memory, given the rarity of next generation successors in peasantry.

9.3 Ethnodemographic Reconfiguration of the Korean Nation?

The national demographic crisis in South Korea has helped reshape South Korea in a fundamentally unexpected direction – namely, multicultural or cosmopolitan reconstruction of families, communities, and society-at-large. Since the early 2000s, as explained in Chapter 6, increasing numbers of South Korea's underclass and often not-so-young bachelors have married foreign brides from various poorer Asian countries. This trend became significant initially between Korean Chinese women (Chaoxianzu) and poor urban men, and then Han Chinese women were introduced to similar South Korean men. From around 2005, many local governments and rural communities began to approach Southeast Asian women – in particular, Vietnamese women – as brides for rapidly increasing rural bachelors whose possibility for attracting Korean brides had practically evaporated. The semi-public campaign of "sending rural bachelors to in-laws' home" (*nongchon chonggak janggabonaegi*, meaning making rural bachelors marry) spread quickly throughout the country (Kim, H. 2014), so South Korean villages suddenly became the very forefront of sociocultural transnationalization or cosmopolitanization. In a great paradox, South Korea's developmental backwater has since led sociocultural cosmopolitanization of the entire nation (see Chapter 6).

The mass arrival of foreign brides from across Asia required fundamental sociocultural readjustments, not only for their Korean spouses and spousal families but also for South Korean society as a whole.

At the urge of civil activists, the South Korean government decided to formally acknowledge and support this marriage transnationalization through an official "multicultural family support" policy. A sort of *transnational reproductive citizenship* is conferred upon foreign brides who fulfill various familial duties of social reproduction such as homemaking, childbearing and childrearing, elderly care, and so forth, often in addition to farm work and other income-earning activities (Chang, K. 2022, ch. 7). In cases of marriage failure, their right to stay in South Korea is rigidly tied to reproductive fulfillment and necessity as mothers of Korean children. A hidden tug-of-war has governed the relationship between the South Korean government and foreign brides in that many of the latter are suspected more as *disguised economic migrants* than motivated reproductive citizens. Above all, their desired level of fertility immediately assimilates that of native South Korean women – a trend not unrelated with the fact that they have married those South Koreans whose developmental or socioeconomic citizenship has been particularly damaged and/or vulnerable in this hyperindustrial society. According to the 2009 national survey, which covered nearly a half of all marriage immigrants, responding foreign brides, in spite of sizable differences between Northeast and Southeast Asian women, expressed their desired number of children at levels hardly distinguishable from native Korean women – 1.1 among Korean Chinese (Chaoxianzu), 1.2 among Han and other Chinese, 1.7 among Vietnamese, 1.9 among Filipina, 1.4 among Mongolians, 1.7 among Thais, 1.8 among Cambodians, etc. (Kim et al. 2010: 393).

In a sense, the "multicultural family support" policy is an intentional strategy for culturally particularizing the complex social and economic problems surrounding foreign brides and their Korean families – instead of coping with more structural issues such as economic instability in farming, sociocultural exclusion of peasants, and so forth (Chang, K. 2013, 2018).[21] At the private level, more problematically, multiculturalism often grinds down to linguistic and cultural impossibilities of effective and harmonious everyday interactions between foreign brides and their Korean spouses, in-laws, and neighbors (Kim, H. 2012, 2014). Paradoxically, such interactive difficulties are often cemented by the unidirectional authoritarian desire of patriarchal Korean families for reinstating the supposedly traditional norms and practices of social reproduction through yet-innocent (or not-yet-modernized) foreign bodies (Chang, K. 2022, ch. 8; see Chapter 6 above).

Despite its accidental or improvised nature and numerous contradictions, however, marriage transnationalization now constitutes very much an integral part of South Korea's proactive *social globalization*. The country's aggressive economic globalization has numerous essential sociodemographic conditions and ramifications. The most fundamental among them is a gradual globalist reconceiving of the Korean nation itself as evidenced by the rapid growth of foreign brides and their mixed-blood children (Kim, H. 2012), the strategic reformulation of over-seven-million overseas compatriotic Koreans' *de facto* citizenship status (Lee, C. 2014), and the circulatory incorporation of Asian labor forces in the South Korean economy (Seol, D. 2014). Marriage transnationalization attests to a critical fact that sociodemographic reproduction is no exception to this all-encompassing process of South Korean globalization.

9.4 Conclusion

Since the early 1960s, South Korea has undergone extremely rapid and fundamental transformation in both demographic and developmental dimensions. The rates of migration/urbanization, fertility, and mortality all kept changing at such unprecedented and incomparable paces that also characterized those of economic growth, industrialization, proletarianization (occupational change from agricultural to industrial sectors), and so forth. This *dual transformation* was no coincidence, as the country's developmental experiences directly involved critical demographic conditions, processes, and consequences.

South Korean development, though dominated by state-business network, relied on human resources in extraordinary scopes and degrees; whereas South Korean citizens – quite often through demographically flexible familial endeavors – rendered their human resources a strategic platform for active developmental participation and gain. Conversely, South Korea's recent economic crisis and restructuring – namely, its post-developmental transition – have both required and caused drastic reformulation of human resources, family relations, and reproductive behaviors, so that earlier demographic trends have been further accelerated in some aspects (e.g. fertility, population aging, etc.) and suddenly slowed down or reversed in other aspects (e.g. natal sex imbalances, divorce, suicide, etc.).

Through half a century of radical sociodemographic changes, the country has dramatically turned from a society known for very high fertility, universal marriage, and rare divorce into one of "lowest-low" fertility, widespread singlehood, and rampant divorce. South Korea's literally *compressed* sociodemographic changes under a socially complex developmental context offer several significant historical and/or theoretical implications, including among others (1) spatial demographic imbalances due to intergenerationally divided urban migration, (2) fertility decline with alternating gender asymmetry, (3) demographic individualization under sustained normative familialism, (4) constant realignment between individual life course and family life cycle, and (5) socioeconomically discrete two-stage population aging.

As these demographic transformations tend fundamentally to undermine the hitherto taken-for-granted social conditions for national economic management and state governance, the so-called "low fertility and aging society" agenda has induced the country to aggressively explore strategic measures for reversing or relieving demographic deficits and imbalances. While such measures are largely targeted at bolstering South Korean women's reproductive citizenship (i.e. offering fertility benefits and reducing childcare burdens for native women), an unprecedented ethnodemographic change has gradually been taking place under a strategically improvised policy of promoting transnational marriages in villages and urban peripheries.

Part III

After Compressed Modernity

─ 10 ─

THE POST-COMPRESSED
MODERN CONDITION

10.1 South Korea in the Post-Compressed Modern Era

The recurring economic, political, and social crises of the so-called West in the twenty-first century have perturbed South Korean society, not only through their globally contagious effects but also in terms of a fundamental civilizational perplexity concerning South Korea's target and approach for national advancement. Catching up with the so-called "advanced nations" (*seonjinguk*) in Europe and North America has been the central paradigm for South Korea's postcolonial development and modernization. But it has become apparent, from the very beginning years of the twenty-first century, that this paradigm is increasingly futile. What they now confront after their phenomenal success in catching up with the West involves not only material affluence and sociocultural pride but also various structural predicaments haunting both Western societies and South Korea alike. Such common predicaments include, among others, rapid deindustrialization and structural joblessness, pervasive political indifference and divisive radicalization, multi-faceted erosion of social citizenship, chronic indebtedness of both poor and middle-class households, demographic shortages and imbalances accompanying "ultra-low" fertility and hyperaging, national and global ecological crises, and so forth (Beck and Grande 2010; Beck 1999; Bauman 2000). South Koreans cannot simply wait and see if the West already has or will soon come up with effective solutions to them. If any, the West may have improvised the so-called neoliberal measures for some of these problems, but this has not been openly acknowledged as such either by the West or South Korea.

The South Korean mishap is further complicated by the particular manners by which South Korea's catch-up development and modernization have been executed. Its postcolonial development and modernization have been narrowly redefined as statist projects of national economic growth and West-oriented institutional assimilation, to which nearly all social, cultural, ecological, as well as economic values and resources have been arbitrarily subordinated. Structural economic inequalities, deficient and defective social welfare, abuse of labor rights, exploitation and alienation of women, rural socioeconomic decay, environmental degradation, sociopolitical authoritarianism, and cultural and philosophical self-erasing have characterized the South Korean path of "successful" modernization and development (Chang, K. 1999). At the very historical moment that South Korean society should embark on fundamentally redressing the costs of such uniquely risky measures, its people are also confronted with the above-indicated common prices to be paid at the supposedly mature stage of development and modernization. This is South Korea's *post-compressed modern* condition.

A crucial irony in post-compressed modern South Korea is that the entrenched political, administrative, techno-scientific, and industrial elites are now taking the problematic consequences of capitalist developmental maturation as a new excuse for prolonging, reviving, or even intensifying the (South Korean-style) risky measures for earlier development and modernization. Reversion to past practices, instead of reform or innovation, has pervasively characterized South Korea's haphazard reactions to the double-fold structural crises in the twenty-first century. In fact, its final years of the twentieth century were devastated by the socioeconomic shocks of the "IMF crisis" that was caused by an unscrupulous reversion of the state to arbitrary developmentalism despite the radically changed global economic environment. As I explain in detail elsewhere (Chang, K. 2019), this tendency has been somewhat obfuscated by the tacit subscription of the South Korean state and its client industrialists and social elites to the neoliberal ideas, policies, and practices derived from the West. However, to be precise, it reflects more an inertia of its own past than a convergence with the new (neoliberal) West.

10.2 The Double-Fold Structural Crises

Many of the particular manners by which South Korea's catch-up development and modernization have been executed and achieved with concomitant structural risks and detriments are comprehensible or detectable in the preceding chapters on key structural properties

178

of compressed modernity (in Part II of this book). Instead of reciting details of each of these structural properties, let us briefly list their particularly problematic risks and detriments and the latest changes and impacts on such risks and detriments as engendered by the country's assimilation with the advanced world. (Chapter 4 is excluded in this recapitulation due to its nature of a broad historical overview.)

Transformative citizenship and its victims   South Korea's state-driven projects of development and modernization have been socially effective in that its citizens have been mobilized and utilized for all sorts of collective transformative purposes. Each of these transformative purposes, however, has selectively and discriminatorily affected its population according to differential material endowments, educational resources, and, not least importantly, sociopolitical affiliations (including home regions in particular). Under this process, the country's development and modernization have produced not only various intended ends of national transformation but also a long and complicated series of *transformative victims*, who have either been alienated and/or exploited. Farmers, women, manual workers, native local communities, and a host of other generic constituents of South Korean society have ended up becoming sequentially victimized subjects. Most recently, the country's aggressive participation in the West-led neoliberal globalization has abruptly assimilated its economy and society into the late modern conditions of (domestic) deindustrialization, joblessness, financialized (debt-based) livelihood, and ever-widening inequalities in income and asset. Not surprisingly, South Korea's neoliberalization has been highly state-driven, with its socioeconomic impacts crucially amplified and complicated by political decisions and engagements. Particularly after the national financial meltdown in the late 1990s, the neoliberal approach to economic crisis management has frequently intensified the sacrificial status of peasants, urban precariat, and youth as a convenient measure for protecting and boosting industrial corporate interests.

Complex culturalism   As agencies of *complex culturalism*, South Korean institutions and citizens have instrumentally, selectively, and flexibly incorporated into themselves various historical and civilizational sources of culture in order to expediently consolidate the postcolonial sociopolitical order and then to maximize socioeconomic development. While such cultural complexity and flexibility may have facilitated South Korea's modernization and development, the country's integrated philosophical and cultural evolution has been critically

179

retarded by structural rifts and chronic confrontations among virtually all agencies of diverse values, ideologies, religions, cultures, and
knowledges. In recent years, the infinitely digitalized presentation
and circulation of these ideational or superstructural substances have
removed nearly all physical constraints to the social expression of
such rifts and confrontations.[1] Often, such rifts and confrontations
are revealed to be materially and politically strategic, rather than
philosophically or spiritually fundamental, and thus remain irresolv-
able through ideational discussions and persuasions alone.[2] Recently,
the mass arrival of foreign brides from across Asia for marrying South
Korean rural bachelors has added to the cultural complexity of South
Korean society at large, not to mention those of hosting bridegrooms,
families-in-law, and rural communities. In many Western societies,
the sustained influx and settling-down of laboring migrants have, on
the one hand, necessitated and induced a conscious public endeavor
for reframing the host societies into organic multicultural communities and, on the other hand, have recently triggered frequent instances
of racist discriminations and attacks on them. The formal exclusion
of foreign guest-workers from South Korea's multiculturalism policy
(solely targeted at foreign brides) is a highly curious practice of showily pursuing a cosmopolitan purpose by a rigidly particularistic or
discriminatory approach. This points to a paradoxical reinforcement
of South Koreans' sociocultural and economic self-centeredness amid
their seemingly enthusiastic promotion of a supposedly cosmopolitan
goal. For a good reason, multiculturalism is often condemned as a
cause for racial/ethnic segregation.

Productionist (ab)use of social reproduction   Various contradicto-
rily juxtaposed international statistics on South Korea's economic
and social conditions – namely, unprecedentedly high rates of
economic growth and industrialization, longest working and studying hours shared with only a few other countries, shocking suicide
rates of all generations unknown among similarly affluent societies,
"lowest-low" fertility rare in societies under political normalcy, and
so forth – have unambiguously shown that the country's "miracle"
development has been achieved in an extreme way by sacrificing and
abusing various basic conditions for social reproduction of human
life and labor. In this respect, South Korean development fails to
constitute a miracle. Some of these social features may be considered
as similar to those of advanced Western societies. For instance, the so-
called "below-replacement fertility" has been observed in Europe and
North America since long before South Korea's fertility fall to that

180

level. As convincingly explained by Beck and Beck-Gernsheim (2002), the instabilities of labor markets, families, and welfare systems have certainly weakened Westerners' desire to organize their lives by the traditional regimes of social reproduction. South Koreans may be no exception to this trend. However, none of the postwar Western states – not to mention social democratic ones – seem to have adopted policy lines or measures for arbitrarily sacrificing and suppressing human citizens' basic conditions of social reproduction. Likewise, the intensities and complexities of South Korea's social reproduction crisis are simply unparalleled among all industrialized nations. This crisis tends to be further aggravated under the latest tendencies of financialized social reproduction under widespread poverty, desperate individuals' voluntarily intensified abuse of social reproduction amid the chronic job crisis, and so forth.

Infrastructural familialism In South Korea's historical and social realities, there have existed highly interesting forms of familial proactivism in the nation's remarkable economic, sociocultural, and even political transformations. Its families have been functioning simultaneously as *developmental family*, *welfare family*, and *social investment family* in effect. Many of the South Korean state's actualized and/or aspired tasks in national economic and social development have been organized, complemented, substituted, or even financed by grassroots citizens' familial efforts and resources. However, the nation's early twenty-first century seems to be marked by drastic declines in its citizens' familial proactivism and accompanying difficulties to the state in relying on their familial norms, relations, and resources to solve various socioeconomic problems. Broadly speaking, South Koreans are now beset with two sets of unprecedented socioeconomic troubles, namely, the so-called "new social risks" ensuing from the nation's sociodemographic maturation and the neoliberal predicaments in employment and livelihood since the "IMF economic crisis" (as part of the Asian financial crisis). Under these problems, South Korea has become a structurally bifurcated society in which a large majority of its citizens are now disenfranchised from the mainstream economy, while being confronted with continually worsening risks in employment, income, housing, health, and so forth. It is these new structural conditions that make rapidly increasing numbers and proportions of grassroots families incapable of servicing social infrastructural utilities for the state's socioeconomic policy efforts. On the one hand, they have been stripped of financial and other material resources for such roles; on the other hand, they have become organizationally and/or

181

normatively weakened (or restructured), so as to relinquish many of the previously taken-for-granted socioeconomic functions and even abstain from marriage and procreation. Without social infrastructural families being earnestly maintained and sufficiently reproduced, the late modern or post-developmental state's public work in economic, social, and educational affairs has turned much more burdensome and difficult.

Compressed demographic transitions The demographic configuration of South Korean society is marked by striking levels of low fertility, high life expectancy, and high urbanization. Perhaps more striking than the current levels of demographic indicators are the rapidities by which South Korean society has changed in these demographic aspects. The South Korean population, until the 1960s, used to be characterized by very high fertility, modest life expectancy, and predominantly rural residence, but only a few decades were taken for its transition to a population of bare replacement-level fertility, substantial old age, and predominantly urban residence. These few decades were the very period of South Korea's capitalist industrial takeoff that was mainly fueled by abundant human resources and, in turn, transformed participating citizens' basic conditions of life. The state's direct population policy was not insignificant in facilitating these demographic transitions, but its successfully executed developmental policy was much more significant in inducing South Koreans to demographically adapt to the new conditions of economic activities and social relations. In fact, their demographic adaptations were no less impressive than sweeping social and economic changes accompanying one of the world's most swift capitalist industrialization. South Koreans' swift demographic adaptations have continued even during the period of drastic economic downturn and restructuring since the late 1990s. Their early experience in aggressively adjusting demographic parameters of life to unprecedented economic opportunities and conditions in the mid-to-late twentieth century has reverberated in their renewed demographic adaptations to economic depressions and instabilities in the early twenty-first century. Such private demographic adaptability of individuals and families, however, has triggered an unprecedentedly grave trend of possible demographic meltdown in rural and, ultimately, entire South Korea. Rural decay, population aging, and even possible population shrinkage are demographic concerns to virtually all advanced nations, but South Korea's such concerns are incomparably intense because of its extremity in these demographic trends and protracted structural

182

factors for them, not to mention the commonly shared conditions of late modern demographics.

10.3 Beyond South Korea

South Korea's "miraculous" achievement in modernization and development has not exempted the country from what Ulrich Beck dubs the risks of "second modernity" – namely, the inherent dysfunctions and increasing failures of modern institutions such as capitalist industry, labor market, public education, science and technology, national government, middle-class family, and so forth. While these onerous risks are only now recognized, South Koreans are struggling with additional predicaments derived from the particular measures and processes of their compressed modernization and development. At the very historical moment that South Korean society should embark on fundamentally redressing the costs of such risky measures of compressed social and economic transformations, its people are confronted with the globally common prices to be paid at the supposedly mature stage of development and modernization.

South Korea's post-compressed modern condition appears no less challenging than its postcolonial condition plagued with poverty and hunger, political rifts, social conflicts and dislocations, and so on. With all technocratic cautions and scientific debates in South Korea on the common risks it shares with the rest of the developed world, its tenaciously conservative political, administrative, techno-scientific, and industrial elites are ironically taking such new risks as a convenient pretext for extending, renewing, or even strengthening the well-known but well-worn measures for compressed development and modernization.

This apparently regressive tendency has often been obfuscated with neoliberal ideas, policies, and/or practices. In fact, the entrenched sections' wide subscription to neoliberalism can be seen as a conveniently disguising justification for their refusal of fundamental reforms to the overworked conservative ideas, policies, and practices for compressed development and modernization (Chang, K. 2012c). That is, what appears most clearly is not so much South Korea's assimilation with the neoliberal West as its ideological and methodological inertia. It may even be the case that the familiarity and acceptability, to South Koreans, of neoliberal ideas, policies, and practices indeed reflect the West's own conservative inertias in socioeconomic affairs despite all noisy discourses on "neoliberalism as reform." In all logical predictions, South Korea's post-compressed modernity, whether neo-liberally framed or not, will not easily be as honorable and beneficial as its compressed modernity. This prospect will stand regardless of whether and how other late modern societies can manage their corresponding historical challenges.

In this respect, South Korea's reputation as a particularly neo-liberalized entity among East Asian societies does not imply that its post-compressed modern dilemma is unique to itself. Nearly all industrialized societies in the region, including Japan, Taiwan, Singapore, and Hong Kong, are beset with serious social risks and problems corresponding to those indicated above in the South Korean context. Even many developed areas in China increasingly display corresponding social challenges (Chang, K. 2017c). Mass media in the region often express great mutual interest in the concerned trends and issues, whereas there have been numerous collaborative international research efforts about them.[3] Such collaborative studies tend to reveal that there are as much significant differences as similarities among the region's neighbors, reflecting wide diversities in their respective compressed modern and post-compressed modern conditions.[4] Relatedly, the customary differentiation between East and West, particularly in sociocultural terms, in explaining their respective post-compressed modern predicaments can be more problematic than pertinent, especially because of the wide national (and subnational) diversities in compressed modernity and concomitantly diverse post-compressed modern conditions in each world.[5] Given that the West in the post-compressed modern era is no more reflexively taken as a commonly aspired future for the once civilizationally and developmentally derailed nations in the East, each society and its citizenry, whether in East or West, should be able to find autonomous answers and solutions to most of their respective social risks and problems in the twenty-first century. It is precisely the widespread difficulty and failure in securing such national or societal measures that have driven post-compressed modern citizens and communities to turn frequently to radically erratic political suggestions and sociocultural perspectives.

NOTES

1 Introduction: Purpose, Debates, and Subjects

1 Statistical indicators in this paragraph are fully presented in "Compressed Modernity in South Korea" (Chang, K. 2016a).
2 *Republic of Korea Policy Briefing*, February 27, 2019 (http://www.korea.kr/news/policyBriefingView.do?newsId=156319329).
3 Particularly notable scholars in this respect include: Amsden (1989) and Lim, H. (1986) on developmental governance, Koo, H. (2001) on working-class formation (2001), Choi, J. (2002) on democratization (2002), Abelmann (2003) on gender and class, Cumings (1981) on postcolonial politics, Moon, S. (2012) and Eckert (2016) on sociopolitical militarism and so forth.
4 For instance, a most consistent effort in this respect has been made by Shin Yong-Ha (1994), a historical sociologist whose intellectual leadership has been critical in the formation of an influential academic school that underscores indigenous historical and sociocultural conditions for contemporary social phenomena.
5 By nature, the contemporary Korean popular songs, called "the K-pop," may be less explicit in such socially discursive engagement. However, the completely globalized esteem of the BTS (Bangtansonyeondan), a latest epitome in this genre, has been substantially based upon its social messages and approaches.
6 The South Korean government has an explicit academic policy of promoting the "international mainstreaming" of national social sciences and overseas Korean studies on the basis of Korean realities and experiences. While its scientific effect yet remains dubious, the Korean wave has certainly helped to promote the transnational popular appreciation of Korean culture, society, and history – not to mention, to the liking of the government, technocracy and likeminded media. On the part of most cultural producers, there are conscious efforts to maintain at least an arm's length distance from such a potentially nationalist, if not chauvinistic, position.
7 Also, contemporary Vietnamese society is increasingly analyzed as another instance of post-socialist compressed modernity. In such studies on China and Vietnam, a possible convergence between post-socialist and late capitalist

185

paths to modernization and development is implicitly suggested in terms of their common compressed modernity.

8 Harvey might be regarded as suggesting a sort of *global-scale compressed modernity* as a distinctive stage of (both modern and postmodern) capitalism. This stage has been further accentuated by global neoliberalism since the 1980s, largely through the same logic and/or crisis of capitalism. Besides, Harvey's work seems to serve as an indispensable precursor to the so-called cosmopolitan turn of sociology led by Ulrich Beck (see Beck and Sznaider 2006), etc.

9 Before the intellectual ascendance of postcolonialism, many sociologists, such as S. N. Eisenstadt (2000), and Paget Henry (Henry and Walter 1995) had pointed out extensive hybridization between indigenous (traditional) and Western (modern) cultures in various instances of late modernization.

10 If postcolonialist literature and scholarship, to the extent that they intellectually and politically represent postcolonial societies or peoples themselves, are taken as social phenomena, it may be said that fundamental transcendence over the West is not entirely absent. For instance, Dipesh Chakrabarty's (1992) critique of (Western) academic history as well as Edward Said's (1978) critique of (Western) literature has not only transcended the epistemological constraints consciously or unconsciously imposed by the West on non-Western (at least by birth) minds but also helped enlighten Western minds about history, morality, and aesthetics.

2 Compressed Modernity: Constitutive Dimensions and Manifesting Units

1 In this regard, David Harvey's (1980) observation on the (global) time–space compression under the accumulation crisis of late modern capitalism should be differentiated from the national, regional, organizational, familial, and personal condensation of time and space under postcolonial compressed modernity.

2 See Ernst Bloch ([1935]1991), *Heritage of Our Times*. As Germany was behind England and France in industrialization, and in modernization in general, Bloch perceived the German social situation as wedged between backward culture and modern industrialism.

3 See Kim, J. (2019) for a lucid account of Korean traditional medicine's arduous struggle in the contemporary health sector under the hegemonic dominance of Western medicine.

4 "Too dynamic" once became a thematic phrase for South Korea among many foreign media correspondents in Seoul during the Roh Moo-Hyun presidency. "Dynamic Korea" was an official catchphrase for attracting international tourism to the country, but these foreign journalists seem to have felt that it was *too* dynamic.

5 Giddens (1990: 18–19) argues, perhaps inspired by Walter Benjamin's critical assessment of modern cities (Gilloch 1997), "In conditions of modernity, place becomes increasingly phantasmagoric: that is to say, locales are thoroughly penetrated by and shaped in terms of social influences quite distant from them."

6 Interestingly, this familial(istic) nature of South Korean modernity seems to

186

have been more persuasively revealed and more effectively communicated in Korean cultural products (that is, dramas, cinemas, and novels that address family relationships and affairs thematically) than in academic social sciences (whose Western dependency chronically inhibits autonomous systematic exploration of the local essential features of social issues and phenomena). See Kim, Y. (2013) for Korean dramas in this regard.

7 See Orta (1999) for an ethnographic discussion of complex personhood. See Abelmann (2003) for a discussion on the South Korean case.

8 Internal multiple (compressed) modernities can be seen as complex local instances of Appadurai's (1990) global "scapes" in postcolonial modernization.

9 See Dirlik (2003, 2004) on "global modernity," and Pieterse (1994) on "globalization as hybridization."

10 In this respect, "provincializing Europe" (Chakrabarty 2000) is a necessary, but not sufficient strategy for analyzing postcoloniality or postcolonial modernity/modernization.

11 Bruno Latour's (1993, 2005) view on social (dis)order in his "practical metaphysics" may have some epistemological affinity with this proposition.

12 If we consider widespread and even endemic manifestations of unintendend and/or unknown consequences in such modernitizations, John Urry's (2003) thesis on "global complexity" can be usefully applied here.

3 Compressed Modernity in the Universalist Perspective

1 Reflexive cosmopolitization underlines the post-national or cosmopolitan stage in reflexive modernization (Chang, K. 2017b). Cosmopolitization differs from cosmopolitanization in its normative and/or ideological neutrality.

2 In liberal societies (such as the U.K. and the U.S.), market economic opportunities (business and labor) and political freedom have sustained the sovereign status of citizens vis-à-vis the state (mostly in charge of infrastructure provision and policing). In social democratic societies (such as Scandinavian countries), market economic opportunities have been complemented by the political right to state-organized social protection. In developmental societies (such as Japan and South Korea), augmentation of market economic opportunities has been conceived as the core responsibility of the state, which in turn has obliged citizens to mobilize private resources for care and protection (Chang 2012a, 2012b).

3 It needs to be pointed out that the internally derived forces of second modernity are much stronger and more diverse for relatively autonomous second modern societies, so that their compressed modernity intensifies in a different direction.

4 See Beck (2002) for his view on terrorism and war in world risk society.

5 See Hobsbawm and Ranger (eds.) 1992, *The Invention of Tradition*.

6 For a highly suggestive analysis in this regard, see Bloch ([1935]1991) .

7 It may not be a coincidence that highly aged (but recently impoverished) historical societies in East Asia – i.e. China and Vietnam – have ultimately come back as effective modernizers.

8 Harvey's (1980) time/space "compression" corresponds to Chang's "condensation."

9 About these diverse components of globalization or reflexive cosmopolit(an)ization, I refer to Beck (1999; 2006), Turner (1994), Turner and Khondker (2010), Mittelman (2000), Mittelman and Othman, eds. (2001), Jameson and Miyoshi, eds. (1998), etc. For a highly persuasive and illustrative account of Australia's neoliberal globalization, see Weiss, Thurbon, and Mathews (2007).

10 Not unrelatedly – that is, due to deindustrialization, financialization, etc. – domestic inequalities have also expanded in many advanced capitalist countries.

11 One of the worst scandals in this regard involves China's toxic and/or bogus commodities. See Chang, K. (2017c).

12 Vietnamese brides in South Korean villages constitute a highly interesting yet arduous instance. See "Baby Boom of Mixed Children Tests South Korea" (*New York Times*, November 28, 2009).

13 Postcolonialism has been a most successful case in this regard (see, for instance, Ashcroft, Griffiths, and Tiffin 2002).

14 China's aggressive hunt for technologically competitive overseas enterprises (including IBM) is a most eye-catching example.

15 In successful cases, this may be called *developmental modernity*.

16 In this situation, Latin American ISI (import substitution industrialization) has been abandoned significantly, and even African subsistence farming has been sacrificed seriously (for export agriculture).

17 The IMF-led structural readjustment programs have been the most disturbing example.

18 American GMO produces are a most telling case in point.

19 See Cumings (1998, 1999) on the thereby shifted Asia/South Korea–U.S. relations.

20 On the Maoist revolution and mass-line modernity, as an exemplary historical case in this respect, see Mark Selden (1971), *The Yenan Way in Revolutionary China*.

21 See Chang, K. (2017c) for the Chinese case.

22 Some of these Western liberals were formally appointed as key policy advisors by the governments of transition countries.

23 Vietnam is a very similar case (see Masina 2006).

24 See Chang, K. (2017c) for an analysis of China as a complex risk society which manifests risk tendencies of highly diverse time–space dimensions.

25 See Sinn and Sinn (1992), *Jumpstart: The Economic Unification of Germany* for the East German experience.

26 The world views of Bruno Latour (1993, 2005) and John Urry (2003) can be usefully accommodated in theoretically justifying this observation.

27 South Koreans' receiving such Chinese delegations, particularly in the early-to-mid 1990s, as a developmentally successful nation was regarded as a highly self-honorable experience in the historical context of almost two millennia, during most of which their ancestors kept sending tributary delegations to imperial China that would often function as civilizational learning task forces as well.

28 Most of each East Asian nation's major universities are extremely eager to elevate their rankings by the major (West-based) global evaluation programs such as THE (Times Higher Education) World University Rankings and QS World University Rankings. This leads to intense pressure on their faculty

and even graduate students to publish major journal articles (as conveniently recognized through SCI, SCIE, SSCI, A&HCI, etc.) and books by Western publishers.

29 In July 2021, even the 100th birthday of the Chinese Communist Party (CCP) was addressed by its leader Xi Jinping (2021) in terms of flagrantly nationalist propaganda and warnings, instead of cosmopolitan pledges that would match China's superpower status in global political and economic affairs achieved through four decades of unprecedented economic development. Between Japan and South Korea, concurrently, their political and legal conflicts over the wartime labor exploitation and sex slavery of Koreans by Japanese military have recently been translated into hostile trade policies by which Japan has attempted to protest South Korea's stern demands for Japan's formal historical recognition of such misdeeds and compensatory responsibilities.

30 There have been intense debates on Park Chung-Hee, the key figure of South Korea's compressed development and modernization, whose personal history of Japanese military education and career is taken as a crucial factor for adopting such economic, sociopolitical, and educational policies as widely resemble those of militaristic Japan before its defeat by the United States (Eckert 2016). Park openly expressed his respect for Japanese and German (Prussian) leaders who had led their nations' revolutionary transformation for catching up with the world's frontline modernizers.

4 Internal Multiple Modernities: South Korea as Multiplex Theater Society

1 This aspect is also emphasized in Therborn's (2003: 295) thesis of "entangled modernities" which indicate "not just the co-existence of different modernities but also their interrelations."

2 See below on the structural nature of postcolonial reflexive modernization in the global context. Japan's reflexive modernization was not postcolonial, but took on a similar nature by recognizing the civilizational and political economic superiority of the West and embarking on West-referenced modernization (or modernitization).

3 In this respect, see Hahm, I. (2006) for a lucid account of South Korean women's "multi-layered modernity."

4 As a socially crucial unexpected phenomenon in this respect, a sort of false primogeniture norm was engendered between the Korean tradition of ritualisitic primogeniture and the Japanese practical family system, called ie. In Chosun, the eldest son's familial authority mostly rest with his function in leading ancestor worship, whereas each sibling's formal aristocratic-bureaucratic status as yangban had to be individually established through state-administered examinations. After Japan's ie system was transposed onto the Korean Confucian primogeniture culture, each family's eldest son began to assume both ritualistic authority and materialistic priority (in terms of disproportionately or exclusively inheriting familial asset, business, etc.). This basically accidental development in family culture would later cause widespread feuds among siblings and between parents and children. For example, as exemplified in Samsung and Hyundai Groups, the business

189

succession conflict among siblings in *chaebol* families has frequently been triggered particularly when the business founder father decided to reject the eldest son as his successor in conglomerate leadership (Chang, K. 2010a).

5 The hotly debated position of many Korean intellectuals and entrepreneurs who behaved as "Japan-collaborators" may be in part characterized or interpreted in terms of their acceptance of Japan as a supranational entity to which Korea (Chosun) had to belong under the new international order of Western hegemony. This would correspond to the position of the pro-American intellectuals and politicians during the Cold War era, accepting the existential exigency of the "free world" as explained below in this chapter.

6 The gender dimension may be added as another instance of colonial dialectical modernity. See Yoo's (2014) recent book on Korean women's resiliently defiant reactions to Japanese colonialism. On the other hand, Japan's colonial family policy and law engendered complicated changes in gender relations, both instituting women's formal legal status in the increasing nuclear families (Lim, S. 2019) and legalizing men's status as "family head" (*hoju*) in the socio-administrative control of Korean population (Yang, H. 2006, 2011).

7 Wonsan General Strike was a landmark episode in this respect. Between January 13 and April 6, 1929, more than two thousand Korean workers affiliated with the Wonsan Labor Association staged one of the most forceful strikes against abusive Japanese (and allied Western) industrialists in the colonial period. Though limited in economic scope, colonial capitalist industrialization helped to form a modern proletarian class of Koreans whose sociopolitical consciousness would strengthen in proportion to the intensity of often racially framed exploitation in Japanese (and some Western) firms.

8 Relatedly, most South Koreans expressed their preference of the socialist economic system in the immediate post-liberation period. In a social survey by the American military occupation authority, citizens in Seoul chose capitalism by 14%, socialism by 70%, and communism by 10% (*Mediatoday*, April 21, 2017; http://www.mediatoday.co.kr/news/articleView.html?idxno=136310).

9 Among South Korea's progressive intellectuals, this socialist or proletarian (ethno)nationalism has long remained a widely influential ideology. In the mid 1990s, some student activists in South Korea tried to reframe their political struggle against military dictatorship and monopolistic developmental capitalism as a pan-Korean project, by associating themselves with the North Korean leadership and openly subscribing to the Juche ideology (Park, C. 2016). This group, often nicknamed NL (national liberation), actually turned into a dominant force in student political movements and subsequently in organized labor movements, causing the ultimate degeneration of both movements. Many of the core figures of NL would convert to (South Korean) New Right, a political position or ideology of justifying whatever conservative ruling powers have existed (including the Japanese colonial rule) and promoting anti-North Korean struggles in terms of democratization, human rights, etc. See Kim, S. (2017) on the Juche ideology.

10 East Asia is an exceptional region in the world history in that the main nations therein have long maintained high degrees of racial homogeneity and continuity within successive state structures. Thus, nationalism in this region is often identified with ethnic consciousness or even racialism (Shin, G. 2006) – in South Korea, in terms of the ideology of *danilminjok* (singular

ethnonation). However, such racial dimension does not exhaust the political, social, and cultural implications of South Korean nationalism, in particular under the turbulent politico-institutional instabilities enmeshed with foreign influences.

11 The recent account by Theodore Hughes (2014) on Korean literature and film in the colonial and postcolonial periods may be read as suggesting various colonial dialectical features in them.

12 (Ethno)nationalist liberalism has generated a particularly forceful impact in sociology, literature and, more recently, cinema. Its key figures include, among others, Han Wan-Sang and Paik Nak-Chung. Politically, it was distinctly illustrated by President Kim Dae-Jung (see Kim, D. 2010), and now by President Moon Jae-In.

13 Reflexive modernization in late modern reality, as argued by Beck and Giddens (Beck, Giddens, and Lash 1994), is a structurally complicated process of social change under the uncontrollable floods of choices that expose modern society and people to more risks than opportunities. See Chang, K. (2017b) for a formal theoretical account of "reflexive modernization" in *The Wiley Blackwell Encyclopedia of Social Theory*. In global perspective, this has been an early modern reality as well.

14 What Pei-Chia Lan (2014) addresses as "glocal entanglements" may correspond to this historical phenomenon.

15 In return for its collusive endorsement of Japan's annexation of Korea, the United States had been allowed to develop wide influences on Koreans in sociocultural affairs – in particular, religion, education, and social work. Many Koreans came to find a sort of safe haven in American-established churches, schools, and welfare organizations during the Japanese colonial rule. Such experiences would help to form a useful popular ground for South Korea's Americanization on all fronts in the post-liberation era.

16 Above all, Seoul National University (SNU) was established, by reorganizing Gyeongseong Imperial University and absorbing some independent colleges, in 1946 after the American comprehensive research university model, with its first president being an American military officer with a PhD. This university would, in turn, become the standard model for other national universities subsequently established in major regional centers. With an overwhelming societal influence, it has served as a nationalist-Americanist institution in the nation's reflexive institutional modernization to date. See *The Fifty Year History of Seoul National University, 1946–1996* (Seoul National University 1996).

17 This has been a core cause for the rise of what is popularly called in South Korea "polifessor" (Noh, S. 2008; Byeon, C. 2012). Polifessors' rampant absenteeism from research and education has even led to parliamentary attempts to regulate them (Sohn, H. 2009). Polifessor is sometimes compared to Confucian scholar-gentry in Chosun, however, in mostly critical views (Byeon, C. 2012). Nonetheless, polifessors would conveniently remind themselves of such scholar-cum-official status as a worthy tradition.

18 This social limit is critically related to the general nature of what may be called *reflexive social sciences* or *reflexively positivist social sciences* in South Korea, characterized by the endemic tendency of measuring the distance between Western standard and South Korean reality, rather than analyzing Korean reality in its own terms.

19 See Lew, S. (2013) and Kim, S. (2011) for solid arguments on the civilizational and institutional protomodernity of Chosun or East Asia in general.

20 In particular, Park Chung-Hee attempted to fortify his rule by the supposedly Confucian ideology of *chunghyo* (loyalty to the nation and piety to parents), implying citizens should serve the nation (embodied in the state leader) like their parents.

21 See *Media Power and Agenda Dynamics* (Park and Chang 2001) about the political nature of South Korean media.

22 Such strategic reverse engineering fundamentally presupposes the long-term consistency in the emulated civilization or system (as well as its internal institutional/ideational coherence). In the immediate post-liberation period, South Korea's preponderant reliance on the American system ironically helped to satisfy such condition, but the cost-minimizing motivation of both the American occupation authority and the South Korean state, the remnant influences of colonial-era Korean elites, and the American prioritization of politico-military stability in the Korean peninsula under the Cold War would soon coalesce to engender chronic structural complexities, inconsistencies, and segmentations in the national model of institutional modernization (Park, T. 2008; Kim, D. 2018; Chang, K. 1999).

23 For instance, the nation's leading comprehensive university, Seoul National University has, as of 2020, 15 undergraduate colleges, which in turn have 82 academic disciplinary departments (http://www.snu.ac.kr/organization). Its general graduate school has 5 areas, 70 departments, and 28 cooperative programs at the Masters level, and 5 areas, 72 departments, and 29 cooperative programs at the PhD level. It also has 12 specialized graduate schools. Each department or graduate program operates basically as an independent institution with mutually segmented educational and research functions, with a faculty-hiring practice of strong inbreeding in terms of undergraduate departmental affiliation. It can hardly be a universal university.

24 There was an earlier trend of *yangbanization* in late Chosun (Kim, S. 2003), however, with a more materially driven purpose of evading state exploitation by various illicitly acquired statuses of *yangban*.

25 The implication of familial neotraditionalization for women has been diametrically different between these two cases (Chang, K. 2018) – namely, overexploitation of South Korean women under extended family relations and rituals, in addition to farm labor as compared with affective romanticization of Western women as the cultural pillar of the modern nuclear family. It should be indicated that Korean women's status norms had also been influenced by the Japanese ideology of *ryosai kenbo* (wise mother, good wife) during the colonial period (Choi, H. 2009), which was not incompatible with Confucian family norms but would normatively reinforce them, with a complicated impact of nurturing a womanly status betrayed by their everyday realties of agricultural and other production labor besides home management. However, it was not institutionally articulated through the patrilineal kinship system but, in fact, accompanied by the colonial legalization of women's formal status in the increasing nuclear families (Lim, S. 2019). Postcolonial neotraditionalization in family culture would help substantially to liquidate the practical effect of women's legal status in everyday life.

26 Even the social orders and relations in South Korea's Protestant churches

are known to be highly Confucian (Gye, J. 2010). Some of them have been hereditarily governed along the male bloodline of their founder priests (Bae, D. 2013; *Hankyoreh* 2017). Familial inheritance of a public status or office is not necessarily Confucian, but Confucian patriarchy has been the main organizational order behind such illicit and impious practices (Im, H. 2000).

27 As a distorted manifestation of this corporate culture, frequent instances of *gieop chongsu*'s physical violence to employees keep making news headlines (e.g. *Hankookilbo* 2017/7/18).

28 In this regard, innumerable South Korean social scientists attended the graduate programs of American universities, often with the public support of the South Korean or the American government, and returned home to lead education, research, and institutional modernization (Kim, J. 2015). It is also indicative that the first president of Seoul National University, South Korea's hegemonic institution of education and research established in 1946, was an American army officer with some academic background.

29 The historico-political origin of the Korean War has been one of the most intensely debated subjects among political scientists and historians across the Pacific ever since the pioneering work of Bruce Cumings (1981).

30 See Han, J. (2003) and Kim, J. (2015) on education; Han, J. (2010) on technology; Lee, B. (2015) on culture; Lee, H. (2009) on economic aid.

31 See Kim, D. (2018) for an interesting observation on the similarity and/ or compatibility between "anti-communist liberalism" in South Korea and neoliberalism in various socioeconomic policies and practices – in particular, suppression of labor rights and social welfare.

32 In the related respect, South Korean troops were mobilized by the United States to fight communist North Vietnam along with American troops during the Vietnam War, by which the United States tried to contain communist expansion in Indochina.

33 This political practice has been branded by critics and media as *gongan tongchi* (rule by public security). Its legal basis is the National Security Law. Many of the core public and collaborative functionaries for this rule, such as public security prosecutors, intelligence officials, and conservative journalists, have been invited or appointed to party, parliamentary, and governmental positions by the successive rightwing political leaders. For instance, it turned out that the recently impeached Park Geun-Hye, Park Chung-Hee's daughter, relied almost exclusively on such public functionaries of *gongan tongchi* during her (incomplete) presidency, who have been imprisoned along with Park for unlawful activities.

34 At the grassroots level, many conservative elderly protesters in recent political rallies against the Moon Jae-In government have been waving not only the South Korean national flag but also the American national flag, displaying their conscious or unconscious identity as free world citizen (or indirect American citizen). They experienced the Korean War in person and/or went through intense Cold War-based political socialization.

35 Nonetheless, two figures from Hyundai, Chung Ju-Yung and Chung Mong-Joon, ambitiously attempted to become the national president. Although neither was successful, they were respectively able to elicit quite wide political support.

36 In Asia, Singapore may be the most distinct state capitalist system, which

193

defines the basic nature not only of economy, but also politics and society. See Chua Beng Huat's *Liberalism Disavowed: Communitarianism and State Capitalism in Singapore* (2017).

37 Rhee's position differed significantly even from that of the conservative Korean Democratic Party (Hangukminjudang), which advocated the situationally necessitated measures of industrial nationalization (until sufficient formation of civilian Korean capital) and land reform (based upon compensation and payment) (Park, T. 2008).

38 Military, as Park's background, is a profession in charge of managing physical interstate relations. Thus, many military-turned-politicians across the world – Park Chung-Hee in particular (Oh, J. 2007) – have displayed strong (ethno)nationalist orientations in other public affairs and policies as well. See Eckert (2016) on the political economic implications of Park's career in the Japanese imperial military.

39 From this position, *chaebol* have been bribing practically anyone with immediate or potential influence on their business interests – politicians, government officials, judges, prosecutors, journalists, scholars, civil activists, and so forth. The forms of such bribing are not entirely illegal and have been evolving ingeniously. Samsung has been most notoriously perceived by South Korean public, spawning such terms as (South Korea as) *Samsung gonghwaguk* (the Samsung republic) and *Samsung janghaksaeng* (Samsung scholarship – reads bribe – awardees). See Song, B. (2007), Ha, S. (2011), Kim, S. (2007). *Chaebol*'s ideological apparatuses such as affiliated economic research institutions and newspapers have remained largely dubious about the hegemonic influence of state capitalist developmentalism and the concomitantly sidelined status of *chaebol*. Instead of propagating any firmly market-liberal position or ideology possibly pivoting around *chaebol*, they have more often preferred to present opportunistic opinions about national economic conditions and policies – that is, demanding or condemning more state intervention and support according to immediate interests of *chaebol* (*Ohmynews* 2007; 2017).

40 This imagination was formally stipulated in the "National Chart of Education," December 5, 1968, which was emphatically declared through Park Chung-Hee's own speech (see Chapter 5, Box 5.1).

41 I explain elsewhere the state-business entrepreneurial merge and its sociopolitical and economic implications for labor relations as part of *developmental liberalism* – the social policy regime of the developmental state (Chang, K. 2019).

42 This phenomenon, called "the Park Chung-Hee nostalgia," even led his daughter, Park Geun-Hye into presidency in 2012. Conversely, her political fall in terms of impeachment accompanying financial and political scandals has critically dampened the Park Chung-Hee nostalgia.

43 This tendency has been particularly noticeable under the currently incumbent Moon Jae-In government, which was formed partly as a broad united front of social movement groups.

44 In no coincidence, Moon Jae-In built a long veritable career as human rights lawyer, serving all such subaltern subjects against illegitimate state violence.

45 These two groups are popularly called NL (National Liberation) and PD (People's Democracy). Also see note 9 in this chapter on NL's historical background and political trajectory.

194

46 The NL group has caused unintended problems to South Korean democracy: first, it has crucially derailed the organized labor movement and its political institutionalization (led by the PD group); second, it has helped extending the lifespan of *gongan tongchi* (the Cold War-based rule with public security means) by openly interacting with North Korea. It seems the conservative conversion of its core members does not genuinely constitute a conversion because of their continued subscription to dogmatic statist authoritarianism.

47 As an endemic side-effect of such statist solution and interaction with the state, many leaders of supposedly liberal social institutions have tried, on the one hand, to establish themselves therein by currying cronyist favor from state officials and politicians and, on the other hand, to access state offices as a personal career ambition, often by manipulating their duties and functions for hidden political purposes. For instance, so many presidents of major South Korean universities have ended up becoming politicians, ministers, or even presidential secretaries.

48 Even academic social sciences used to be heavily monitored and controlled in conjunction with the National Security Law.

49 The three most subscribed newspapers, *Chosun*, *JoongAng*, and *Dong-A*, have commonly been proactive in maintaining or reviving anti-communism and anti-North Korea ideology in formal politics. They are popularly abbreviated as *Chojoongdong* by critical citizens.

50 For instance, on the day of her impeachment from presidency, Park Geun-Hye's three most powerful administrative staff – the Blue House chief of staff (Kim Ki-Choon), the presidential head secretary in civil affairs (Woo Byung-Woo), as well as the prime minister (Hwang Kyo-Ahn) – were all former *gongangeomsa* (public security prosecutors).

51 Amsden, in her authoritative treatise on South Korean development, *Asia's next giant: South Korea and Late Industrialization* (1989), argues that some of these informal economic rules and forms have significant developmental effects.

52 Chang Ha-Sung, the key figure in this shareholder accountability movement, once served as the chief secretary of policy affairs in Blue House (the presidential office) accompanying President Moon Jae-In's recognition of his contribution to economic reform. See Chang's *Capitalism in Korea* (2014) for a comprehensive self-account of his economic reform agendas and ideas. Interestingly, his cousin at the University of Cambridge, Chang Ha-Joon (2012) holds a contrasting position about *chaebol* by emphasizing their strategic developmental utility (*Hankyoreh*, September 20, 2012), which echoes Alice Amsden's view.

53 See Choi, J. (2019) for a vivid account of contemporary South Korean society's "collective rituals" in addressing *minjujuui* (democracy), *seongjangjuui* (growthism), *minjokjuui* (ethnonationalism), and *genderjuui* (genderism).

54 Such propagandic approach to modernization induced ordinary South Koreans to get normatively immersed in it. Geundaehwa (meaning modernization) was very popular as a store name, along with Hyundae (meaning modern), Gukje (meaning international), and so forth.

5 Transformative Contributory Rights: Citizen(ship) in Compressed Modernity

1 Cumings (2005) characterizes the Japanese rule in Korea as "administrative colonialism," perhaps as opposed to European colonial rules elsewhere that were often directly driven by private entrepreneurial interests and activities.

2 The United States military government office announced an act on the establishment of Seoul National University on August 22, 1946, and appointed an American military officer, Dr. Harry Bidwell Ansted, as its inaugural president.

3 This helped intensify the rent-seeking nature of formal educational certification, and ignited private educational investment by cost-benefit conscious citizens (Chang, K. 2010a, Chapter 3).

4 Barack Obama has been one of the most fervent enthusiasts for South Koreans' education zeal as well as work ethic. In his public speeches, particularly after the subprime national economic crisis, Obama time and again exhorted Americans to emulate South Koreans in educational devotion and achievement (Chang, K. 2022, ch. 6).

5 The expansion of educational opportunities was often accompanied by the strengthening of political control through education (Seth 2012).

6 Any mismanagement of the educational competition systems – in particular, the college entrance examination system – would result in a serious political dent in the incumbent government's popularity and even necessitate dismissal of the education minister. Its performance as the "exam policing state" (Chang, K. 2010a, ch. 3; Chang, K. 2022, ch. 6) has always been one of the political priorities.

7 At Seoul National University, as of 2012, 45 percent of its faculty had PhDs from American universities, comprising 79 percent of all faculty with foreign PhDs (*Yonhapnews*, July 6, 2012).

8 According to SEVIS, South Korea used to send the biggest group of foreign students to American colleges and universities, even dwarfing India and China. China later caught up with both India and South Korea.

9 Other East Asian societies, including Japan, Taiwan, Singapore, Hong Kong, and post-Mao China, share similar characteristics of *hakbeolsahoe* (e.g. Morris and Sweeting, eds. 1995), but South Korea has been quite distinct even to the eyes of other East Asians.

10 See Kariya (2013) on a similar situation in Japan.

11 Such remedial policies include: the *sinjisigin* (new brain) campaign under Kim Dae-Jung, abolition of education-based discriminations under Roh Moo-Hyun, anti-discriminatory hiring of high-school graduates under Lee Myung-Bak, and education credential-blind hiring in public sectors under Moon Jae-In. These successive governmental efforts reflect the increasing political sensitivity of educationally caused inequalities under the chronic employment crisis for youth.

12 "The fourth industrial revolution" was first presented by Klaus Schwab, founder of the World Economic Forum, at the third Davos Forum in 2016, as a broad indication of the accelerated fusion of "physical, digital and biological worlds" and its economic, social, human, and academic consequences

(Schwab 2017). The South Korea government, under Moon Jae-In, almost instantaneously picked it up as a new developmental catchphrase, leading to its wide official, journalistic, and social circulation long before most other countries became familiarized with it (https://www.4th-ir.go.kr/). It was as early as in October 2017 that a grand task force, the Presidential Committee on the Fourth Industrial Revolution, was set up with a top executive authority (https://www.4th-ir.go.kr/article/detail/258?boardName=internalData&category=).

13 The recent upgrading of professional education in law, medicine, welfare, and education, among others, has also been modeled after American professional graduate schools. This implies, on the one hand, a significant weakening of the short-coursed nature of educationally certified professional jobs and, on the other hand, a substantial increase in the financial burden for professional education.

14 During the so-called "IMF economic crisis" of 1997 to 1998, ironically, a reversely collectivist doctrine of *gotong bundam* (pains-sharing) forced wage workers and other grassroots citizens to accept, again as citizenship duties, mass dismissal and pay-cut in order to "save the national economy first" (Chang, K. 2019, ch. 3).

15 Upon seizing state power through a coup, Park Chung-Hee rounded up major business figures for corruption charges as an effort to build a politico-moral platform for his authoritarian rule. Even when these figures were later pardoned in exchange for committed participation in the state-led development programs, they remained extremely cautious in order not to irritate Park for ascetic issues. See Kim, H. (2004) for detailed accounts of the Park-era politics and economy.

16 According to OECD's (2020b) public data, South Korea's public spending on welfare still remains at a lowest level among industrialized countries. For instance, as of 2018, its social expenditure as a proportion of GDP remained at 11.1% as compared to the OECD average at 20.1% ("OECD Data: Social expenditure – aggregated data"). As of 2000, the corresponding figures were 4.5% and 17.4%, so there has been some significant catchup despite a substantial remaining gap.

17 See Bertrand Badie's (2000) discussion of similar situations across the world.

18 In 1960, a student-led political eruption successfully subverted the Rhee dictatorship, but was immediately accompanied by Park's coup.

19 The patriarchal nature of civil society and labor movements has been a hotly debated issue. Despite the initial role of female factory workers in proletarian struggle, the main beneficiary of democratization was their male counterparts in heavy industries, public sectors, etc. (Koo, H. 2001). Even new social movements have been structurally gender-divided, so that mostly female activists and citizens of life-world movements would feel segregated and even discriminated by mostly males counterparts of politically oriented movements (Moon, S. 2012).

20 In a New Year interview with *Kyunghyang Shinmun* (January 1, 2013). Choi Jang-Jip, South Korea's eminent political scientist, criticized dominant politicians in the main opposition party (the Democratic United Party) for their "movementist perspective on democracy" that, according to him, had led to a great political failure in embracing grassroots' realities and sentiments.

21 This elitism has been criticized as "the attitude of monopolizing truth"

(*Sisain*, January 2, 2013). The deceased president, Roh Moo-Hyun was particularly controversial for such political posture, igniting the conservative political and media elites' ferocious anger and alienating politically moderate citizens who would cast their political votes for the conservative party's candidates in many subsequent years. More recently, many progressive intellectual politicians with envious economic and/or educational backgrounds have been derogatorily branded as *Gangnam jwapa* (implying hypocritical bourgeois leftist).

22 When the Moon Jae-In administration was inaugurated in 2017, most key positions in the presidential office were occupied by former activists in democracy, unification, economic justice and other social movements. This made influential conservative media very uncomfortable.

23 See Han Sang-Jin's (2009) thesis on *jungmin* (middling grassroots) in this regard.

24 Despite all its economic side-effects, South Korea's globalization – mostly in neoliberal directions – has been explicitly negated or resisted by very few social groups. In this respect, the practical importance of English, as a means of (neoliberal) cosmopolitan citizenship, began to be even further emphasized, after decades of its primacy in public education. Local governments competed in constructing "English villages" that were supposedly designed to enable intensive experiential learning of English in a simulative physical setting of English-spoken societies. Unfortunately, these lavish facilities have been severely underutilized, so their usage is gradually changing into tourist purposes.

25 In frequent media articles and political speeches, Japan's earlier pessimism about South Korea's aggressive globalism has recently turned into an envious awe.

26 In this respect, it is indicative that virtually none among influential opinion leaders, many of whom serve as newspaper columnists, have openly opposed globalization. Most columns on globalization have either advocated globalization or scolded responsible figures and institutions for not being sufficiently prepared for successful globalization. Ever since the Kim Young-Sam government kicked off its *segyehwa* (globalization) campaign in the early 1990s, a sort of *globalization fetishism* has dominated South Korean society despite its painful economic experience during "the IMF crisis." South Korea's globalization since the 1990s has not necessarily severed it from its earlier developmental strategy, characterized by active trade-based international economic participation and aggressive technological and educational integration with the West (see Chapter 4).

27 For instance, virtually all universities have embraced globalization as their developmental direction, as exemplified by "global" campuses, studies, faculty members, and so forth. These initiatives are often eligible for the government's special budget for educational globalization.

28 See Nancy Abelmann's highly indicative work on this trend at the family level (Abelmann 2004; Kang and Abelmann 2011).

29 South Korea's military engagement in the Vietnam War has been the only (partial) exception in this regard.

30 Above all, South Korea has not yet joined the United Nations Human Rights Treatises that require each receiving state to guarantee, among others, migrant workers' rights to live with their family (Lee, K. 2008). In reality,

many foreign workers do live with children, whose illegal residential status denies them access to education, health care, and general welfare.

31 Many pregnant South Korean women have tried to secure American or Canadian citizenship for their unborn children by strategically travelling to the U.S. or Canada for imminent delivery. This maternal behavior, called *wonjeongchulsan* (expedition delivery), is much more frequent if a male fetus has been detected. This is because, with American or Canadian citizenship, the boy will be able to avoid military conscription in South Korea and also enjoy pleasant life in North America. Although this trend apparently irritates the American and Canadian immigration authorities and many local as well as South Korean citizens, it has not been effectively curbed.

32 As of early 2013, according to my interview of a key national officer, the South Korean government briefly considered the merger of the so-far separated policy programs for foreign workers and for marriage migrants. The merger has not taken place to date.

33 According to official statistics of the Ministry of Foreign Affairs and Trade (June 20, 2012), the corresponding numbers as of 2011 were as follows: 2.70 million (including 0.37 million South Korean nationals) in China; 2.18 million (including 1.08 million South Korean nationals) in the U.S.; 0.90 million (including 0.58 million South Korean nationals) in Japan; 0.22 million (including negligible South Korean nationals) in Russia; 0.17 million (including negligible South Korean nationals) in Uzbekistan; 0.11 million (including negligible South Korean nationals) in Kazakhstan; 0.23 million (including 0.13 million South Korean nationals) in Canada; 0.13 million (including 0.10 million South Korean nationals) in Australia, etc.

34 For instance, The Overseas Koreans Foundation, the government's official arm for its overseas Korean policy, annually hosts World Korean Business Convention (Segyehansangdaehoe) since 2002 in different South Korean cities (http://www.hansang.net/portal/PortalView.do). In parallel, World Chinese Entrepreneurs Convention (Shijiehuashangdahui) have been held biennially since 1991 (http://www.11thwcec.com.sg/en/index.html).

35 Chaoxianzu (Korean Chinese) have been particularly active in this regard. Many South Korean firms operating in China have critically relied upon Chaoxianzu's managerial, cultural as well as linguistic service labor (Piao, K. 2006); whereas, in conjunction with South Korea's rapid population aging, Chaoxianzu migrants have offered affordable care labor for many families with ill or handicapped elderly (Hong and Kim 2010).

36 See Sung, M. (2010) on different political nuances of "defector" and "refugee" as used in South Korea.

6 Complex-Culturalism vs. Multiculturalism

1 See Chapter 4 on South Koreans' postcolonial cultural *neotraditionalization*, as opposed to retraditionalization.

2 See Kim, M. (2010, 2018) for lucid research on the relationship between South Korea's catchup development and political cultural complexity.

3 Such analyses of compressed modernity in South Korea's popular culture include: Martin-Jones (2007) and Baik, P. (2012) on South Korean films;

Keblinska (2017), Lee, K. (2004), and Abelmann (2003) on South Korean dramas; Regatieri (2017) and Jang and Kim (2013) on K-pop.

4 In the early evening shows of South Korean television stations, such as "Six O'clock My Hometown" (www.kbs.co.kr), rural elderly peasants are almost daily interviewed as to their rustic life styles and morals.

5 For instance, see the weekly television show, entitled "Multicultural Mother-in-Law and Daughter-in-Law Biographic Notes" (Damunhwa Gobuyeoljeon), by *EBS* (https://home.ebs.co.kr/gobu/main).

6 Accordingly, the hitherto dominant ideology of *danilminjok* (one homogeneous ethnic nation) disappeared from public discourse almost overnight.

7 Koichi Iwabuchi, in *Recentering Globalization: Popular Culture and Japanese Transnationalism* (2002), presents the concept/theory of "borrowed nostalgia" in order to explain the transcultural nature of Japanese people's self-tailored consumption of other Asian cultures. It is "a condition that finds people constituting memory on the basis of mass-mediated cultural forms originating from elsewhere" (Iwabuchi 2018). Relatedly, Kim, S. (2012) characterizes East Asia as a hybrid community.

8 Many students from multi-ethnic families have complained about being called "Hey, multicultural(s)!" by their friends and, sometimes, teachers. See "Multiculturals, raise your hands" (*OhmyNews*, August 11, 2016) and "'Hey, multicultural' . . . the homeroom teacher calls my friend like this" (*Seoul Times*, July 30, 2018).

7 Productive Maximization, Reproductive Meltdown

1 See Ochiai (2011) for a broad, demographically focused account of social reproduction failures under East Asia's compressed modernity.

2 In *German Ideology*, Marx briefly referred to social reproduction as one of the two historical moments of capitalism, but he did not elaborate further on such materialist conception of social reproduction, spawning wide theoretical, ideological, and political confusions thereafter (Marx and Engels 1970).

3 Productionism should be differentiated from productivism. The former is the developmentalist emphasis on the primacy of economic production (vis-à-vis consumption, welfare, etc.) for national development, whereas the latter is the neoliberal insistence on the economically productive nature of noneconomic affairs (such as welfare, education, etc.). More broadly, productivism can be considered as a philosophical underpinning of the modern economy – and, according to Giddens (1990), of modernity in general – as incorporated in liberal economics and other system-oriented social sciences. Productionism is, in a sense, a crude form of productivism, and their mutual distinction blurs particularly at the macro aggregate level. For instance, national economic growth is a goal or indicator of both productionism and productivism

4 Like welfare state typologies, we may propose to classify social reproduction regimes according to various criteria, including the economic production versus social reproduction relationship. Generally, different types of the welfare states may have correspondingly different types of social reproduction regimes.

5 South Koreans' average daily length of sleep has for many years remained the OECD's shortest (*Chosunilbo*, February 16, 2017).

6 The developmental sacrificing of social reproduction was inherently linked to the governmental condemnation of consumption (vis-à-vis saving and investment) as a barrier to national economic development. As Laura Nelson (2000) persuasively shows, South Korean women, as supposed chief agencies (or culprits?) of consumption, were thereby subjected to intense public pressure for managing consumption frugally. Women's roles in social reproduction and consumption are structurally enmeshed because many parts of social reproduction involve consumption. Thus, the governmental pressure on women against consumption may also have helped justify its productionist approach to development and modernization and concomitant sacrificing of social reproduction.

7 In this context, production was routinely defined as politics in state socialist societies, with work units serving as the formal basis for political studies.

8 See *Chen Village* by Chan and Madsen (1984) for a lucid account of this situation. I referred to the Chinese state's reliance on the traditional, communitarian, and/or familial norms and relations of villagers in rural production and welfare for segregative urban-centered development as *ruralism* or *ruralist development* (Chang, K. 2005). Ruralism is a sustained tendency before and after Deng Xiaoping's liberal reform.

9 Family-reliant rural reform instantly prompted Chinese villagers to yearn for more children (as future familial economic hands) than allowed under the strict family planning policy of the state (Chang, K. 1996). As the Chinese state refused to step back from strict fertility control (despite this policy's contradiction with its family-reliant rural reform policy), demographic confrontation became one of the thorniest areas of state-peasant conflict.

10 Gordon White (1998: 188) pointed out the peripatetic nature of the social policy regimes of East Asia's developmentalist countries. In fact, their overall developmental experiences can be seen this way.

11 These two systems of political economy can be simplistically compared as follows: in a *liberally liberal* society, bourgeoisie as the dominant class will insist on minimal social spending in order to minimize its financial burden of tax; whereas in a *developmental liberal* society, the developmental state will try to minimize social spending in order to maximize economic or developmental investment within a given budget.

12 I elsewhere present several general characteristics of developmental liberalism – (Chang, K. 2019, ch. 2). Each of these characteristics has critical ramifications for social reproduction and its relationship with economic production. Also see note 18 in Chapter 8.

13 Nancy Abelmann's (1997, 2003) influential research has shown this attribute of South Korean families in regard to women's daily lives and discourses.

14 See Chang, K. (2018), Chapter 5 on elderly suicide as a type of individualization.

15 See a series of influential work by Nancy Abelmann in this respect (Abelmann 2003, 2004; Kang and Abelmann 2011).

16 The pragmatic position of peasant parents in flexibly diverting rural familial resources for urban-headed/based children is characterized as *indirect exit* in my earlier work (Chang, K. 2010a, ch. 6).

17 On July 7, 1993, under his neoliberal advisors' urge, President Kim Young-Sam came to enrage the entire peasant community by heedlessly (or frankly?) commenting:

The decrease in rural population is an unavoidable trend, and no measure is available to block it perforce. At the current level of 14%, our country's rural population, as compared to advanced countries such as the United States with rural population at 3%, has not overcome the backward country pattern. Thus, rural population should be further reduced along the advancing (*seonjinhwa*) of rural communities, such as mechanized farming, etc.

(*Korea Economic Daily*, July 7, 1993)

It took only several years thereafter that Kim's such remark, based upon an erroneous identification of rural population as farmers (that were less than 10% of the national population and proportionally smaller than those of many "advanced countries") and an internationally incompatible classification of many practically urban places of *eup* (administrative rural towns) as rural, was accompanied by a desperate exploration of rural jobs by many of those suddenly discharged from employment during the "IMF crisis," for which the Kim Young-Sam government was chiefly responsible. Even after this unprecedented financial crisis was gradually stabilized, there has developed a steady trend of *gwinong* (return to farming) and *gwichon* (return to village) as individualized quests of many, mostly aged urbanites (Kim and Lee 2017)).

18 See "South Korea's FTA territory expansion ... manufacturing industry in high expectation, agriculture and animal husbandry in deep worry" (*Yonhapnews*, September 23, 2014).

19 This degenerative class culture has been no less serious among peasants (Chang, K. 2010a, ch. 6).

20 The sharing of household work by South Korean husbands is notoriously limited. Interestingly, the working women's share of household work is even higher than that of fulltime housewives (Chang, K. 2010a, ch. 5). This appears to be the material outcome of a class-specific gender culture by which husbands in lower social strata tend to make their wives work more regularly in the economy and more intensely in the households than those in higher strata. Economic, educational, and cultural factors seem to be complexly coalesced behind this depressive phenomenon.

21 According to "A Questionnaire Survey on Citizens' Perception about the Class Upward Mobility Ladder," a comprehensive social survey by Hyundai Economic Research Institute (2017), those South Koreans who thought "Class upward mobility is unlikely even if individuals make hard efforts" kept increasing from 75.2% in 2013 to 81.0% in 2015 and 83.4% in 2017.

22 For a useful collection of accounts of new social risks in the European context, see Taylor-Gooby, ed. (2004).

23 A newspaper article was entitled very suggestively, "white-headed son ... serving daughter-in-law ... early retired husband ... 'depressed middle-age' housewives are in distress" (*Hankyoreh*, August 1, 2011). Here, "white-headed" means "unemployed," and "serving daughter-in-law" is the opposite of the traditional support relationship between a mother-in-law and a daughter-in-law.

24 See Fine (2012) for a succinct account of various trends of financialization in the neoliberal context.

25 Many indebted young women have ended up being forced into prostitution

202

by their private usury creditors (many of whom operate businesses involving prostitution) (Kim, J. 2015).

26 Among these, the Bangladesh-learned Miso micro-finance program for small businesses is particularly interesting (Chang, K. 2016b).

8 Social Institutional Deficits and Infrastructural Familialism

1 South Koreans' situationally induced family-centeredness is conceptualized as *situational familialism*, as opposed to *ideational familialism* based upon traditional norms and/or sociocultural values and *institutionalized familialism* embedded in family-centered social institutions and public policies (Chang, K. 2018, ch. 1).

2 While South Koreans' family-centeredness, or familialism (*gajokjuui*), has often been highlighted by scholarly accounts, media descriptions, and cultural productions (such as novels, cinemas, and dramas), this attribute has not been addressed with sufficiently systematic conceptual, theoretical, and analytical instruments for objective understanding. In this respect, Nancy Abelmann's devoted and influential work on South Korean family, women, and youth has been invaluable (Abelmann 1997, 2003, 2004). On the other hand, some scholars and social critics have offered interesting critical appraisals of South Koreans' familialism, such as Lee, D. (2001), *Familialism is Savage*, Kim, H. (2017), *The Strange Normal Family: Imagining Autonomous Individual and Open Community*, and Kim, D. (2020), *South Koreans' Energy, Familialism: Family as Protective Shield for Individuals and Scaffolding for Status Rise*.

3 Another, though arguable, dimension of infrastructural familialism involves communal and national sociopolitical allegiances based upon familially derived identities and interests – for instance, hometown-based political partisanship (reproducing regional rivalry politics), family-line-based legal citizenship (embodying hereditary ethnonational membership), and so forth (Chang, K. 2004).

4 It should be pointed out that South Koreans' private values about family relations, goals, and duties are highly complex and plural by closely reflecting dynamic historical and social conditions. About four main lines of family values have been identifiable: Confucian, instrumentalist, affectionate, and individualistic familialisms (see Chang, K. 2010a, ch. 2).

5 See Han, N. (1984), Cho and Ahn (1986), and Cho and Lee (1993) for succinct reviews of sociological family studies in Korea.

6 In this way, modern South Korea has become a neo-Confucian society, even without systematic political and/or cultural succession of Confucian norms and rules in formal arenas. This distinguishes South Korea from Southeast and West Asian societies respectively under formalized Buddhist and Islamic cultural-religious hegemony.

7 The exceptionally lengthy politico-civilizational stability of Korea, along with China, has been sustained by the relative solidity of egalitarian family farming as institutionalized by various versions of *gyunjeon* (equal land) (Kim, S. 1998).

8 Economists like Georgescu-Roegen (1960) explain the predominance of family farming in almost all late-developing countries in terms of maximized social employment and total product as opposed to individualized profit of

a capitalist production unit. Also, the Chayanovian characteristics of family-based peasantry (Chayanov 1986) have largely been relevant in Korea as well.

9 In this regard, Meillassoux (1981) argues that the familial mode of peasant production and reproduction as incorporated into the capitalist economy brings about a dual structure of capitalist expropriation.

10 See Task Force in Rural Policy for the New Economy Long-Term Plans, Republic of Korea (1995).

11 A large part of South Korea's globally noted household debt reflects the unwilling dependence of such self-employed people on consumer loans under most banks' reluctance to offer them favorable business loans (Kim, D. 2015).

12 A sort of endogamy within the *chaebol* community further reinforces the exclusive structure of corporate control with some interlocking effect, while exogamy with state elite families is sought when political protection of business interests is crucial (SED 1991).

13 As of 2018, South Korea's social expenditure accounted for only 11.1% of GDP, as compared to 20.1% among all OECD member countries combined ("OECD Data: Social expenditure – aggregated data"; https://stats.oecd.org/Index.aspx?DataSetCode=SOCX_AGG). The corresponding figures in earlier years were: 2.7% and 16.4% in 1990, 4.5% and 17.4% in 2000, 8.2% and 20.6% in 2010.

14 This is a key component of *developmental liberalism* as the developmental state's social policy paradigm. See Chang, K. (2019), *Developmental Liberalism in South Korea*, Chapter 2.

15 In this sense, the liberal state of early industrial capitalism was *pro-industrial liberal*, if not developmental liberal. This trait would be revitalized in the neoliberal era in terms of family value debates (Somerville 1992).

16 It is no coincidence that the Asian value debate has been most strongly staged in societies that used to be governed under the (successful) developmental state regimes – Singapore, Taiwan, Malaysia as well as South Korea. For instance, Singapore has moved as far as to enact the "filial piety" law, whereas South Korea has implemented the same policy line in various indirect ways (i.e. applying a strict means test for adult children before providing welfare benefits for their aged parents). A political discussion of the filial piety law did take place in South Korea in 1996, but its state (after democratization) has not been as authoritative as the Singaporean counterpart in social policy (Park, K. 2007). A potential societal backlash has prevented any further political move for the morality-based welfare law. Nonetheless, the Asian value debate seemed tantamount to the family value debate in the Anglo-American West under neoliberalism in that both ideological drives were meant to articulate many social problems accompanying industrial or financial capitalism as private responsibilities (Chang, K. 1997) and thereby reinforce the conservative pro-capitalist social order and political economy.

17 Relatedly, Samuel Preston argues that the family-reliant Japanese welfare system has been much less costly and more effective than the separate institution-based American welfare system (Preston and Kono 1988). Even in contemporary China, liberal economic reform came to necessitate a central role of each private family in providing material as well as emotional relief for various needy groups (Chang, K. 1992).

18 As detailed in *Developmental Liberalism in South Korea* (Chang, K. 2019), the developmentally induced liberal approach to social policy, *developmental liberalism*, has various consistent features: namely, depoliticization/technocratization/developmental obfuscation of social policy; developmental cooptation of social policy constituencies; state-business entrepreneurial merge and direct state engagement in labor relations; familial reconstitution of social citizenship; welfare pluralism and demobilization of civil society. In a manner of speaking, developmental cooptation of ordinary citizens and familial reconstitution of their social citizenship constitute two sides of a coin: as the state has attempted to concentrate its resources in economic development (and minimize social expenditure) and make a maximum proportion of citizens participate in and benefit from it, the citizenry have been exhorted to accept full responsibility for social protection and reproduction of their own family members, as epitomized in the public slogan of "family protection first, social welfare later" (*seongajeongboho, husahoebokji*).

19 See Kim, K. (2017), Han, S. (2020), and Lew, S. (2013) for various accounts of the importance of Confucian culture in South Korean development. See Park, H. (2014) for the Confucian modernization discourse in conjunction with the "multiple modernities" perspective.

20 This tendency among young South Korean women was analyzed as "individualization without individualism" (Chang and Song 2010).

21 According to Davies and Mehta (2013), educationalization is defined as "the way in which practices, processes, and forms associated with schooling increasingly penetrate other social spheres, as well as the ways in which formal schooling is assigned more responsibility for social problems that originate in those spheres." Also see Depaepe (2008), Depaepe and Smeyers (2008), etc.

22 As shown earlier in Table 5.1, as of 2018, 69.57% of those aged 25–34 in South Korea had tertiary education, far ahead of the next group of OECD member countries such as Russia (62.66%), Canada (61.75%), and Japan (60.73%). The OECD average was only 44.48%.

23 According to *Education at a Glance: OECD Indicators*, the private share of the public educational expenses in South Korea was consistently the highest in the 2000s among all member countries of the OECD, while the recent demographic shrinkage of its youth population has gradually but slightly lowered such ranking (OECD 2001–2019).

24 In a survey by the ROK Ministry of Health and Welfare, 49 percent of youth aged 12–17 years complained of sleep shortage, all due to study burdens (*YTN*, August 25, 2019; https://www.ytn.co.kr/_ln/0103_20190825222424 2005).

25 Relatedly, while not formally documented in terms of public statistics, South Koreans' educationally caused stress, either as current students or as former students currently affected by their previous educational (under)achievements, may easily be the world's worst. For instance, as their biggest regret in life, many adults indicate "not having been able to learn" (by attending school), "not having studied hard as student," and so forth.

26 In an implicit comparison to *chaebol* (family-controlled business conglomerates in South Korea), many family-controlled private schools have been derogatorily called *jokbeolsahak*. The Ministry of Education has

been subjected to wide intellectual and media criticism about chronic corruption in conjunction with its under-the-table endorsement of private schools' practical profit-seeking. See Chung, D. (2017) on the case of Sangji University.

27 Accordingly, most teachers' colleges have required very high levels of credentials and exam scores from applicants, who are increasingly women.

28 For instance, see "Education pledges that should be presented by the presidential candidates" (*DTNews* 24, April 18, 2017) on the last presidential election in 2017.

29 This policy direction has been steadfastly reinforced under the current Moon Jae-In government.

30 It was Rhyu Si-min, a minister of welfare in the Roh Moo-Hyun government, who officially promoted "the social investment state" as a supposedly new approach in social welfare. Unfortunately, his ministry term was only about fifteen months, leaving no significant impact in that direction.

31 This tendency was analyzed as *defamiliation* in my earlier work (Chang, K. 2010a, ch. 8).

9 The Demographic Configuration of Compressed Modernity

1 Another scheme for institutionalizing basic social citizenship during the U.S. military occupation period was the almost instantaneous establishment of primary public education throughout the country (Seth 2002).

2 The figures for 2010 and 2019 are the respective proportions of farm household population.

3 See Jun, K. (1996) for an illuminating account of urban migrants' adaptive demographic behavior based upon life history data. On the other hand, the maintenance of universal and stable marriage into the urbanized period, coupled with socially inclusionary economic growth, should be seen as a crucial basis for sustained population growth.

4 Ochiai (2010), after comparing Japan to South Korea and other late developed societies in terms of the relative durations of this stable period, concludes that Japan's demographic transitions have been "semi-compressed" as compared to the "compressed" experiences of South Korea, etc.

5 Above all, South Korea's rapid integration with China and other populous Asian economies has fundamentally redefined the sociodemographic basis of South Korean capitalism, setting a regionally based path for quasi-Lewisian industrialization in which industrial capital, instead of rural labor, has transnationally migrated in order to utilize much cheaper labor forces and directly capture consumers in other countries. Within the country, as carefully observed by Kong, T. (2012), the industrial exigencies of technological catch-up and sectoral upgrading have been embodied in existing human resources (i.e. employees) to a much less extent than has been the case in Germany, Japan, etc.

6 Socially speaking, the crisis-accelerated restructuring of the South Korean economy has been both postindustrial and post-developmental in that the rapid evaporation (or overseas relocation) and casualization of industrial employment, despite the continuing state insistence on developmental governance, have implied practical disenfranchisement of increasing numbers of

ordinary South Koreans from what may be called *developmental citizenship* (Chang, K. 2012b).

7 For various national situations of lowest-low fertility in Asia, see *Ultra-Low Fertility in Pacific Asia: Trends, Causes and Policy Issues*, edited by Gavin Jones, Paulin Tay Straughan, and Angelique Chan (2009). Peter McDonald's (2009) comparative appraisal of Asian fertility in this book is particularly useful.

8 Park Eun-Tae, the chair of the 2013 IUSSP Congress, was quoted by *Munhwailbo* as warning that the South Korean population would be halved by 2060 unless special measures are taken (www.munhwa.co.kr, June 27, 2013).

9 The striking prevalence of elderly suicides even made a *New York Times* headline ("As Families Change, Korea's Elderly Are Turning to Suicide") in its international affairs section (February 17, 2013).

10 Japan has often been looked at by South Korean media as a precursor to these trends. For instance, *MBC*, "The Dark Side of Aging in Japan, 'Killing by Illness Caregiver' – More Than 236 Cases for 10 Years" (May 18, 2012).

11 Male workers' mishaps frequently had a chain effect on female workers, who were asked to sacrifice first in labor reshuffling (Chang, K. 2019, ch. 3). However, the proportion of female workers at each workplace was generally low, so such gendered buffering was in no sense significant.

12 Kim, D. (2005) argues that the second fertility transition in South Korea began from 1985. While I do not disagree, it is important to acknowledge the particular velocity of fertility decline since the "IMF economic crisis."

13 I addressed this dilemma of South Korean families in terms of *risk family* (Chang, K. 2011), as compared to Ulrich Beck's (1992) "risk society." Relatedly, perhaps a new theory of intergenerational and inter-gender risk flows could be developed systematically. See Ochiai (2011) who extends this perspective to comparatively address the broader Asian situation in terms of "unsustainability" of familialist social practices and state policies.

14 This social intransigence is clearly evidenced by the still widespread social hostility and governmental indifference to *mihonmo* (unmarried mothers) (Kim et al. 2012). South Korean demographers occasionally indicate the importance of out-of-wedlock births in sustaining European fertility and hint at the necessity for a similar change in South Korea. However, the fundamental sociocultural nature of such non-marital or post-marital fertility has not been carefully analyzed or discussed yet.

15 According to Lee et al. (2011), 34 percent of all households were categorized as such.

16 This is part of the broader social phenomenon I describe as *unbalanced family nucleation* (Chang, K. 2010a, ch. 2).

17 According to an international social survey publicized in early 2011, South Korea differed from all other countries covered in the survey in terms of the unusually high proportion of women who felt unhappiest in their middle age (*Chosun Ilbo*, January 14, 2011).

18 In these court cases, most aged parents have sadly lost their suits due to the ad hoc nature of their contentions (*SBS*, April 20, 2013).

19 Besides, the intra-generation inequalities in income and wealth are incomparably higher among the elderly population than among any other age group

(Sohn, B. 2009). This reflects the extremely class-divisive nature of the developmental economic order and the blunt political neglect or suppression of social securities, particularly with regard to old age, since the early years of capitalist industrialization.

20 It was 47 in 1947 (*MBC*, August 29, 2008).

21 As explained earlier, in Chapter 6, another dimension of particularization is to exclude foreign guest workers from the multicultural family support policy (Seol, D. 2014).

10 The Post-Compressed Modern Condition

1 As a highly interesting development in this respect, YouTube has become extremely popular among aged conservative activists in South Korea because they can conveniently create, copy, and circulate various contents of their particular preference and ideology on this digital platform (*Kyunghyang Shinmun* 2018).

2 This contradiction was acutely revealed in the Park Geun-Hye government's "*munhwagye* (culture world) blacklist" incident, by which her key political appointees as well as herself ended up in court with prison terms. The blacklist of (politically) critical or unfriendly figures in culture was complemented by a practical *whitelist* of collaborative figures in culture (Jung, I. 2017).

3 See Chan, Zinn, and Wang, eds. (2016), *New Life Courses, Social Risks and Social Policy in East Asia*, and Ochiai and Aoi, eds. (2014), *Transformation of the Intimate and the Public in Asian Modernity*, as exemplary collaborative studies in this regard.

4 Among other trends, such differences are particularly pronounced in the way each East Asian society and its people have relied upon what is analyzed as *infrastructural familialism* in Chapter 8 in this book with mutually distinct trends of individualization (Chang and Song 2010).

5 See Turner and Khondker (2010), *Globalization in East and West*, as a particularly careful study of globalization in this respect.

REFERENCES

Abelmann, Nancy. 1997. "Women's Class Mobility and Identities in South Korea: A Gendered, Transnational, Narrative Approach." *Journal of Asian Studies* 56(2): 398–420.

— 2003. *The Melodrama of Mobility: Women, Talk, and Class in Contemporary South Korea*. Honolulu: University of Hawaii Press.

— 2004. "Class and Cosmopolitan Striving: Mothers' Management of English Education in South Korea." *Anthropological Quarterly* 77(4): 645–672.

Amsden, Alice. 1989. *Asia's Next Giant: South Korea and Late Industrialization*. New York: Oxford University Press.

Appadurai, Arjun. 1990. "Disjuncture and Difference in the Global Cultural Economy." *Theory, Culture and Society* 7(2/3): 295–310.

Apter, David E. 1965. *The Politics of Modernizaton*. Chicago: University of Chicago Press.

Ashcroft, Bill, Gareth Griffiths, and Helen Tiffin. 2002. *The Empire Writes Back: Theory and Practice in Post-Colonial Literatures*, 2nd edn. New York: Routledge.

Badie, Bertrand. 2000. *The Imported State: The Westernization of the Political Order*. Stanford: Stanford University Press.

Bae, Dawk Mahn. 2013. "Hereditary Succession of South Korean Churches: The Distorted History" (in Korean). *Theology and Mission* 43: 69–102.

Baik, Peter. 2012. "South Korean Cinema and the Experience of Compressed Modernity." Presented at the Conference on "World Cinemas, Global Networks" at the Center for International Education, University of Wisconsin-Milwaukee, April 29, 2012.

Baran, Paul A. 1957. *The Political Economy of Growth*. New York: Monthly Review Press.

Baudrillard, Jean. [1981]1994. *Simulacra and Simulation*. Ann Arbor: University of Michigan Press.

Bauman, Zigmund. 2000. *Liquid Modernity*. London: Polity.

Beck, Ulrich. [1984] 1992. *Risk Society: Towards a New Modernity*. London: Sage.

— 1994. "The Reinvention of Politics: Towards a Theory of Reflexive Modernization." Beck, Ulrich, Anthony Giddens and Scott Lash, *Reflexive*

Modernization: Politics, Tradition and Aesthetics in the Modern Social Order, pp. 1–55. Stanford: Stanford University Press.

— 1999. *World Risk Society*. Cambridge: Polity.

— 2002. "The Silence of Words and Political Dynamics in the World Risk Society." *Logos* 1(4): 1–18.

— 2006. "Living in the World Risk Society." *Economy and Society* 35(3): 329–345.

Beck, Ulrich and Edgar Grande. 2007. *Cosmopolitan Europe*. Cambridge: Polity.

— 2010. "Varieties of Second Modernity: The Cosmopolitan Turn in Social and Political Theory and Research." *British Journal of Sociology* 61(3): 409–443. Beck, Ulrich and Elisabeth Beck-Gernsheim. 2002. *Individualization: Institutionalized Individualism and Its Social and Political Consequences*. London: Sage.

Beck, Ulrich and Natan Sznaider. 2006. "Unpacking Cosmopolitanism for the Social Sciences: A Research Agenda." *British Journal of Sociology* 57(1): 381–403.

Beck, Ulrich, Anthony Giddens, and Scott Lash. 1994. *Reflexive Modernization: Politics, Tradition and Aesthetics in the Modern Social Order*. Stanford: Stanford University Press.

Beck, Ulrich, Wolfgang Bonss, and Christoph Lau. 2003. "The Theory of Reflexive Modernization: Problematic, Hypotheses and Research." *Theory, Culture and Society* 20(2): 1–33.

Bloch, Ernst. [1935]1991. *Heritage of Our Times*. Berkeley: University of California Press.

Brun, Ellen and Jacques Hersh. 1976. *Socialist Korea: A Case Study in the Strategy of Economic Development*. New York: Monthly Review Press.

Byeon, Chang-Gu. 2012. "Korea's Sun-bi Spirits and the Realization of a Just Society: Focusing on the Behaviors of Politicians and Polifessors" (in Korean). *National Thought* 6(4): 131–156.

Byun, Yong-Chan, Kim Dong Hoe, and Lee Song Hee. 2010. *A Study of the Relationship between Marriage Behavior Changes and Fertility* (in Korean). Seoul: Korea Institute for Health and Social Affairs.

Caldwell, John C. 1982. *Theory of Fertility Decline*. London: Academic Press.

Chakrabarty, Dipesh. 1992. "Provincializing Europe: Postcoloniality and the Critique of History." *Cultural Studies* 6(3): 337–357.

— 2000. *Provincializing Europe: Postcolonial Thought and Historical Difference*. Princeton: Princeton University Press.

Chan, Anita and Richard Madsen. 1984. *Chen Village: A Recent History of a Peasant Community in Mao's China*. Berkeley: University of California Press.

Chan, Raymond, Jens Zinn, and Lih-Rong Wang, eds. 2016. *New Life Courses, Social Risks and Social Policy in East Asia*. London: Routledge.

Chang, Ha-Joon. 1994. *The Political Economy of Industrial Policy*. Basingstoke: Palgrave Macmillan.

Chang, Ha-Sung. 2014. *Capitalism in Korea: Beyond Economic Democratization, to a Just Economy* (in Korean). Seoul: Heybooks.

Chang, Kyung-Sup. 1992. "China's Rural Reform: The State and Peasantry in Constructing a Macro-Rationality." *Economy and Society* 21(4): 430–452.

— 1996. "Birth and Wealth in Peasant China: Surplus Population, Limited Supplies of Family Labour, and Economic Reform." Alice Goldstein and Wang Feng, eds. *China: The Many Facets of Demographic Change*, pp. 21–46. Boulder: Westview Press.

— 1997. "The Neo-Confucian Right and Family Politics in South Korea: The Nuclear Family as an Ideological Construct." *Economy and Society* 26(1): 22–42.

— 1999. "Compressed Modernity and Its Discontents: South Korean Society in Transition." *Economy and Society* 28(1): 30–55.

— 2004. "The Anti-Communitarian Family? Everyday Conditions of Authoritarian Politics in South Korea." Chua Beng Huat, ed. *Communitarian Politics in Asia*, pp. 57–77. London: Routledge.

— 2005. "*Ruralism* in China: Reinterpretation of Post-Collective Development." *International Journal of Asian Studies* 2(2): 291–307.

— 2009. *Family, Life Course, and Political Economy: The Micro-Foundations of Compressed Modernity* (in Korean). Seoul: Changbi.

— 2010a. *South Korea under Compressed Modernity: Familial Political Economy in Transition*. London: Routledge.

— 2010b. "The Second Modern Condition? Compressed Modernity as Internalized Reflexive Cosmopolitisation." *British Journal of Sociology* 61(3): pp. 444–464.

— 2011. "Developmental State, Welfare State, Risk Family: Developmental Liberalism and Social Reproduction Crisis in South Korea" (in Korean). *Korea Social Policy Review* 18(3): 63–90.

— 2012a. "Different Beds, One Dream? State–Society Relationships and Citizenship Regimes in East Asia." Chang Kyung-Sup, and Bryan S. Turner, eds. *Contested Citizenship in East Asia: Developmental Politics, National Unity, and Globalization*, pp. 62–85. London: Routledge.

— 2012b. "Developmental Citizenship in Perspective: The South Korean Case and Beyond." Chang Kyung-Sup and Bryan S. Turner, eds. *Contested Citizenship in East Asia: Developmental Politics, National Unity, and Globalization*, pp. 182–202. London: Routledge.

— 2012c. "Predicaments of Neoliberalism in the Post-Developmental Liberal Context." Chang Kyung-Sup, Ben Fine, and Linda Weiss, eds. *Developmental Politics in Transition: The Neoliberal Era and Beyond*, pp. 71–90. Basingstoke: Palgrave Macmillan.

— 2013. "Particularistic Multiculturalism: Citizenship Contradictions of Marriage Cosmopolit(an)ization." Proceedings of the International Conference on "Life and Humanity in Late Modern Transformation: Beyond East and West," organized by SNU Center for Social Sciences, Korea Institute for Health and Social Affairs, and Korean Sociological Association, May 30–31, 2013, Seoul National University.

— 2014. "Asianization of Asia: Asia's Integrative Ascendance through a European Aperture." *European Societies* 16(3): 1–6.

— 2016a. "Compressed Modernity in South Korea: Constitutive Dimensions, Historical Conditions, and Systemic Mechanisms." Youna Kim, ed. *The Routledge Handbook of Korean Culture and Society: A Global Approach*, pp. 31–47. London: Routledge.

— 2016b. "Financialization of Poverty: Proletarianizing the Financial Crisis in Post-Developmental Korea." *Research in Political Economy* 31: 109–134.

211

— 2017a. "Compressed Modernity." *The Wiley Blackwell Encyclopedia of Social Theory, Volume I.* Hoboken: Wiley Blackwell (https://doi.org/10.1002/9781118430873.est0839).

— 2017b. "Reflexive Modernization." *The Wiley Blackwell Encyclopedia of Social Theory, Volumes IV.* Hoboken: Wiley Blackwell (https://doi.org/10.1002/9781118430873.est0835).

— 2017c. "China as a Complex Risk Society: Risk Components of Post-Socialist Compressed Modernity." *Temporalités*, number 26 (Special Issue: "'Compressed Modernity' and Chinese Temporalities") (https://journals.open-edition.org/temporalites/3810).

— 2018. *The End of Tomorrow? Familial Liberalism and Social Reproduction Crisis* (in Korean). Seoul: Jipmundang.

— 2019. *Developmental Liberalism in South Korea: Formation, Degeneration, and Transnationalization.* Basingstoke: Palgrave Macmillan.

— 2020. "Developmental Pluralism and Stratified Developmental Citizenship: An Alternative Perspective on Chinese Post-Socialism." *Citizenship Studies* 24(7), 856–870.

— 2022. *Transformative Citizenship in South Korea: Politics of Transformative Contributory Rights.* New York: Palgrave Macmillan.

Chang, Kyung-Sup and Song Min-Young. 2010. "The Stranded Individualizer under Compressed Modernity: South Korean Women in Individualization without Individualism." *British Journal of Sociology* 61(3): 540–565.

Chang, Kyung-Sup, Chin Meejung, Sung Miai, and Lee Jaerim. 2015. "Institutionalized Familialism in South Korean Society: Focusing on Income Security, Education, and Care" (in Korean). *Journal of the Korean Family Studies Association* 27(3): 1–38.

Chayanov, A. V. (1986) [1925] *Theory of the Peasant Economy.* Madison: University of Wisconsin Press.

Chin, Meejung. 2013. "Portrait of Unmarried One-Person Households in Early Adulthood: Delayed Transition or Achieved Individualization." Proceedings of the International Conference on "Life and Humanity in Late Modern Transformation: Beyond East and West," organized by SNU Center for Social Sciences, Korea Institute for Health and Social Affairs, and Korean Sociological Association, May 30–31, 2013, Seoul National University.

Cho, Dong-Sung. 1991. *A Study of Korean Chaebol* (in Korean). Seoul: Maeil Economic Daily.

Cho, Myung-Rae. 2003. "The Trend and Prospect of Urbanization: The Past, Present, and Future of South Korean Cities" (in Korean). *Economy and Society* 60: 10–39.

Cho, Sung-Nam and Dong-Won Lee. 1993. "Towards Relevant Scholarship: Family Sociology in South Korea." *Current Sociology* 41(1): 25–39.

Cho, Seok-Gon and Oh Yu-Seok. 2003. "The Formation of the Preconditions of Compressed Growth: Focusing on the Preparation of the Accumulation System of South Korean Capitalism in the 1950s" (in Korean). *Trend and Prospect* 59: 258–302.

Cho, Uhn and Ahn Byoung-chol. 1986. "The Sociology of the Family: Recent Trends in Research and Theoretical Orientation" (in Korean). *Korean Journal of Sociology* 20(2): 103–118.

Choe, Hong-Ki. 1991. "Confucianism and Family" (in Korean). *Journal of the Korean Family Studies Association* 2: 207–228.

Choi, Hyaeweol. 2009. "'Wise Mother, Good Wife': A Transcultural Discursive Construct in Modern Korea." *Journal of Korean Studies* 14(1): 1–33.

Choi, Jang-Jip. 2002. *Democracy after Democratization: Crisis and Conservative Origin of Korea's Democracy* (in Korean). Seoul: Humanitas.

Choi, Jongryul. 2019. *Sociology of Show: How South Korean Society Reflects on Itself* (in Korean). Seoul: Maybook.

Choi, Sun-Young. 2020. "Life Course Rearrangement and Marriage Behavior Changes of Korean Women" (in Korean). PhD dissertation, Department of Sociology, Seoul National University.

Choi, Sun-Young and Chang Kyung-Sup. 2004. "The Modern Reconstruction of the Sexual Division of Labor: Changes of 'Korean Women's Ex-Employment during Family Formation'" (in Korean). *Social Research* 2(2): 173–203.

— 2016. "The Material Contradictions of Proletarian Patriarchy in South Korea's Condensed Capitalist Industrialization: The Instability in the Working Life Course of Male Breadwinners and Its Familial Ramifications." Raymond Chan, Jens Zinn, and Lih-Rong Wang, eds. *New Life Courses, Social Risks and Social Policy in East Asia*, pp. 149–166. London: Routledge.

Chosunilbo (www.chosun.com).

Chu, Byeong-Wan. 2011. *Multicultural Society and Global Leader* (in Korean). Seoul: Daegyo.

Chua, Beng Huat. 2012. *Structure, Audience and Soft Power in East Asian Pop Culture*. Hong Kong: Hong Kong University Press.

— 2017. *Liberalism Disavowed: Communitarianism and State Capitalism in Singapore*. Singapore: National University of Singapore Press.

Chung, Duck-Cho. 1991. "Korean Family Welfare Policy" (in Korean). *Korean Family Welfare Policy and Elderly Problem* (Proceedings of the First Seminar of the Korea Family Welfare Policy Institute), pp. 5–42.

Chung, Dae-Hwa. 2017. *Sangji University Democratization Struggle 40 Years: Lively Records of the Struggle and Experimentation for the Future of South Korean Private Schools* (in Korean). Seoul: Hanul.

Cumings, Bruce. 1981. *The Origins of the Korean War: Liberation and Emergence of Separate Regimes, 1945–1947*. Princeton: Princeton University Press.

— 1984. "The Origins and Development of the Northeast Asian Political Economy: Industrial Sectors, Product Cycles, and Political Consequences," *International Organization* 38(1): 1–40.

— 1987. "The Legacy of Japanese Colonialism in Korea." Ramon H. Myers, and Mark R. Peattie, eds. *The Japanese Colonial Empire, 1895–1945*, pp. 478–496. Princeton: Princeton University Press.

— 1997. *Korea's Place in the Sun*. New York: Norton.

— 1998. "The Korean Crisis and the End of 'Late' Development." *New Left Review* 231: 43–72.

— 2005. "State Building in Korea: Continuity and Crisis." Matthew Lange, and Dietrich Rueschemeyer, eds. *States and Development: Historical Antecedents of Stagnation and Advance*, pp. 211–236. New York: Palgrave Macmillan.

Dahrendort, Ralf. 1959. *Class and Class Conflict in Industrial Society*. Stanford: Stanford University Press.

Danuri (http://www.liveinkorea.kr/kr/), January 11, 2013.

Davies, Scott, and Jal Mehta. 2013. "Educationalization." James Ainsworth, ed., *Sociology of Education: An A-to-Z Guide*. London: SAGE (https://sk.sagepub.com/reference/sociology-of-education/n127.xml).

213

Depaepe, Marc, ed. 2008. *Educational Research: The Educationalization of Social Problems*. Berlin: Springer.

Depaepe, Marc, and Paul Smeyers. 2008. "Educationalization as an Ongoing Modernization Process." *Education Theory* 58(4): 379–389.

Dirlik, Arif. 2003. "Global Modernity: Modernity in an Age of Global Capitalism." *European Journal of Social Theory* 6(3): 275–292.

— 2004. "Spectres of the Third World: Global Modernity and the End of the Three Worlds." *Third World Quarterly* 25(1): 131–148.

Dong-A Ilbo (www.donga.com).

Dong-A Science (www.dongascience.com).

Donzelot, Jacques. 1979. *The Policing of Families*. New York: Pantheon.

Dore, Ronald. 1973. *British Factory, Japanese Factory: The Origins of National Diversity in Industrial Relations*. Berkeley: University of California Press.

DTNews 24. 2017. "Education Pledges That Should Be Presented by the Presidential Candidates" (in Korean), April 18, 2017.

e-Narajipyo. 2020a. "The Number and Population of Agricultural Households" (http://www.index.go.kr/potal/main/EachDtlPageDetail.do?idx_cd=2745).

— 2020b. "The Population Structure by Age and Gender" (http://www.index.go.kr/potal/main/EachDtlPageDetail.do?idx_cd=1010).

— 2020c. "The Trends in Birth and Death" (http://www.index.go.kr/potal/main/EachDtlPageDetail.do?idx_cd=1011#quick_05).

EBS. 2020. " Multicultural Mother-in-Law and Daughter-in-Law Biographic Notes" (Damunhwa Gobuyeoljeon; https://home.ebs.co.kr/gobu/main).

Eckert, Carter J. 2016. *Park Chung Hee and Modern Korea: The Roots of Militarism, 1866–1945*. Cambridge: Harvard University Press.

Edaily (www.edaily.co.kr).

Eisenstadt, Shmuel. 2000. "Multiple Modernities," *Daedalus* 129(1): 1–29.

Eun, Ki-Soo. 2013. "Pathways to Post-Patriarchal Society: Global Convergence of Gender (Non-)Preference and East Asian Particularities." Proceedings of the International Conference on "Life and Humanity in Late Modern Transformation: Beyond East and West," organized by SNU Center for Social Sciences, Korea Institute for Health and Social Affairs, and Korean Sociological Association, May 30–31, 2013, Seoul National University.

Evans, Peter. 1995. *Embedded Autonomy: States and Industrial Transformation*. Princeton: Princeton University Press.

Evans, Peter, Dietrich Rueschemeyer, and Theda Skocpol, eds. 1985. *Bringing the State Back in*. Cambridge: Cambridge University Press.

Fanon, Frantz. [1963]2004. *The Wretched of the Earth*. New York: Grove Press.

Financial News (http://www.fnnews.com).

Fine, Ben. 2012. "Neo-Liberalism in Retrospect? – It's Financialization, Stupid." Chang Kyung-Sup, Ben Fine, and Linda Weiss, eds. *Developmental Politics in Transition: The Neoliberal Era and Beyond*, pp. 51–69. Basingstoke: Palgrave Macmillan.

Frank, Andre Gunder. 1967. *Capitalism and Underdevelopment in Latin America: Historical Studies of Chile and Brazil*. New York: Monthly Review Press.

Geertz, Clifford. 1973. *The Interpretation of Cultures*. New York: Basic Books.

Georgescu-Roegen, Nicholas. 1960. "Economic Theory and Agrarian Economics." *Oxford Economic Papers* 12(1): 1–40.

Giddens, Anthony. 1990. *The Consequences of Modernity*. Stanford: Stanford University Press.

Gilloch, Graeme. 1997. *Myth and Metropolis: Walter Benjamin and the City*. Cambridge: Polity.

Goode, Willam. 1963. *World Revolution and Family Patterns*. New York: Free Press.

Gye, Jae-Gwang. 2010. "Influence of Confucian Culture on the Formation of the Korean Church Leadership: Focus on the Influence of Confucian Authoritarianism" (in Korean). *Theology and Practice* 22(2010/2): 77–106.

Ha, Seung-Wu. 2011. "Samsung Republic, Are We Citizens?" (in Korean). *Silcheon Munhak* 103: 163–172.

Hahm, In-Hee. 2006. "The Korean War, Families and the Women's Multi-layerd Modernity" (in Korean). *Society and Theory* 9: 159–189.

Han, Hong-Gu. 2002. "Has Korean Civil Society Had History?" (in Korean). *Citizen and World* 1(2002/2): 91–110.

Han, Jin-Geum. 2010. "A Study in Technical Assistance Training Program of U.S. Aid Agency in 1950s" (in Korean). *Korean History Studies* 56: 437–495.

Han, Jun-Sang. 1996. *The Youth Issue* (in Korean). Seoul: Yonsei University Press.

— 2003. *The Recollection of Modern South Korean Education* (in Korean). Seoul: Korea Academic Information.

Han, Nam-Je. 1984. "The Outcomes and Problems of Family Research" (in Korean). *Korean Journal of Sociology* 18(2): 46–70.

Han, Sang-Jin. 2009. "The Dynamics of Middle-Class Politics in Korea: Why and How Do the Middling Grassroots Differ from the Propertied Mainstream?" (in Korean). *Korean Journal of Sociology* 43(3): 1–19.

— 2020. *Confucianism and Reflexive Modernity: Bringing Community Back to Human Rights in the Age of Global Risk Society*. Leiden: Brill.

Hankiss, Elemer. 1988. "The "Second Society": Is There an Alternative Social Model Emerging in Contemporary Hungary?" *Social Research* 55(1/2): 13–42.

Hankookilbo (www.hankookilbo.com).

Hankyoreh (www.hani.co.kr).

Hao, Lingxing. 2013. "Compressed Modernity in the Life Course of a Cohort of Taiwanese Youth: Teen Sex and First Marriage." Presented at the Taiwan Youth Project Conference, Academia Sinica, Taipei.

Hareven, Tamara. 1982. *Family Time and Industrial Time: The Relationship Between the Family and Work in a New England Industrial Community*. New York: Cambridge University Press.

Harvey, David. 1980. *The Condition of Postmodernity*. Oxford: Blackwell.

Henry, Paget and Emile Walter. 1995. "Comparing Peripheral Cultural Systems: India and the Caribbean." *Caribbean Quarterly* 41(1): 1–24.

— 2020. "After Neoliberalism and Post-structuralism: Postcolonial Studies, Diaspora, and Globalization." Ashmita Khasnabish, ed. *Postcoloniality, Globalization, and Diaspora: What's Next?*, pp. 27–50. Lanham: Lexington Books.

Hobsbawm, Eric John. 1994. *The Age of Extremes: The Short Twentieth Century, 1914–1991*. London: Penguin.

Hobsbawm, Eric John and Terence O. Ranger, eds. 1992. *The Invention of Tradition*. Cambridge: Cambridge University Press.

215

Hochschild, Arlie. 1990. *The Second Shift: Working Parents and the Revolution at Home*. New York: Avon Books.

Hong, Sae Young and Gum Ja Kim. 2010. "A Study of the Acculturation Meaning among Chinese-Chosun Residential Care Attendants in Long-Term Care Settings" (in Korean). *Journal of the Korea Gerontological Society* 30(4): 1263–1280.

Hughes, Theodore. 2014. *Literature and Film in Cold War South Korea: Freedom's Frontier*. New York: Columbia University Press.

Humphries, J. 1982. "Class Struggle and the Persistence of the Working-Class Family." Anthony Giddens, and David Held, eds. *Classes, Power, and Conflict*, pp. 470–490. Berkeley: University of California Press.

Huntington, Samuel. 1968. *Political Order in Changing Societies*. New Haven: Yale University Press.

Hwang, Yeojung. 2013. "The Stress of Students" (in Korean). ROK National Statistical Office, ed. *Korean Social Trends 2013*, pp. 119–126.

Hyundai Economic Research Institute. 2017. "A Questionaire Survey on Citizens' Perception about the Class Upward Mobility Ladder" (in Korean). Special survey report.

Im, Dong-Jin and Park Jin-Kyeong. 2012. "An Empirical Study of Policy Participants' Attitude and Preference on the Multiculturalism and the Multicultural Policy in Korea: Focused on Public Servants, Service Providers, Experts" (in Korean). *Journal of the Korean Association of Policy Sciences* 16(2): 29–62.

Im, Heui-Sook. 2000. "The Hereditary Succession Problem of South Korean Churches and Its Feminist Theological Critique" (in Korean). *Korean Feminist Theology* 43(2000/9): 93–107.

Isin, Engin F. and Bryan S. Turner. 2007. "Investigating Citizenship: An Agenda for Citizenship Studies." *Citizenship Studies* 11(1): 5–17.

Iwabuchi, Koichi. 2002. *Recentering Globalization: Popular Culture and Japanese Transnationalism*. Duke: Duke University Press.

— 2018. "Nostalgia for a (Different) Asian Modernity: Media Consumption of 'Asia' in Japan." *Genius* (https://genius.com/Koichi-iwabuchi-nostalgia-for-a-different-asian-modernity-media-consumption-of-asia-in-japan-annotated).

Jackson, Stevi. 2015. "Modernity/Modernities and Personal Life: Reflections on Some Theoretical Lacunae." *Korean Journal of Sociology* 49(3): 1–20.

Jameson, Fredric and Masao Miyoshi, eds. 1998. *The Cultures of Globalization*. Durham: Duke University Press.

Jang, Wonho and Youngsun Kim. 2013. "Envisaging the Sociocultural Dynamics of K-Pop: Time/Space Hybridity, Red Queen's Race, and Cosmopolitan Striving." *Korea Journal* 53(4): 83–106.

Jeon, Jae-Ho. 1999. "Nationalism in the Park Chung-Hee Regime (1961–1979): The Change of Discourse and its Cause" (in Korean). *Journal of the Korean Political Science Association* 32(4): 89–109.

Jeong, Jin-sang. 1995. "The Dismantlement of the Social Estates during the Liberation Periods: A Case Study of Two Villages in Jinyang-gun" (in Korean). *Social Science Research* 13(1): 331–351.

Ji, Joo Hyoung. 2011. *The Origin and Formation of Neoliberalism in South Korea* (in Korean). Seoul: Book World.

Jones, Gavin, Paulin Tay Straughan, and Angelique Chan, eds. 2009. *Ultra-Low Fertility in Pacific Asia: Trends, Causes and Policy Issues*. London: Routledge.

216

Joo, Jeongsuk. 2011. "Transnationalization of Korean Popular Culture and the Rise of "Pop Nationalism" in Korea." *Journal of Popular Culture* 44(3): 489–504.

Joongang Ilbo (www.joins.com).

Jun, Kwang-Hee. 1996. "The Fertility Adaptation Process of Rural-to-Urban Migrant Residents: An Analysis of Life History Data" (in Korean). *Journal of Institute for Social Sciences* 7: 39–57.

Jung, In Sook. 2017. "The Ideology and Reality of Arm's Length Principle in Culture/Arts Funding Policy: Focused on the Blacklist Case" (in Korean). 54(3): 7–40.

Kang, Jiyeon and Nancy Abelmann. 2011. "The Domestication of South Korean Pre-College Study Abroad in the First Decade of the Millennium." *Journal of Korean Studies* 16(1): 89–118.

Kang, Myung Hun. 1996. *The Korean Business Conglomerate: Chaebol Then and Now*. Berkeley: Institute of Asian Studies, University of California.

Kang, Myung Koo. 1999. "Postmodern Consumer Culture without Postmodernity: Copying the Crisis of Signification." *Cultural Studies* 13(1): 18–33.

— 2011. "Compressed Modernization and the Formation of a Developmentalist Mentalite." Hyung A. Kim and Clark W. Sorensen, eds. *Reassessing the Park Chung Hee Era, 1961–1979: Development, Political Thought, Democracy, and Cultural Influence*, pp. 166–186. Seattle: University of Washington Press.

Kariya, Takehiko. 2013. *Education Reform and Social Class in Japan: The Emerging Incentive Divide*. London: Routledge.

KBS. 2020. "Six O'Clock My Home Village" (Yeoseotsi Naegohyang; http://program.kbs.co.kr/1tv/culture/sixhour/pc/index.html).

Keblinska, Julia. 2017. "Mediated Nostalgia: Touching the Past in *Reply 1994*." *Journal of Japanese and Korean Cinema* 9(2): 124–140.

Ki, Kwang-Seo. 2012. "A Study on Land Reform in South Korea during the Korean War" (in Korean). *Studies in Korean Early Modern and Contemporary History* 62: 7–32.

Kim, Bong-Hwan. 2009. "Career Guidance Tasks for Unbalanced Preferences of Youth for Certain Vocations" (in Korean). *Career Education Studies* 22(4): 63–83.

Kim, Chang-Nam. 2014. *Understanding of Popular Culture* (in Korean). Seoul Hanul Academy.

Kim, Chi-Wan. 2017. "Children's Education Prior to Old-Age Preparation? Old-Age Measure vs. Children's Education Expenses" (in Korean). *Life and Talk*, December 4, 2017 (https://www.lifentalk.com/1635).

Kim, Dokyun. 2015. "The Duality of Self-Employment Debt and Its Increase after the Exchange Crisis" (in Korean). *Economy and Society* 108: 73–107.

Kim, Dong-Choon. 1997. *National Division and Korean Society* (in Korean). Seoul: Yeoksabipyongsa.

— 2002. "Confucianism and Korean Familialism: Is Familialism a Product of Confucian Values?" (in Korean). *Economy and Society* 55: 93–118.

— 2018. "Anti-Communist Liberalism as an Origin of the Korean-Style Neo-Liberalism: Continuity of Anti-Communist and Developmental State to Neo-Liberalism" (in Korean). *Economy and Society* 118: 240–276.

— 2020. *South Koreans' Energy, Familialism: Family as Protective Shield for Individuals and Scaffolding for Status Rise* (in Korean). Seoul: Pieona.

Kim, Dong-No. 2007. "Colonial Modernity and Transformation of Peasant Movement during the Colonial Period" (in Korean). *Korean Journal of Sociology* 41(1): 194–220.

— 2010. "Nationalism and Political Strategy of Korean Political Leaders: A Comparison of Park Chung-hee and Kim Dae-jung" (in Korean). *Phenomenon and Recollection* 111(2010/9): 203–224.

Kim, Doo-Sub. 2005. "Theoretical Explanations of Rapid Fertility Decline in Korea." *Japanese Journal of Population* 3(1): 1–25.

Kim, Han-Sang. 2013. "Cold War and the Contested Identity Formation of Korean Filmmakers: On *Boxes of Death* and Kim Ki-yŏng's USIS Films." *Inter-Asia Cultural Studies* 14(4): 551–563.

Kim, Hee Joo, Jong Hee Kwon, and Hyeong Suk Choi. 2012. "A Case Study on Discrimination Experienced by Unmarried Mother" (in Korean). *Korean Journal of Family Welfare* 36: 121–155.

Kim, Hee Kyung. 2017. *The Strange Normal Family: Imagining Autonomous Individual and Open Community* (in Korean). Seoul: Dongasia.

Kim, Hung-Ju. 1992. "The Realities of Agricultural Labor and the Family Problems of Peasants at the Current Stage" (in Korean). *Rural Society* 2: 85–144.

Kim, Hyewon. 2018. "Domesticating Hedwig: Neoliberal Global Capitalism and Compression in South Korean Musical Theater." *Journal of Popular Culture* 51(2): 421–445.

Kim, Hyun-Sun. 2006. "National, Semi-National, and Non-National: The Principles and Process of Nation Formation in South Korea" (in Korean). *Social Research* 12: 77–106.

Kim, Hyun Mee. 2012. "The Emergence of the 'Multicultural Family' and Genderized Citizenship in South Korea." Chang Kyung-Sup, and Bryan S. Turner, eds. *Contested Citizenship in East Asia: Developmental Politics, National Unity, and Globalization*, pp. 203–217. London: Routledge.

— 2014. "The State and Migrant Women: Diverging Hopes in the Making of 'Multicultural Families'." Chang Kyung-Sup, ed. *South Korea in Transition: Politics and Culture of Citizenship*, pp. 147–160. London: Routledge.

Kim, Hyung-A. 2004. *Korea's Development under Park Chung Hee: Rapid Industrialization, 1961–79*. London: Routledge.

Kim, Jeongseop and Lee Junghae. 2017. "The Recent Reality of Farming Return and Village Return and Its Implications" (in Korean). *Rural Policy Focus*, number 151. Naju: Korea Rural Economic Institute.

Kim, Jongyoung. 2015. *The Ruled Ruler: Studying in the U.S. and the Birth of South Korean Elites* (in Korean). Seoul: Dolbegae.

— 2019. *Hybrid Oriental Medicine* (in Korean). Seoul: Dolbegae.

Kim, Ju-Hee. 2015. "Financialization of Korea's Sex Industry and the 'Securitization' Process of Women's Bodies" (in Korean). PhD dissertation in Department of Gender Studies, Ewha Womans' University.

Kim, Ju-Suk. 1994. *Woman and Family in the South Korean Countryside* (in Korean). Seoul: Hanul Academy.

Kim, Kyong-Dong. 2017. *Confucianism and Modernization in East Asia: Critical Reflections*. Basingstoke: Palgrave Macmillan.

Kim, Kyung-Il. 1992. *The History of Labor under Japanese Imperialism* (in Korean). Seoul: Changbi.

Kim, Myoung Soo. 2010. "Catch-up Economic Growth and Cultural Complexity in Korea" (in Korean). *Review of Culture and Economy* 13(2): 307–341.

— 2018. *The Cultural Origin of South Korean Economic Development: Catchup Development, Developmental State, and Cultural Hybridity* (in Korean). Seoul: Jipmundang.

Kim, Nora. 2012. "Multiculturalism and Politics of Belonging: The Puzzle of Multiculturalism in Korea." *Citizenship Studies* 16(1): 103–118.

Kim, Sang-Jo. 2007. "Samsung Republic: A Government over the Government Produced from the Financial Crisis" (in Korean). *Hwanghae Review* 56: 25–44.

Kim, Sang-Jun. 2003. "Yangbanization of the Entire Country: The Confucian Equalization Mechanism in Late Chosun" (in Korean). *Society and History* 63: 5–29.

— 2011. *Sweat of Mencius, Blood of the Sacred Kings: Confucian Civilization and Universal Human Values* (in Korean). Seoul: Acanet.

Kim, Seung-Kwon et al. 2010. *The 2009 National Survey Study of the Actual Conditions of Multicultural Families* (in Korean). Ministry of Health, Welfare, and Family, Ministry of Justice, Ministry of Gender Equality, and Korea Institute for Health and Social Affairs.

Kim, Seung Kuk. 2012. "East Asian Community as Hybridization: A Quest for East Asianism." Jan Nederveen Pieterse, and Jongtae Kim, eds. *Globalization and Development in East Asia*, pp. 98–116. London: Routledge.

Kim, Soo-Jung and Kim Eun Yi. 2008. "Media Discourse on Asian Women's International Marriage: The Korean Case" (in Korean). *Korean Journal of Journalism and Communication Studies* 43: 385–426.

Kim, Sung-Han. 1998. *A Study of China's Land Institution History: The Gyunjeonje in the Middle Age* (in Korean). Seoul: Sinseowon.

Kim, Sung-Kyung. 2017. "Juche (Self-Reliance) in North Korea." *The Wiley Blackwell Encyclopedia of Social Theory, Volume III*. Hoboken: Wiley Blackwell (https://doi.org/10.1002/9781118430873.est0820).

Kim, Sunhyuk. 2000. *The Politics of Democratization in Korea: The Role of Civil Society*. Pittsburgh: University of Pittsburgh Press.

Kim, Taekyoon. 2019. *Critical International Development Studies on Korea* (in Korean). Seoul: PKBoo.

Kim, Youna. 2013. "Korean Wave Pop Culture in the Global Internet Age: Why Popular? Why Now?" Youna Kim, ed. *The Korean Wave: Korean Media Go Global*, pp. 75–92. London: Routledge.

KimGoh, Yeonju. 2013. *Our Mother, Why? Understanding Mother Humanly Curious* (in Korean). Seoul: Dolbegae.

Kojima, Hiroshi. 2009. "Family Formation Behaviors of Couples in International Marriages: A Comparative Analysis of Japan and Taiwan." Hong-Zen Wang and Hsin-Huang Michael Hsiao, eds. *Cross-Border Marriages with Asian Characteristics*, pp. 107–146. Taipei: Center for Asia-Pacific Area Studies, Academia Sinica.

Kong, Jung-Ja. 1990. "The Marriage Patterns of *Chaebol* Families" (in Korean). Women's Research Group on Korean Society, ed. *A Study of the Korean Family*, pp. 37–59. Seoul: Kachi.

Kong, Suk-Ki. 2012. "Politics of Cosmopolitan Citizenship: The Korean Engagement in the Global Justice Movements." *Citizenship Studies* 16(1): 69–84.

Kong, Tat Yan. 2000. *The Politics of Economic Reform in South Korea: A Fragile Miracle*. London: Routledge.

— 2012. "Neoliberal Restructuring in South Korea Before and After the Crisis." Chang Kyung-Sup, Ben Fine, and Linda Weiss, eds. *Developmental Politics in Transition: The Neoliberal Era and Beyond*, pp. 235–253. Basingstoke: Palgrave Macmillan.

Koo, Hagen. 1993. "Strong State and Contentious Society." Hagen Koo, ed. *State and Society in Contemporary Korea*, pp. 231–249. Ithaca: Cornell University Press.

— 2001. *Korean Workers: The Culture and Politics of Class Formation*. Ithaca: Cornell University Press.

— 2016. "The Global Middle Class: How Is It Made, What Does It Represent?" *Globalizations* 13(4): 440–453.

Korea Economic Daily (www.hankyung.com).

Korea Higher Education Research Institute (KHEI). 2014. "57% of the Overseas Doctoral Degrees between 1945 and 2013 Are American Degrees" (in Korean). Press release based upon the Ministry of Education data (http://khei.re.kr/post/2099).

Korea Statistical Information System (KOSIS). (http//kosis.kr).

Korea Statistical Office (KSO). 2020. "The Tentative Result of Birth and Death Statistics in the Survey of Population Changes in 2019" (in Korean). Media brief.

Korean Family Studies Research Group (KFSRG). 1992. *The Family Problems of Urban Low-Income Groups* (in Korean). Seoul, Hau.

Kornai, Janos. 1992. *The Socialist System: The Political Economy of Communism*. Oxford: Oxford University Press.

Kung, I-Chun. 2009. "The Politics of International Marriages: Vietnamese Brides in Taiwan." Hong-Zen Wang and Hsin-Huang Michael Hsiao, eds. Cross-Border Marriages with Asian Characteristics, pp. 177–188. Taipei: Center for Asia-Pacific Area Studies, Academia Sinica.

Kwon, Tai Hwan. 1977. *Demography of Korea: Population Change and Its Components, 1925–66*. Seoul: Seoul National University Press.

— 2003. "Demographic Trends and Their Social Implications." *Social Indicators Research* 62/63: 19–38.

Kyunghyang Shinmun (www.khan.co.kr).

Lan, Pei-Chia. 2014. "Compressed Modernity and Glocal Entanglement: The Contested Transformation of Parenting Discourses in Taiwan." *Current Sociology* 62(4): 531–549.

— 2016. "Compressed Parenthood in Taiwan." *Global Dialogue: Newsletter for the International Sociological Association*, 6 (2), (June) (http://isa-global-dialogue.net/compressed-parenthood-in-taiwan/).

Laslett, Barbara and Johanna Brenner. 1989. "Gender and Social Reproduction: Historical Perspectives." *Annual Review of Sociology* 15: 381–404.

Latour, Bruno. 1993. *We Have Never Been Modern*, translated by Catherine Porter. Cambridge: Harvard University Press.

— 2005. *Reassembling the Social: An Introduction to Actor-Network Theory*. Oxford: Oxford University Press.

Lee, Bong-Beom. 2015. "The Cold War and the Aid, the Dynamism of the Construction of the Cold War Culture during the Aid Age: The Aid from American Private Foundations and Korean Culture in 1950s–60s" (in Korean). *Korean Studies* 39: 221–276.

Lee, Cheol-Sung. 2019. *The Generation of Inequality: Who Has Made South Korean Society Unequal* (in Korean). Seoul: Munhakgwajiseongsa.

Lee, Chul-Woo. 2014. "How Can You Say You're Korean? Law, Governmentality, and National Membership in South Korea." Chang Kyung-Sup, ed. *South*

Korea in Transition: Politics and Culture of Citizenship, pp. 93–110. London: Routledge.

Lee, Deuk-Jae. 2001. *Familialism Is Savage* (in Korean). Goyang: Sonamu.

Lee, Hee Jae. 2011. "The Nature of the Change in the Confucian Rituals during the Japanese Colonial Occupation Period: Focusing on Family Rituals in 'The Standard Rules of Rituals' in the 1930s" (in Korean). *Japan Studies* 15: 565–584.

Lee, Hyeon Jung. 2012. "'The Parent–Child Suicide Pact' and the Concept of the Family in East Asia: A Cross-Cultural Approach of South Korea, China, and Japan" (in Korean). *Korean Studies* 40: 187–227.

Lee, Hyun-jin. 2009. *The American Economic Aid Policy to the Republic of Korea, 1948–1960* (in Korean). Seoul: Hyean.

Lee, Kwang-Kyu. 1990. *Family and Clan in Korea* (in Korean). Seoul: Mineumsa.

Lee, Kyung Sook. 2008. "The Study on Implementation of International Human Rights Norms to Protect Rights of Migrant Workers: United Nations International Human Rights Treaties and Migrant Workers Convention" (in Korean). *Legal Studies* 11(2): 189–221.

Lee, Keehyeung. 2004. "Speak Memory! *Morae Sigye* and the Politics of Social Melodrama in Contemporary South Korea." *Cultural Studies, Critical Methodologies* 4(4): 526–539.

Lee, Seoung-Won. 2008. "The Critical Review on Democracy in the Era of Globalization: With the Case of the Enactment of Two Revised Bills on 'Overseas Koreans' and 'Citizenship' in South Korea" (in Korean). *Economy and Society* 79: 88–111.

Lee, Sang-Young, Noh Yong-Hwan, and Lee Gi-Ju. 2012. "Policy Issues and Directions for a Rapid Increase in Suicides in Korea" (in Korean). KIHASA Research Report 2012–64. Seoul: Korea Institute for Health and Social Affairs.

Lee, Sophia Seung-Yoon, Baek Seung Ho, Kim Migyoung, and Kim Yoon Young. 2017. "Analysis of Precariousness in Korean Youth Labour Market" (in Korean). *Journal of Critical Social Policy* 54: 487–521.

Lee, Young Boon, Yong Woo Lee, Hee Jung Choi, Hwa Young Lee. 2011. "An Explorative Study on Coresident Adult Children in Korea" (in Korean). *Korean Journal of Family Welfare* 31: 5–30.

Lew, Seok-Choon. 2013. *The Korean Economic Developmental Path: Confucian Tradition, Affective Network*. Basingstoke: Palgrave Macmillan.

Lewis, W. Arthur. 1954. "Economic Development with Unlimited Supplies of Labour." *Manchester School of Economics and Social Studies* 22(1): 139–191.

Lie, John. 1998. *Han Unbound: The Political Economy of South Korea*. Stanford: Stanford University Press.

— 2012. "What is the K in K-pop? South Korean Popular Music, the Culture Industry, and National Identity." *Korea Observer* 43(3): 339–363.

Lim, Hyun-Chin. 1986. *Dependent Development in Korea, 1963–1979*. Seoul: Seoul National University Press.

Lim, Sungyun. 2019. *Rules of the House: Family Law and Domestic Disputes in Colonial Korea*. Berkeley: University of California Press.

Lipton, Michael. 1977. *Why Poor People Stay Poor: Urban Bias in World Development*. Cambridge: Harvard University Press.

Lyotard, Jean-François. [1979]1984. *The Postmodern Condition: A Report on Knowledge*. Minneapolis: University of Minnesota Press.

McDonald, Peter. 2009. "Explanations of Low Fertility in East Asia: A Comparative Perspective." Gavin Jones, Paulin Tay Straughan, and Angelique Chan, eds. *Ultra-Low Fertility in Pacific Asia: Trends, Causes and Policy Issues*, pp. 23–39. London: Routledge.

Martin-Jones, David. 2007. "Decompressing Modernity: South Korean Time Travel Narratives and the IMF Crisis." *Cinema Journal* 46(4): 45–67.

Marx, Karl and Frederick Engels. [1945–46] 1970. *The German Ideology*. New York: International Publishers.

Masina, Pietro. 2006. *Vietnam's Development Strategies*. London: Routledge.

MBC (Munhwa Broadcasting Corporation). 2012. "The Dark Side of Aging in Japan, 'Killing by Illness Caregiver' – More Than 236 Cases for 10 Years," May 18, 2012.

Media Today (www.mediatoday.co.kr).

Meillassoux, Claude. 1981. *Maidens, Meal and Money: Capitalism and the Domestic Community*. New York: Cambridge University Press.

Minjushinmun. 2011. "'I Sell My Kidney Because of No Money for Food': The Reality of Internet 'Illegal Trade of Human Organs'" (in Korean), August 23, 2011 (http://www.iminju.net/news/articleView.html?idxno=3391).

Mittelman, James H. 2000. *The Globalization Syndrome: Transformation and Resistance*. Princeton: Princeton University Press.

Mittelman, James H. and Norani Othman, eds. 2001. *Capturing Globalization*. London: Routledge.

Mobrand, Erik. 2019. *Top-Down Democracy in South Korea*. Seattle: University of Washington Press.

Moon, Seung-Sook. 2012. "Local Meanings and Lived Experiences of Citizenship: Voices from a Women's Organization in South Korea." *Citizenship Studies* 16(1): 49–68.

Morris, P. and A. Sweeting, eds. 1995. *Education and Development in East Asia*. New York: Garland.

National Archives of Korea (https://theme.archives.go.kr/next/koreaOfRecord/charterNaEdu.do).

National Statistical Office (NSO), Republic of Korea. 1996, *Changes in Social and Economic Indicators since Liberation* (in Korean).

— 1998. *Economic and Social Change in the Fifty Years of the Republic of Korea Seen through Statistics* (in Korean).

— 2020. *The Statistical Yearbook on Population Dynamics 2019* (http://www.index.go.kr/potal/stts/idxMain/selectPoSttsIdxSearch.do?idx_cd=2430).

Nelson, Laura C. 2000. *Measured Excess: Status, Gender, and Consumer Nationalism in South Korea*. New York: Columbia University Press.

New York Times (www.nytimes.com).

Noh, Si-Pyeong. 2008. "Polifessor and Think Tank" (in Korean). *Korean Administration Forum* 122(2008/6): 65–72.

Ochiai, Emiko. 2010. "Reconstruction of Intimate and Public Spheres in Asian Modernity: Familialism and Beyond." *Journal of Intimate and Public Spheres* (pilot issue): 1–22.

— 2011. "Unsustainable Societies: The Failure of Familialism in East Asia's Compressed Modernity." *Historical Social Research* 36(2): 219–245.

— 2014. "Care Diamonds and Welfare Regimes in East and Southeast Asian Societies." Ochiai Emiko and Hosoya Leo Aoi, eds. *Transformation of the Intimate and the Public in Asian Modernity*, pp. 164–189. Leiden: Brill.

Ochiai, Emiko and Hosoya Leo Aoi, eds. 2014. *Transformation of the Intimate and the Public in Asian Modernity*. Leiden: Brill.

Oh, Je Yeon. 2007. "Nationalism Separation between Park Chung-Hee Regime and University Students in Early 1960`s: With Focus on "Nationalistic Democracy"" (in Korean). *Memory and Prospect* 16: 285–323.

Ohmynews. 2007. "Chaebol-Affiliated Research Institutes, Supporting Subsidiary Companies with Research Reports?" (in Korean). September 24, 2007.

— 2016. " Multiculturals, Raise Your Hands" (in Korean), August 11, 2016.

— 2017. "Inequality Revolved by Change in the Wage System? A Strange Logic of the *Chaebol*-Affiliated Economic Research Institute" (in Korean), July 4, 2017.

Organisation for Economic Cooperation and Development (OECD). 2011, 2019. *Education at a Glance: OECD Indicators*. Paris: OECD (https://data.oecd.org/eduatt/population-with-tertiary-education.htm).

— 2019. *OECD Employment Outlook 2019*. Paris: OECD Publishing.

— 2011, 2019. *Education at a Glance: OECD Indicators*. Paris: OECD (https://data.oecd.org/eduatt/population-with-tertiary-education.htm).

— 2020a. "OECD Data: Population with Tertiary Education" (https://data.oecd.org/eduatt/population-with-tertiary-education.htm).

— 2020b. "OECD Data: Social Expenditure – Aggregated Data" (https://stats.oecd.org/Index.aspx?DataSetCode=SOCX_AGG).

Orta, Andrew. 1999. "Syncretic Subjects and Body Politics: Doubleness, Personhood, and Aymara Catechists." *American Ethnologist* 26(4): 864–889.

Overseas Koreans Foundation. 2020. "World Korean Business Convention (*Segyehansangdaehoe*)" (http://www.hansang.net/portal/PortalView.do).

Paik, Peter Y. 2012. "South Korean Cinema and the Experience of Compressed Modernity," Presented at the Conference on "World Cinemas, Global Networks," Center for International Education, University of Wisconsin-Milwaukee, April 29, 2012.

Park, Chai Bin and Nam-Hoon Cho. 1995. "Consequences of Son Preference in a Low-Fertility Society: Imbalance of the Sex Ratio at Birth in Korea." *Population and Development Review* 21(1): 59–84.

Park, Chan-Su. 2016. "'Born in 1986', NL is Presently Ongoing" (in Korean). *Hankyoreh*, April 29, 2016.

Park, Hee. 2014. "Multiple Modernities and the Discourses on Confucian Modernization in East Asia" (in Korean). *Journal of Asian Studies* 17(2): 113–151.

Park, Kangwoo. 2014. "The College Wage Premium in Korea. 1974–2011: A Supply and Demand Factor Decomposition" (in Korean). *Journal of Industrial Economics and Business* 27(1): 477–505.

Park, Keong-Suk. 2003. *Aging Society, An Already Realized Future* (in Korean). Seoul: Euiam Publishing.

— 2007. "Meaning of the Discourses of Filial Piety Law in a Moral and Political Economy" (in Korean). *Journal of the Korean Family Studies Association* 19(3): 31–52.

Park, Mee-Hae. 1991. "Patterns and Trends of Educational Mating in Korea." *Korea Journal of Population and Development* 20(2): 1–16.

Park, Myoung-Kyu and Chang Kyung-Sup. 1999. "Sociology between Western Theory and Korean Reality: Accommodation, Tension, and a Search for Alternatives." *International Sociology,* 14(2): 139–156.

Park, Myung-Lim. 1996. *Outbreak and Origins of the Korean War* (in Korean). Seoul: Nanam Publishers.

Park, Seung-Gwan and Chang Kyung-Sup. 2001. *Media Power and Agenda Dynamics* (in Korean). Seoul: Communication Books.

Park, Tae Gyun. 2008. "The First Korean Government and the U.S. in 1948" (in Korean). *Citizen and the World* 14: 95–109.

Parsons, Talcott and Neil Smelser. 1956. *Economy and Society*. New York: Free Press.

Piao, Kuangxing. 2006. "Labor Flux of Korean Chinese and Social Changes in Global Era" (in Korean). PhD dissertation, Department of Sociology, Seoul National University.

Pieterse, Jan Nederveen. 1994. "Globalization as Hybridisation." *International Sociology* 9(2): 161–184.

Preston, Samuel and Shigemi Kono. 1988. "Trends in Well-Being of Children and the Elderly in Japan." Diana Palmer, John Logan Palmer, and Timothy M. Smeeding, eds. *The Vulnerable*, pp. 277–307. Washington, DC: Urban Institute Press.

Rajkai, Zsombor, ed. 2016. *Family and Social Change in Socialist and Post-Socialist Societies*. Leiden: Brill.

Redding, S. Gordon. 1990. *The Spirit of Chinese Capitalism*. Berlin: Walter de Gruyter.

Regatieri, Ricardo Pagliuso. 2017. "Development and Dream: On the Dynamics of K-Pop in Brazil." *Development and Society* 46(3): 505–522.

Republic of Korea. 2019. "Policy Briefing" (in Korean), February 27, 2019. (http://www.korea.kr/news/policyBriefingView.do?newsId=156319329).

Rhyu, Mina. 2005. "'Collaboration and Frustration' to Japanese Colonial Government: Focusing on the Relationship of Kyonghagwon, Hyangyo and Munmyo" (in Korean). *Korean Culture* 36: 157–191.

Riskin, Carl. 1987. *China's Political Economy: The Quest for Development since 1949*. Oxford: Oxford University Press.

Rostow, W. W. 1959. "The Stages of Economic Growth." *Economic History Review* 12(1): 1–16.

Ryoo, Woongjae. 2008. "Globalization, or the Logic of Cultural Hybridization: The Case of the Korean Wave." *Asian Journal of Communication* 19(2): 137–151.

Safa, Helen Icken, ed. 1982. *Towards A Political Economy of Urbanization in Third World Countries*. Delhi: Oxford University Press.

Said, Edward. 1978. *Orientalism: Western Conceptions of the Orient*. New York: Pantheon.

SBS (www.sbs.co.kr).

Schein, Louisa. 1997. "Gender and Internal Orientalism in China." *Modern China* 23(1): 69–98.

Schmid, Andre. 2010. "Colonialism and the 'Korea Problem' in the Historiography of Modern Japan: A Review Article." *Journal of Asian Studies* 59(4): 951–976.

Schwab, Klaus. 2017. *The Fourth Industrial Revolution*. New York: Penguin.

Segyeilbo (https://www.segye.com).

Selden, Mark. 1971. *The Yenan Way in Revolutionary China*. Cambridge: Harvard University Press.

Seok, Sang-Hoon. 2013. "An Analysis of the Current Conditions and Causes of Elderly People's Poverty and Income Inequality" (in Korean). Seoul: Korea Employment Information Service

Seol, Dong-Hoon. 2014. "The Citizenship of Foreign Workers: Stratified Formation, Fragmented Evolution." Chang Kyung-Sup, ed. *South Korea in Transition: Politics and Culture of Citizenship*, pp. 131–146. London: Routledge.

Seoul Economic Daily (SED). 1991. *Chaebol and Gabol: Korean High Society Seen Through Marriage Network* (in Korean). Seoul: Jisiksanupsa.

Seoul National University. 1996. *The Fifty-Year History of Seoul National University, 1946–1996, Volumes 1 and 2* (in Korean). Seoul: Seoul National University Press.

Seoul Times. 2018. "'Hey, Multicultural' . . . the Homeroom Teacher Calls My Friend like This" (in Korean), July 30, 2018.

Seth, Michael. 2002. *Education Fever: Society, Politics, and the Pursuit of Schooling in South Korea*. Honolulu: University of Hawaii Press.

— 2012. "Education Zeal, State Control and Citizenship in South Korea." *Citizenship Studies* 16(1): 13–28.

SEVIS. 2020. "U.S. Student and Exchange Visitor Program" (www.ice.gov/sevis/).

Shibata, Haruka. 2009. "The Gap between Social Policy Modernization and Lifestyle Modernization in Compressed Modernity: Cross-National Time-Series Analyses of Social Spending and Total Fertility Rate on 30 Western and Asian Countries, 1990–2007." Presented at the International Conference on "Compressed Modernity and Social Policy: Cross-National Time-Series Analysis on Western and Asian Countries," July 24–25, 2009, Kyoto University.

— 2010. "The Possibility of Social Policy for Preventing Suicide in Compressed Modernity." Presented at the 3rd Next-Generation Global Workshop of the Kyoto University Global Center of Excellence Program on "Reconstruction of the Intimate and Public Spheres in 21st Century Asia," December 11–12, 2010, Kyoto University.

Shim, Doobo. 2006. "Hybridity and the Rise of Korean Popular Culture in Asia." *Media, Culture and Society* 28(1): 25–44.

Shin, Gi-Wook. 1997. *Peasant Protest and Social Change in Colonial Korea*. Seattle: University of Washington Press.

— 2006. *Ethnic Nationalism in Korea: Genealogy, Politics, and Legacy*, Stanford: Stanford University Press.

Shin, Kwang-Yeong. 2013. "Economic Crisis, Neoliberal Reforms, and the Rise of Precarious Work in South Korea." *American Behavioral Scientist* 57(3): 335–353.

Shin, Yong-Ha. 1994. "A Suggestion for the Development of 'Unique Korean Sociology'" (in Korean). *Korean Journal of Sociology* 28(1): 1–12.

— 2001. *Ethnonational Movement and Social Movement in Early Modern Korea* (in Korean). Seoul: Munhakgwajiseongsa.

Shorter, Edward. 1988. "Grand Theories of Family Change: Modernization Theory." Presented at the Seminar on "Theories of Family Change," International Union for the Scientific Study of Population (IUSSP).

Sinn, Gerlinde and Hans-Werner Sinn. 1992. *Jumpstart: The Economic Unification of Germany*. Cambridge: MIT Press.

Sisain (http://www.sisainlive.com).

Sohn, Byong Don. 2009. "Income Inequality of the Aged: Trends and Factor Decomposition" (in Korean). *Journal of Korean Gerontological Society* 29(4): 1445–1461.

Sohn, Hee-Kwon. 2009. "Constitutional Review of the Bills for Regulating the Polifessor" (in Korean). *Education Issue Studies* 35: 141–163.

Somerville, Jennifer. 1992. "The New Right and Family Politics." *Economy and Society* 21(2): 93–128.

Song, Baek-Seok. 2007. "'Samsung Republic Phenomenon' and the Limits of the Capitalist State" (in Korean). *Korean Political Science Review* 41(1): 57–79.

Song, Ho-Keun. 2016. "The Formation of Citizen and Civil Society in South Korea: The Deficiency in Citizenship and Excess 'National'" (in Korean). *The Horizon of Knowledge,* volume 20 (May 2016):1–19.

Suh, Jae-Jin. 1995. *Another North Korean Society: A Study of the Duality of Social Structure and Social Consciousness* (in Korean). Seoul: Nanam.

Suh, Jae-Jung and Mikyoung Kim, eds. 2017. *Challenges of Modernization and Governance in South Korea: The Sinking of the Sewol and Its Causes.* Basingstoke: Palgrave Macmillan.

Sung, Minkyu. 2010. "The Psychiatric Power of Neo-Liberal Citizenship: The North Korean Human Rights Crisis, North Korean Settlers, and Incompetent Citizens." *Citizenship Studies* 14(2): 127–144.

Task Force in Rural Policy for the New Economy Long-Term Plans, Republic of Korea. 1995. "New Economy Long-Term Plan – Programs for Task Implementation: Long-Term Plans for Agriculture, Forestry, and Fishery" (in Korean). Policy discussion paper.

Taylor-Gooby, Peter, ed. 2004. *New Risks, New Welfare: The Transformation of the European Welfare State.* Oxford: Oxford University Press.

Therborn, Göran. 2003. "Entangled Modernities." *European Journal of Social Theory* 6(3): 293–305.

Turner, Bryan S. 1994. *Orientalism, Postmodernism, and Globalism.* London: Routledge.

— 2001. "The Erosion of Citizenship." *British Journal of Sociology* 52(2): 189–209.

— 2014. "Asian Citizenship and Beyond: Contradictions between Democracy and Demography." Chang Kyung-Sup, ed. *South Korea in Transition: Politics and Culture of Citizenship*, pp. 181–188. London: Routledge.

— 2016. "We Are All Denizens Now: On the Erosion of Citizenship." *Citizenship Studies* 20(6/7): 679–692.

Turner, Bryan S. and Habibul Haque Khondker. 2010. *Globalization East and West.* London: Sage.

Turner, Bryan S., Chang Kyung-Sup, Cynthia F. Epstein, Peter Kivisto, J. Michael Ryan, William Outhwaite, eds. 2017. *The Wiley Blackwell Encyclopedia of Social Theory. Volumes I–V.* Hoboken: Wiley Blackwell.

Urry, John. 2003. *Global Complexity.* Cambridge: Polity

Wade, Robert. 1990. *Governing the Market: Economic Theory and the Role of Government in East Asian Industrialization.* Princeton: Princeton University Press.

Walder, Andrew. 1986. *Communist Neo-Traditionalism: Work and Authority in Chinese Industry.* Berkeley: University of California Press.

Wando Times. 2013. "'Uncomfortable' Because of Being Mobilized for Various Multicultural Family Events" (in Korean). January 9, 2013 (http://wandonews.com/news/articleView.html?idxno=192595).

Wang, Hong-Zen and Ching-Ying Tien. 2009. "Who Marries Vietnamese Bride? Masculinities and Cross-Border Marriages." Hong-Zen Wang and Hsin-Huang

REFERENCES

Michael Hsiao, eds. *Cross-Border Marriages with Asian Characteristics*, pp. 13–38. Taipei: Center for Asia-Pacific Area Studies, Academia Sinica.

Wang, Zhan. 2015. "Risk in the Compressed Modernity: Focusing on Knowledge and Consensus of the 'Beijing Smog'" (in Japanese). *Journal of International Media, Communication, and Tourism Studies* 20: 95–114.

Weber, Max. 1946. *From Max Weber: Essays in Sociology.* New York: Oxford University Press.

Weiss, Linda. 1995. "Governed Interdependence: Rethinking the Government-Business Relationship in East Asia." *Pacific Review* 8(4): 589–616.

— 1998. *The Myth of the Powerless State.* Ithaca: Cornell University Press.

Weiss, Linda, Elizabeth Thurbon, and John Mathews. 2007. *National Insecurity: The Howard Government's Betrayal of Australia.* Crows Nest: Allen & Unwin.

White, Gordon. 1998. "Social Security Reforms in China: Towards an East Asian Model?" Roger Goodman, Gordon White, and Huck-ju Kwon, eds. *The East Asian Welfare Model: Welfare Orientalism and the State*, pp. 175–198. London: Routledge.

Whittaker, D. Hugh, Timothy J. Sturgeon, Toshie Okita, and Tianbiao Zhu. 2020. *Compressed Development: Time and Timing in Economic and Social Development.* Oxford: Oxford University Press.

Xi, Jinping. 2021. "Speech at a Ceremony Marking the Centenary of the Communist Party of China." *China Xinhua News*, July 1, 2021 (http://www.xinhuanet.com/english/special/2021-07/01/c_1310038244.htm).

Xu, Honggang and Yuefang Wu. 2016. "Lifestyle Mobility in China: Context, Perspective and Prospects." *Mobilities* 11(4): 509–520.

Yang, Hyunah. 2006. "Vision of Postcolonial Feminist Jurisprudence in Korea: Seen from the 'Family-Head System' in Family Law." *Journal of Korean Law* 5(2): 12–28.

— 2011. *Reading the Korean Family Law: At the Intersection of Tradition, Coloniality and Gender* (in Korean). Seoul: Changbi.

Yi, Jeong-Duk. 2015. "Compressed Economic Growth and Compressed Modernity in East Asia," Presented at the Joint Meeting of East Asian Anthropological Association (EAAA) and Tawan Society for Anthropology and Ethnology (TSAE) on "Multiple Landscapes of Anthropology," National Chengchi University, October 3–4, 2015.

Yi, Jeong-Duk et al. 2017. *The Compressed Modern Life World in South Korea: The Concept of Compressed Modernity and the Compressed Experiences* (in Korean). Seoul: Knowledge and Conscience.

Yi, Ki-baek. 1984. *The New History of Korea*, translated from Korean by Edward W. Wagner with Edward J. Shultz. Cambridge: Harvard University Press.

Yoo, Seong Ho. 1996. "Determinants of the Independent Living Arrangements among Korean Elderly and their Adult Children: A Theoretical Investigation" (in Korean). *Journal of the Korea Gerontological Society* 16(1): 51–68.

Yoo, Theodore Jun. 2014. *The Politics of Gender in Colonial Korea: Education, Labor, and Health, 1910–1945.* Berkeley: University of California Press.

Yoon, Hong-Sik. 2008 "The Expansion of New Social Risks and the Base Draft of the Policy of the Lee Myung-Bak Government: Focusing on the Area of Women and Family (Welfare) Policies" (in Korean). *Monthly Welfare Trends* 113 (March 2008): 23–27.

Yoon, In-Jin. 2008. "The Development and Characteristics of Multiculturalism in South Korea – With a Focus on the Relationship of the State and Civil Society" (in Korean). *Korean Journal of Sociology* 42(2): 72–103.

— 2012. "Circumstantial Citizens: North Korean 'Migrants' in South Korea." Chang Kyung-Sup and Bryan S. Turner, eds. *Contested Citizenship in East Asia: Developmental Politics, National Unity, and Globalization*, pp. 218–239. London: Routledge.

— 2016. "Characteristics and Changes of Koreans' Perceptions of Multicultural Minorities" (in Korean). *Journal of Diaspora Studies* 10(1): 125–154.

Yoon, Sang Woo. 2008. "A Critical Assessment of Social Policy and the Welfare State during the Post-Democratic Era in Korea: Focusing on 'Social Citizenship'" (in Korean). *Social Science Research* 16(1): 346–387.

Yoon, Seungjoo. 2017. "Eastern Spirit, Western Instrument." *The Wiley Blackwell Encyclopedia of Social Theory, Volume II*. Hoboken: Wiley Blackwell (https://doi.org/10.1002/9781118430873.est0849).

YTN (www.ytn.co.kr).

Yui, Kiyomitsu. 2012. "Multiple Modernities, Compressed Modernity and Hybrid Modernity: Theories of Modernities in Fundamental Reconsideration with Asian Perspective." Presented at the 40th World Congress of the International Institute of Sociology (IIS), Delhi, February 16–19, 2012.

Zaretsky, Eli. 1973. *Capitalism, the Family, and Personal Life*. New York: Harper & Colophon Books.

Zhang, Liang. 2013. "Individualization and Rural Society Reconstruction in the Process of Modernization." *Zhejiang Social Sciences* 2013(3) (https://en.cnki.com.cn/Article_en/CJFDTotal-ZJSH201303002.htm).

INDEX

modernity (*cont.*)
  means-end reversal under 87
  modernity-tradition entanglements
    10
  and social reproduction 126
  see also compressed modernity;
    multiple modernities;
    postcolonial modernity; reflexive
    institutional modernity; second
    (late) modernity; Western
    modernity
modernization
  early 38–41
  and economic development 138–9,
    177–8, 179
  and infrastructural familialism 141,
    143, 145
  socialist 44–5
  theory 30–3
Moon Jae-In 72, 78, 98, 117, 138
Moon, Seung-Sook 7
mortality rates 17
multiculturalism 108
  ad hoc multiculturalism and
    reproductive globalization
    114–18
  and cloakroom cosmopolitanization
    122–4
  and complex culturalism 15–16,
    109–14, 118, 180
  multicultural family support policy
    15, 17, 101–2, 109, 117–18, 120,
    120–1, 122, 171
  and transnational marriages 16,
    74–6, 85, 101–2, 108–9, 114–21,
    122–4, 171
multiple modernities
  thesis of 53
multiplex theater society
  South Korea as 14, 78, 82–5

national citizenship 105
national development
  condensed 16
  and infrastructural familialism 143

national developmentalism
  and compressed modernity 126
  and state-capitalist modernity 70–3
national modernity 53
nationalism
  developmental 93
  methodological 11
neoliberal citizenship 99–102
neoliberal economic globalism 14,
    73–6, 77–8, 81–2
neoliberal economic restructuring
  Third World countries 43, 44
neoliberal globalization 54, 86, 179
  and demography 159–60
neoliberalism
  and the post-compressed modern
    condition 183–4
newly industrializing countries 41
new social risks 135–6, 181, 202
North Korea 79, 103, 108, 144
  defectors/refugees in South Korea
    104, 105
  and free world modernity 68, 69
  socialist postcolonial development
    158
  state socialism 45
nuclear families 166, 167
nude aging 169

Ochiai, Emiko 7
OECD (Organisation for Economic
  Co-operation and Development)
  73
  tertiary education in OECD
    countries 91
Orientalism 24, 113

Pacific War 54, 55, 56, 66
Parasite (movie) 5
Park Chung-Hee 88, 97, 141
  authoritarian developmental
    governance 158
  and capitalist industrialization 54
  and developmental citizenship 94,
    95

rural areas 27
  aged population 161, 169
  compressed demographic
    transitions in 182
  exodus from 125
  extinction of familial peasantry
    132–3
  foreign brides from 119–20
  migrating family members from 28,
    144
  rural-to-urban migrant labor 17,
    141, 158
  see also peasantry; transnational
    marriages
rural–urban divide
  developmental and demographic
    162–3
Russia
  post-socialist transition 45–6, 47
  and South Korean globalization
    103, 104
  state socialism in Soviet Russia 44,
    45

Said, Edward 24
second (late) modernity 11, 18, 35,
  183
  and reflexive cosmopolit(an)ization
    36–7, 39–48
secondary organizations
  modernization and development 27
self-centered globalism 16, 110, 114,
  121
self-employment 146, 147–8
Seoul
  Japan-built Western buildings 89
Seoul National University 90
Singapore 48, 160, 164, 184
social globalization
  and transnational marriages 172
social identity
  and tranformation-embedded
    interests 87
social investment families 155, 156,
  181

the social investment state 154–5
social reproduction 16–17, 125–6,
  125–39, 127
  in China 129
  crisis of 127
  and developmental liberalism 129,
    130–2
  and economic production 125–6,
    127–8, 139
  and the familial peasantry 132–3
  and family structure 167
  financialization of 137–8
  and industrial working life history
    134–5
  labor of foreign brides 100,
    118–19, 120–1, 124
  and peasant families 132–4
  and post-socialist transition
    societies 128–9
  productionist (ab)use of 180–1
  and Stalinist socialism 128
  and women in urban poor families
    135–6
social welfare
  and familial self-welfare 149–51
socialism 59, 127–8
  socialist revolutions 32
  see also transition societies (post-
    socialist)
sociocultural globalization 15, 87,
  105
sociocultural transnationalization
  170–1
Soviet Union 44, 45
space (place)
  compression/complication 20, 23–4,
    29
  condensation/abridgement 20, 22–3
Stalinist socialism 127–8
state-capitalist modernity 14, 76, 79,
  80–1, 84, 117
  and national developmentalism
    70–3
state-socialist countries
  economic production 127–8

CPSIA information can be obtained
at www.ICGtesting.com
Printed in the USA
JSHW031731100422
24607JS00001B/86

9 781509 552887